# East Asia's Potential for Instability & Crisis

*Implications for the United States and Korea*

**Edited by**
**JONATHAN D. POLLACK**
**HYUN-DONG KIM**

Center for Asia-Pacific Policy / The Sejong Institute

# RAND

# PREFACE

The contributions to this volume are revised versions of papers first presented at a joint conference on "East Asia's Potential for Instability and Crisis—Implications for the United States and Korea," jointly sponsored by RAND's Center for Asia-Pacific Policy and The Sejong Institute. The conference was held at RAND, Santa Monica, California, on February 27-28, 1995.

The conveners of the meeting (Jonathan D. Pollack and Hyun-Dong Kim) asked each paper writer to assess the possibilities for major political, economic, or security realignment in East Asia, and then to assess the potential implications of such destabilizing change for the United States and Korea. Analysis focused on five issues: (1) political and/or economic scenarios in China that severely impeded or reversed Chinese and regional stability; (2) arms acquisitions within East Asia that undermined regional stability and the incentives for collaboration among the major regional powers; (3) a breakdown in efforts to develop new arrangements for the global trading system; (4) future developments on the Korean peninsula or between Korea and the United States that severely eroded U.S.-ROK alliance cohesion; and (5) a political or economic crisis in the U.S.-Japan relationship that called into question the future viability of the U.S.-Japan alliance.

Through comparative assessment of these five areas, the conference was intended to identify areas of difference and commonality between analysts from RAND and from Sejong, to highlight issues for consideration by American and Korean policymakers, and to suggest potential directions for future research.

# FOREWORD

The publication of this volume culminates the first formal collaboration between RAND's Center for Asia-Pacific Policy and The Sejong Institute. The contributions to this symposium attest to the goals of our two institutions. By rigorous analysis of complex political, economic, and security issues, RAND and Sejong hope to contribute to post-Cold War policy deliberations very much needed in the United States as well as Korea. Our two countries have much to learn from one another; it is in that spirit that we see the need for heightened dialogue and debate on both sides of the Pacific.

We believe that this volume furnishes important and timely insights into the policy challenges faced by both countries; we also believe it testifies to the value of continued research collaboration between RAND and Sejong.

James A. Thomson                                    Bae Ho Hahn
President and Chief Executive Officer               President
RAND                                               The Sejong Institute

# CONTENTS

# TABLES

East Asia has been an extraordinary success story over the past several decades. By numerous measures—dynamic economic growth, greatly increased levels of intraregional trade, increased political openness, regional stability, and the avoidance of major armed conflict—the region as a whole has exhibited far more "pluses" than "minuses." If anything, these trends have been reinforced in the post-Cold War world. In comparison to many geographic regions, for example, the Balkans, sub-Saharan Africa, Central Asia and the Caucasus, and the Caribbean, the well being and steady advancement of East Asia seem palpable. These circumstances have greatly benefited the United States and Korea, enabling both countries to sustain close collaboration with one another while also forging increased political, economic, and institutional ties with other states in the region.

There are many reasons to believe that these trends will persist into the next century. But what if they do not? When and how might optimistic assessments about East Asia's future be altered in strategically significant ways? What are the possible implications should optimistic estimates be invalidated? There are at least six classes of events that, should they materialize in whole or in part, would have the capability to undermine or destabilize prevailing political, economic, and security patterns:

- major internal political or economic changes within one or more states that reconfigure the incentives of different countries to sustain collaboration with their neighbors;

- destabilizing internal conflicts that could have spillover consequences elsewhere in the region;

- a political crisis in alliance ties or in the pattern of relations among two or more regional powers and/or their external security partners;

- a major crisis or outright military hostilities across national boundaries or within disputed territories;

- a militarily significant increase in the defense capabilities of one or more states that reconfigures the prevailing security perceptions and patterns within the region;

- a serious challenge to the maintenance of the global trading system that undermines support for economic and technological interdependence.

Any of these outcomes would have major implications for the region and for the future of the U.S.-ROK relationship; should more than one occur simultaneously or should one development trigger additional negative consequences, the ramifications could prove even more far reaching.

To assert such possibilities, however, is not to predict that any are inevitable. But the fact that various negative outcomes are conceivable warrants the attention of analysts as well as policymakers. It would not be prudent to assume that present regional patterns will persist indefinitely, or that states will be able to adapt and adjust successfully to potential policy change. To be sure, decisionmakers must always allow for the possibility of abrupt and unanticipated policy developments. However, in recognizing such possibilities, it is necessary to pose some basic questions:

- What sequence of events or developments could lead to a scenario of destabilizing change?

- What are the potential indicators or causal factors that could point to a highly negative outcome, and how prevalent or likely are any of these factors at present?

- How would a particular scenario affect the interests and policy calculations of the United States and Korea?

- What can or should U.S. and Korean policymakers do (in conjunction with other states or on a bilateral basis) to render major instability or an outright crisis less likely, or to address such a crisis should it occur?

To assess these issues, analysts from RAND and The Sejong Institute focused on five specific issues that were judged particularly significant for the region as a whole and for U.S.-Korean relations in particular. The intention was not to rank order these concerns, or to achieve consensus on the likelihood of one or another scenario. Rather, comparative assessment sought to highlight some of the salient concerns evident in both countries, and to identify areas of potential divergence, especially in relation to the consequences that could flow from destabilizing change. The areas on which attention focused were:

- leadership scenarios in post-Deng Xiaoping China that would impede or reverse the future prospects for Chinese and regional stability;

- arms acquisitions within East Asia that could undermine regional stability and the incentives for future collaboration among regional powers;

- a failure to reach satisfactory agreement on the parameters of the future global trading system, leading to a major reconfiguration of interregional and intraregional economic ties;

- policy developments on the Korean peninsula that could trigger highly negative effects in the U.S.-Korean alliance;

- a political or economic crisis in the U.S.-Japan relationship that severely erodes alliance cohesion and the viability of future cooperation.

All paper writers and conferees agreed that these five areas—especially if more negative trends emerged—would define much of the character of the emergent East Asian system. But the range of opinion presented in the papers and during conference discussion underscored differences of perspective between Korea's position as a middle power still divided between South and North and the global role of the United States. To be sure, American power is no longer as dominant as during the Cold War, though with the Soviet Union's collapse the United States still retains a singular capability to shape global political, economic, and security norms.  By comparison, Korea views its interests and strategies from a more local if increasingly assertive perspective, reflecting both its economic emergence and its democratization.  But the United States, though still attentive to the concerns of its regional partners, necessarily defines its policy options in more global terms.

The principal concern for Korean and American decisionmakers is where, when, and how the respective policy orientations of the two countries intersect.  Under "normal" conditions—that is, in the absence of destabilizing events or a major crisis—there are no insuperable obstacles to close policy coordination.  But alliance bonds could be weakened under a variety of circumstances and conditions.  For example, Korea might undertake military acquisitions that the United States judges undermining of complementarity and interoperability in weapons systems and roles and missions.  A second such possibility would be unilateral moves by the United States on trade policy that Korea deems disadvantageous to its own economic interests (e.g., diminished market access to the United States, or steps that see Korea's much smaller economy dwarfed by Japan's regional predominance or by a fledgling Chinese sphere of economic influence).  A third possibility would reflect a pronounced divergence in U.S. and Korean policy calculations in relation to future U.S. or ROK dealings with North Korea, or a post-unification U.S. regional policy that Korean policymakers believe is overly tilted toward Japan or China without adequate regard for Korean interests.

Specifying such possibilities is not to predict them, nor did analysts engage in worst case analysis.  Indeed, conceived in broad terms, both countries retain ample reason to sustain close interaction and collaboration.  But the analysis in several areas (in particular, the discussions on international economic policy, U.S.-Korean alliance ties and the future of U.S.-Japan relations) highlight the possibility (if not the certainty) of political outcomes that could severely disrupt future alliance strategies.  Whether as part of a conscious effort to reconfigure the terms of the U.S.-ROK relationship or as an unintended consequence of actions taken in related policy areas, such change could needlessly damage the political bonds that have been nurtured over the decades, to the pronounced detriment of the interests of both states.

In view of the judgments of the authors and in light of conference discussions, several principal implications for U.S. and Korean policymakers seemed evident. First, neither country can afford to take its alliance partner for granted. After more than four decades of maintaining the political status quo on the peninsula, the ground may now be shifting in Korea. This process of change will ultimately reconfigure both the political character of the peninsula, and the expectations that Korea and the United States have of one another. Such change will presuppose a new alliance bargain mindful of America's global obligations but commensurate with Korea's own capabilities and political maturation. This bargain cannot emerge unilaterally. Thus, as the prospect of a new relationship between South and North becomes more clearcut, or should unification abruptly and unexpectedly take place, the United States and Korea will require new "terms of reference" for the alliance. The time to turn to this challenge is now, rather than after such developments have transpired. Ongoing efforts and exchanges at both a governmental and policy analytic level can and should contribute to this process of future-oriented assessment.

Second, both countries need to define their interests in regional as well as peninsular terms. There has been a repeated tendency in both countries to examine policy needs in an overly restrictive fashion. This may have been understandable when Korea and the United States were focused principally on the peninsular confrontation, but this is far less the case today, and will be even less the case in the future. Even before unification, Korea has emerged as a political and economic actor of far greater consequence than in the past. A more appropriate perspective, therefore, is for both countries to identify their complementary as well as their potentially divergent interests, treating East Asia in more comprehensive terms. Without a conscious effort by both countries to remain mindful of the fuller spectrum of their respective policy concerns, debate could be too narrow, and needlessly divisive. There is clearly a role for policy analysts in both countries to shape a more comprehensive and differentiated view of U.S. and Korean interests, which also needs to be imparted to policymakers in both countries.

Third, without assuming the worst, the stability and success of the region—especially in comparison to the upheavals elsewhere in the globe—could engender undue complacency about the future. It is incumbent on both countries to remain realistically prepared for the future. Despite continued cause for optimism, the analysis in this volume highlights a wide spectrum of possibilities and contingencies that could develop amidst a broader process of political, economic, and security realignment. Some negative scanarios discussed in this volume suggest the possibility of sharp discontinuities, especially in the political processes within various states. Other possibilities highlight directions or tendencies that are already developing, especially in terms of the shifting balance of economic and military capabilities. The challenge of leadership is to point the way toward a preferred future. The contribution of policy analysis is to highlight the pitfalls and consequences that could accompany this process, and to offer insights and longer-term perspectives to assist decisionmakers. There is reason to be hopeful about the longer-term, but only if America and Korea are both fully prepared for policy challenges that could yet confront them, either under "predictable" or "unpredictable" scenarios. It is toward a fuller understanding of such challenges that analysts in Korea and the United States must commit themselves in earnest.

# ACKNOWLEDGMENTS

Special thanks go to Rachel Swanger for ably facilitating the conversion of the conference papers into a coherent volume, and to Barbara Wagner, who labored long, hard, and cheerfully to prepare the manuscript for final publication. Finally, the Sejong Institute and the RAND Center for Asia-Pacific Policy wish to express their gratitude to the Korea Foundation for its financial support of this publication.

# CONTRIBUTORS

Jin-Young Chung is Director of the International Political Economy Program at The Sejong Institute.

Hyun-Dong Kim was Director of the Foreign Policy and Security Studies Program of The Sejong Institute. He is now pursuing a career in Korean politics.

Jae-Cheol Kim is a Fellow in the Area Studies Program of The Sejong Institute.

Taehyun Kim is Director of the Foreign Policy and Security Studies Program of The Sejong Institute.

Hong Pyo Lee is a Fellow in the Area Studies Program of The Sejong Institute.

Myonwoo Lee is a Fellow in the Area Studies Program of The Sejong Institute.

Norman D. Levin is a Senior Policy Analyst in the International Policy Department, RAND.

Julia Lowell is an Economist in the International Policy Department, RAND.

Jonathan D. Pollack is Senior Advisor for International Policy, RAND.

Courtney Purrington is a Political Scientist in the International Policy Department, RAND.

Michael D. Swaine is Co-Director of the Center for Asia-Pacific Policy, and a Senior Policy Analyst in the International Policy Department, RAND.

Ashley Tellis is a Political Scientist in the International Policy Department, RAND.

# Section I

# China's Future

The first conference session was devoted to three papers on China, with particular attention to the outcome of the impending succession process. (The papers by Jae-Cheol Kim and Hong Pyo Lee have been merged in the conference volume.) There was a broad congruence of views on the probable outcome of the succession to Deng Xiaoping, with Jiang Zemin likely to emerge as Deng's successor, at least in the early post-Deng period. But the RAND participants seemed more prepared to entertain the possibility of discontinuous scenarios, principally in the mid-to longer term. Both research teams recognized China's incentives for a stable outcome in the succession process, and a parallel Chinese interest in maintaining its outwardly oriented development policies of the past decade and a half. But there was clear concern about whether the current successor leadership would be able over the longer run to maintain a working consensus across a broad spectrum of issues and societal pressures they may yet confront.

Analysts from RAND and Sejong both recognized the potential weakness of political arrangements in a government based on men rather than on laws or institutions. Under such circumstances, the capacity of leaders less confident of their authority to manage looming social, political, and institutional changes is far from certain. Some participants called attention to the increased reliance on nationalism as an integrative theme for the new leadership. Over the longer run, the challenge posed for a successor leadership intent on building its authority could prove very difficult, and might lead to a more polarized political environment.

Several conferees called attention to the contradiction between China's growing economic links with the outside world and the lack of a self-confident successor leadership able to effectively manage its external political ties. Though under some circumstances the necessity of such external ties might move the Chinese toward a more collaborative policy orientation, in other contexts Chinese behavior might be far less cooperative. The consequences of China's military modernization are particularly important in this context. Though a more robust Chinese military capability would not necessarily predict a more risk-prone foreign policy, it could result in a more politically assertive state, which could entail challenges to Beijing's smaller neighbors, including Korea.

The implications of the shifting situation in North Korea also stimulated much discussion, in particular how increased signs of instability in the North might influence future Chinese policy calculations. Several participants argued that under some circumstances (and for their own interests, rather than those of the North Korean leadership), the Chinese might well be intent on preserving the present system in North Korea, if only to ensure that nominally socialist systems persist in some form in Korea as well as China. This raised possible circumstances that could be less favorable to the interests of the Republic of Korea.

Although no final consensus was reached on these issues, all agreed that China's political future—including potential challenges to the regime's legitimacy and authority—was likely to prove among the decisive policy factors in East Asia over the coming decade. This would be especially critical should the momentum behind China's rapid economic development begin to falter.

# Chapter One

# LEADERSHIP SUCCESSION IN CHINA: IMPLICATIONS FOR DOMESTIC AND REGIONAL STABILITY

Michael D. Swaine

## INTRODUCTION

As a rapidly developing economic and military power with expanding links to the outside world, China's future evolution arguably constitutes the most critical variable influencing the Asia-Pacific security environment. However, China today faces many internal problems, especially an impending passage of the remaining revolutionary era leaders, possibly resulting in a very unstable leadership transition. The outcome of this process could exert a major, indeed decisive, impact on China's future domestic order and Chinese policy toward the region.

This paper assesses the likelihood that the process of leadership succession underway in China will undermine domestic and regional stability. It is divided into three major sections. The first section analyzes the major factors that could produce leadership instability during the succession. The second section identifies and assesses several scenarios of leadership and regime instability that might result from the succession process. The final section examines the implications that major alternative succession scenarios might present for China's policy toward the Asia Pacific region.

## SOURCES OF LEADERSHIP INSTABILITY

China's current political-military leadership system exhibits several basic features that could produce significant domestic instability in the aftermath of the death of Deng Xiaoping. The first feature is intrinsic to the nature of a Leninist system. The second feature is rooted in the characteristics of the post-Tiananmen successor leadership. The third feature derives from the policy issues facing a post-Deng leadership.

## The Succession Dilemma

The most fundamental flaw confronting the Chinese leadership system is the absence of any institutionalized or regularized process for wielding and transferring supreme political power. As with other Leninist regimes, political power at the pinnacle of the system resides in the individual, not in legal norms, formal institutions, or regularized procedures.[1] Hence, the dominant leader in this system emerges through a process of contention among various aspirants to power.

To be successful in this struggle, a contender must possess, to varying degrees, at least four essential attributes:

- Bonds of loyalty and trust with colleagues and subordinates in party, state, and army organs, established through long-term personal relationships or blood ties;

- Political skills to co-opt, convince, or coerce less powerful colleagues to either support him or acquiesce to his exercise of power;

- The ability to utilize party, state, and military bureaucracies and procedures to serve his political ends;

- The ability to devise successful policies to cope with or avoid major problems that could divide the leadership or undermine the system.

In order to survive and succeed politically, a leader must usually compensate for an insufficiency in one or more of these attributes by possessing others in abundance. For example, a leader with weak personal networks must compensate for this constraint by possess-

---

[1]This factor is reinforced, in the Chinese case, by a long history of individual rule and the general emphasis in Chinese culture on a monistic political structure.

ing an extremely high capability to manipulate the bureaucracy, to persuade others, and to formulate effective policy solutions.[2]

The transfer of power in such a system entails a fundamental dilemma for the incumbent leader and for his presumed successor. In the absence of any institutionalized process of leadership selection, the dominant leader invariably seeks to choose his own successor, in order to preserve political order after his death and to maximize the chances that his policies will continue and his reputation will remain unblemished. Yet this process rarely succeeds, for two closely related reasons: (1) the dominant leader cannot transfer his own political skills and resulting authority to his designated successor, so the latter must build his own authority; and (2) the designated successor is almost invariably prevented by the dominant leader from building authority in the pre-succession stage, because the latter usually fears that his protégé would seek to overthrow him if he is allowed to amass too much power. As a result, the dominant leader either purges his designated successor before the latter has a chance to assume power or the successor fails to consolidate his position after the death of his mentor and is overthrown. This, in turn, tends to precipitate an open and potentially paralyzing struggle among the remaining aspirants to power, which can threaten the leadership arrangements and the stability of the entire system.

Both of these outcomes occurred in China during and immediately following the Mao Zedong era.[3] In the eighties, Deng Xiaoping made great efforts to increase the likelihood that his designated successors,

---

[2]Given the critical importance of personal relations in China, however, any individual who possesses few personal "guanxi" ties will usually be at a major disadvantage in comparison to those who command extensive personal networks, regardless of his capabilities in other areas.

[3]Liu Shaoqi and Lin Biao, both designated successors to Mao Zedong, were overthrown by the Great Helmsman during the upheaval of the Cultural Revolution of the sixties and seventies. Although a powerful party and government leader, Liu was condemned for allegedly advocating revisionist practices that undermined Mao's rule. Lin Biao, a famous military officer, Defense Minister, and critical backer of Mao during the height of the Cultural Revolution, died in a plane crash in Mongolia while trying to flee China, allegedly after having failed in an effort to seize power from the Chairman. In the late seventies, Hua Guofeng ascended to China's most powerful party, state and military posts as Mao Zedong's personally chosen successor. Yet he lacked most of the personal attributes necessary to consolidate power and was soon displaced and eventually overthrown by Deng Xiaoping.

first Hu Yaobang and subsequently Zhao Ziyang, would attain and consolidate power in a smooth and stable manner. Yet Deng ultimately succumbed to the suspicions generated by the succession dilemma and proved unwilling to fully relinquish power to either man. He purged both leaders during the final years of the decade, with Zhao falling from power during the Tiananmen upheavals of April-June 1989.[4] These actions reaffirmed that power in China remained highly personalized and in the hands of the gerontocrats, and that any successor's ability to build authority in the system while Deng remained alive would remain highly circumscribed.

### The Successor Leadership

It is no surprise that the current post-Tiananmen successor leadership suffers from many political shortcomings, both as a group and individually. In contrast to the revolutionary "generalists" of the Mao Zedong generation, who enjoyed extensive personal links to colleagues throughout the party, state, and military apparatus, the successors are all "bureaucratic technocrats" with relatively narrow experience in party or government administration and limited personal contacts elsewhere in the leadership structure. Especially important, none of the major candidates for the succession enjoy strong, direct ties to the military leadership, an essential attribute of past dominant leaders. Moreover, none appear to possess the vision and overall prestige of revolutionary leaders such as Mao Zedong, Zhou Enlai, or Deng Xiaoping. In sum, as a group, the successor leadership possesses weaker factional bases, far lower popular prestige, less control over the major institutions of rule and perhaps a lower ability to cope with major problems than their predecessors.

An assessment of the leading contenders for the succession further illustrates these shortcomings. Four members of the Politburo Standing Committee will likely wield the greatest influence in the formal leadership structure after the death of Deng Xiaoping: Jiang Zemin, Li Peng, Qiao Shi, and Zhu Rongji. Although each man con-

---

[4]Zhao Ziyang had attained a significant level of leadership authority during the mid-eighties. However, during the Tiananmen crisis, Deng and his retired elderly colleagues soon pushed Zhao aside and made all the critical decisions of that period, ignoring all "normal" party procedures.

trols significant political resources, each also exhibits critical deficiencies that could limit his ability to consolidate power as a dominant leader.

Jiang Zemin (born 1926) is clearly the leading figure among the four. Anointed by Deng as "the core of the third generation of leaders" (the first being led by Mao and the second by Deng), Jiang is most closely associated with Deng's reform policies, which enjoy strong, although certainly not unanimous, support throughout the leadership and society. Perhaps more important, Jiang also holds all three of China's top party, state, and military posts (i.e., General Secretary of the Chinese Communist Party (CCP), President of the People's Republic of China (PRC), and Chairman of the Central Military Commission) and reportedly heads several small leadership groups that exercise executive power in key policy arenas such as financial and economic affairs, Taiwan affairs, and political-legal affairs.

Such a concentration of formal power facilitates Jiang's efforts to build authority in all four of the critical areas mentioned above, i.e., by expanding his network of personal contacts, his influence over personnel selection and the agenda setting process, his control over key bureaucratic levers, and his knowledge of critical policy issues. For example, Jiang has worked especially hard to improve his ties to the military leadership since 1990, while generally portraying himself as supportive of professional military interests. He may also have established a base of support within the People's Armed Police (PAP), a key organ charged with the maintenance of domestic stability and a crucial buffer between society and the regular military. In addition, Jiang has reportedly attempted to increase his stature within the country by playing a more prominent role in the international arena as head of state. Jiang may also enjoy significant support outside of Beijing, as a result of long service in the Shanghai area as a leading party and government official.

While significant, Jiang's advantages are greatly counterbalanced by several major weaknesses. First, according to observers in Beijing, Deng believes that Jiang Zemin has amassed excessive power and taken some actions of which he disapproves. If true, this could severely undermine Jiang's authority as Deng's hand-picked successor, providing ammunition to potential rivals. Second, despite strenuous efforts, Jiang has not yet developed a strong power base in key party, state, and military organs. For example, PLA officers in the central military departments in Beijing insist that Jiang's links to the PLA remain very weak. Third, by many accounts Jiang is not a particularly competent administrator or problem solver. Many Chinese familiar with Jiang's career view him as a political opportunist, adept principally at reading and responding to the shifting political winds. While perhaps useful for survival under Deng's shadow, such qualities do not inspire confidence and loyalty toward him as an independent figure.

Li Peng (born 1928) is often viewed as Jiang's major rival in the successor leadership. Li possesses three major political assets. First, as Premier of the State Council, he is the formal leader of the government and thus a key player in critical economic and institutional policy areas. Second, Li is chairman of the small leading group responsible for foreign affairs and thus probably a major architect of the foreign policy successes China has enjoyed in recent years. Third, Li probably enjoys the support of a few surviving hard-line elders such as Peng Zhen, as well as ideologues within the party propaganda apparatus who regained positions of influence after Tiananmen. But the April 1995 death of Chen Yun, a very influential elder leader and Deng's major rival during the reform period, is a clear setback for Li.

Despite some potential advantages, Li Peng labors under major political weaknesses. First and foremost, Li is an extremely unpopular figure, largely because of his close association with the suppression of the Tiananmen demonstrators in June 1989. Second, like Jiang Zemin, Li Peng is considered a man of modest administrative abilities. Many knowledgeable observers believe that Li rose through the party and state hierarchy largely by virtue of his stature as the adopted son of the late Premier Zhou Enlai and through the personal support of powerful patrons such as Chen Yun. Third, with a narrow background as a state economic cadre, Li has few political roots among China's increasingly important regional leaders. Fourth, nothing in Li Peng's career as a technical cadre and state official suggests that he enjoys significant connections to the military. Finally, Li is past retirement age for senior officials and is coming to the end of his tenure as Premier, thus suggesting that he will need to relinquish formal control over the government bureaucracy. Together, such major shortcomings indicate that Li

Peng's political destiny might be that of a spoiler at best, i.e., able to obstruct others but not able to wield supreme power in his own right.

Qiao Shi (born 1924) is perhaps the most enigmatic figure within the successor leadership.  Although a strong supporter of Deng's reforms, his political loyalties and intentions are extremely difficult to ascertain.  Qiao has generally stayed out of the public limelight.  However, his career history suggests that he wields considerable influence behind the scenes and possesses significant political and institutional resources.  He has held many influential and sensitive leadership posts within key central party bureaucracies, especially in the areas of party intelligence/security and political/legal affairs.  Such positions, and the personal ties that they undoubtedly engendered, provided Qiao with access to the critical functions of internal party surveillance and control and the personnel selection process.  In addition, Qiao has reportedly added to his power base through service as head of the National People's Congress.  Finally, unlike Jiang Zemin and Li Peng, Qiao Shi is widely viewed as a very capable administrator.

Despite his bureaucratic connections and administrative capabilities, Qiao also suffers from major political shortcomings.  First, the absence of any clear, strong political affiliations with the party leadership probably makes it difficult for others to assess his loyalties and hence engenders distrust.  Second, Qiao has few apparent ties to important institutions outside the central party and state organs, which greatly limits his personal network.  In particular, as with the other senior leaders, he enjoys few if any direct ties to the military, although his lengthy service as head of the CCP Political and Legal Affairs Commission may have provided him with some links to the People's Armed Police, since that apparatus has major responsibility for party activities within the PAP.

Zhu Rongji (born 1928) possesses many important political attributes.  As a former long-term industrial cadre and a strong proponent of economic reform, his power base is centered largely in the crucial economic arena.  Indeed, in recent years, he has served as the leading official in charge of the reform effort, with a particular responsibility for reestablishing central control over the financial sector.  Zhu may also enjoy regional support in the Shanghai area as a result of several years service as a leading party and state official, similar to Jiang Zemin. In addition, while mayor of Shanghai, Zhu developed a reputation as a tough, uncompromising administrator acceptable to foreigners. He also gained support from some pro-democracy elements because of his moderate stance toward Shanghai demonstrators during the spring 1989 protests and his subsequent attempts to shield Shanghai intellectuals from the conservative crackdown of 1989-90.

Yet Zhu Rongji has perhaps the greatest number of political deficiencies of any leading candidate for the succession. His considerable capability in dealing with foreigners, as well as his apparent popularity in Western circles as an open-minded leader, may work against him, given the widespread fear of external influence and the xenophobic strain still evident in the Chinese political system. In addition, Zhu is known for mistreating his subordinates, which has undoubtedly alienated many potential supporters. He is also regarded as an excessively ambitious figure among mainstream party cadres. Finally, as with his colleagues, Zhu enjoys few links to the military.

In sum, none of the above four individuals appears to display a sufficient level of the essential attributes that would permit one of them to attain and maintain dominance over the post-Deng political scene.

## Beyond the Inner Circle:  Surviving Elders, Once Defeated Challengers, and Princelings

Aside from the internal problems of the successor leadership, several major political outsiders could also undermine the prospects for a smooth and stable transition after Deng's death. As suggested above, several aged, formally retired yet still influential party and military cadres such as Peng Zhen, Bo Yibo, Song Ping, Wan Li, and Deng Liqun remain on the scene and will likely survive Deng. One or more of these individuals might seek to replace one of the designated successors such as Jiang Zemin with their own candidate for supreme leadership.

The current leadership situation is also complicated by the continued presence on the political scene of assorted "failed" aspirants to supreme power who may be looking for another opportunity to reenter politics.  Most notable among this group is former PRC President and CMC First Vice Chairman Yang Shangkun.  Yang (along with his younger half-brother, former General Political Department head Yang Baibing) was removed from power at the 14th Party Congress in the Fall of 1992 for purportedly attempting to develop a factional network designed to control the post-Deng succession and overthrow Jiang Zemin.  Although currently off the formal political stage, one or both Yangs could attempt a comeback in a post-Deng setting. Indeed, Yang Shangkun has been increasingly visible in recent months, having visited several critically important cities and regions. As an elder revolutionary, he retains considerable prestige and extensive organizational contacts.  Moreover, he is still respected in some leadership circles as a skillful party administrator and a leader of the reform effort in the mid-eighties, including military reform.

A further complication is presented by the continued presence in the political wings of former party leader Zhao Ziyang.  Zhao was a major proponent of radical reform, decentralization, and the open door in the eighties and a vocal opponent of the use of military force during the Tiananmen crisis.  Hence, he could conceivably play an important political role in any post-Deng succession struggle as a lightning rod for various progressive (or purely ambitious) forces opposed to Jiang Zemin or Li Peng.  After Deng's death, such individuals might attempt to align with (or use) Zhao in an effort to force a reversal of verdicts on Tiananmen and thereby fatally compromise the position of Li and Jiang.

Finally, the influential sons and daughters of China's senior party leadership could also destabilize the succession process.  Some of these individuals, known as "princelings," occupy important posts within leading party, state, and military organs.  Few are currently viewed as politically ambitious figures in their own right; most are concentrating on making money.  However, this situation could change rapidly after the passing of Deng and other Party elders.  For example, many "princelings" could become targets of veiled (or open) criticism, as the excessively privileged (and often corrupt) sons and daughters of party and military officials, thus precipitating conflict among the successors.  Recent turnover in the Beijing Municipal Party apparatus, including the resignation of First Secretary Chen Xitong in the aftermath of attacks on high level corruption, could be a harbinger of future steps, and could suggest vulnerabilities of some within "princeling" circles. Under such circumstances, senior "princelings" could seek to manipulate or influence potential successors or ally with some leaders to block or replace others.

## Potential Policy Challenges

In addition to the above systemic weaknesses and internal leadership problems, a number of specific policy issues have the potential to seriously destabilize the post-Deng succession. Such a destabilization could occur in one of two ways: (1) policy issues might evolve into crises that divide the successor leadership, or (2) a putative successor might seek to "manage" or control an issue in a manner that prompts strong resistance from his colleagues.

Perhaps the most important potential policy problems are in the economic arena. In order to reduce persistent inflationary pressures and yet assure continued high levels of growth, future Chinese leaders will likely seek to: (1) raise efficiency by drastically increasing the level of privatization in the economy, thereby loosening controls over land, labor, and capital; and (2) increase the economic resources and policy levers available to the central government by strengthening national control over the tax collection system and enhancing the state's fiscal capabilities. Such actions would threaten the monopoly power of the party and further aggravate relations between central and local authorities in China, already a major source of tension in the system. Differences within the successor leadership over how to handle such critical issues could precipitate open conflict among them.[5]

A second set of critical problems relates to China's defense modernization effort. Continued improvements in the military's force structure, organizational efficiency, and warfighting capability will require: (1) major decreases in the number and size of China's main ground force units; (2) significant adjustments in the balance among China's air, naval, and land forces; (3) far less interference in purely

---

[5]Specifically, such economic issues could exacerbate latent differences within the top leadership over the pace and extent of economic reform. One viewpoint stresses the maintenance of a strong public sector in the economy and greater government controls, especially at the central level. Another viewpoint supports a much more rapid pace of advance and a larger private sector.

military affairs by party-directed political commissars, and (4) major increases in government funds for critical areas such as weapons procurement and military research and development.  In addition, the continued decline in military morale, along with increasing military corruption, will likely demand greater attention in the future.  All of these issues are highly controversial and could precipitate major leadership conflict.

The third set of problems falls within the foreign and security policy realm.  On the broadest level, continued economic and military modernization could increase pressures to resolve important debates over critical aspects of China's security strategy, such as the relative emphasis placed on continental versus maritime orientations and the proper definition of critical strategic boundaries.  More narrowly, latent differences over China's stance toward Taiwan, the Spratly Islands in the South China Sea, and other highly sensitive regional issues linked to Chinese nationalist sentiments could also incite conflict among the successors, especially if external events were to exacerbate tensions in these areas.  Recent adverse developments in U.S.-China relations, though partly reflecting Chinese anger at the U.S. issuing of a visa to Taiwan President Lee Teng-hui, very likely derive from the interplay of different leadership forces, suggesting the growing connections between the succession process and China's foreign and security policy orientation.

Finally, conflict among the successor leadership could be precipitated or aggravated by sensitive social issues.  The future handling of the Tiananmen Incident is perhaps the most important such issue.  The actions of the leadership in suppressing the massive demonstrations of April-June 1989 and declaring them a counter-revolutionary rebellion continue to generate great controversy within Chinese society.  In a post-Deng setting, pressures could grow to reassess these events.  Some members of the successor leadership unconnected to Tiananmen (e.g., Zhu Rongji) might press for at least a partial reversal of the official verdict in order to undermine the position of hardliners associated with the crisis (e.g., Li Peng), increase their general popularity, and elicit support from potential sympathizers within the bureaucracy.  Others would likely seek to defend the official verdict.  This dispute could easily generate intense conflict among the successors.

## SCENARIOS OF LEADERSHIP CONFLICT

The above features of leadership politics and the policy environment in China suggest that the death of Deng Xiaoping could precipitate a severe struggle among the successors in many different ways. At least four possible scenarios come to mind. They are not mutually exclusive; indeed, some could occur simultaneously, or in sequence.

First, Deng's death might release a floodgate of opposition to Jiang Zemin within the current leadership. Remaining members of the gerontocracy, supported by specific followers in the Politburo Standing Committee, could ally against Jiang, charging him with disloyalty to Deng Xiaoping, political incompetence, etc. This scenario assumes that the level of opposition to Jiang within the senior levels of the leadership is very high, and had been held in check only through Deng's continued presence.

Second, Jiang Zemin might move against his most powerful colleagues and political opponents, thus precipitating open conflict. A Leninist system provides a weak basis for enduring bonds of trust among leaders. Thus, strong incentives exist for any successor to oust his erstwhile colleagues and seize exclusive power. Following Deng's death, Jiang Zemin could attempt to consolidate his control over the political apparatus by placing trusted outsiders in high posts while removing any potential challengers from leading organs in Beijing, thereby provoking a general leadership struggle. Recent moves by Jiang against the CCP apparatus in Beijing suggest that he is pursuing such a strategy even prior to Deng's death. Jiang's actions also indicate that the increasing infirmity of various Party elders is enabling Jiang to more fully consolidate his power position.

Third, influential outsiders might yet mount a challenge against Jiang and his closest associates, seeking an alliance with other potential successors. This scenario assumes that former senior officials such as Yang Shangkun or Zhao Ziyang, or individual princelings, enjoy significant support within critical institutions or among the senior levels of the elite. The Tiananmen issue could serve as a catalyst for such a challenge from the outside.

Fourth, Jiang Zemin might fail to handle a key challenge to the leadership or the political system. As noted above, effectiveness in handling major policy problems is a critical requirement for success, especially if a putative successor has a limited personal network of supporters and limited influence over key bureaucracies. Jiang might prove totally incapable of dealing effectively with major challenges to the regime after Deng's death, thus precipitating an effort to oust him from power.

Any of these scenarios could result in severe and open conflict within the successor leadership. But would such conflict precipitate widespread political and social unrest destabilizing to the entire regime? This would depend, in large part, upon two critical factors: (1) the general socio-economic environment; and (2) the role played by key institutions such as the military.

Historically in China, political legitimacy has been closely associated with a strong, unified central government under the control of a single, wise leader. Hence, a weak, irresolute center mired in conflict connotes illegitimacy and a lack of virtue among the leadership. Such a government engenders popular contempt and invites challenges from the outside. The chances of such an outcome are heightened at present due to the low level of respect accorded the communist regime in general and the widespread anxieties and concerns about the future evident within the populace and among many officials. Numerous citizens are especially angered by the growing corruption of cadres at all levels of the party and government, and are concerned that economic reform might stall, or produce greater hardships as privatization efforts move forward. Jiang Zemin's recent attacks on high level corruption reflect his effort to identify with this popular resentment, though it remains to be seen whether he will be able to direct any such campaigns to his full advantage.

But resentment against the regime would become particularly intense if the economy were in decline. The ability to maintain high levels of economic growth and rising living standards for the people has become the principal remaining source of legitimacy for the Chinese government. If the regime is failing in this task as leadership conflict breaks out (indeed, economic failure could be a cause of that conflict), the likelihood of popular protest would increase exponentially.

Given the demoralized and ineffectual state of the party apparatus, the Chinese military remains the last potential institutional bulwark against social instability that could result from an open, paralyzing succession struggle. Unified military intervention would be especially likely if several influential retired military elders were still active. These individuals might pressure their "subordinates" within the formal military hierarchy to directly intervene, and would probably also serve to maintain unity within the military.

Military involvement in leadership politics might not promote order and stability, however. Historically, senior military figures have enjoyed close personal contacts with their counterparts in the party apparatus. Indeed, the two groups originally formed a single cohort of party-army revolutionaries. As a result, at times, key military figures such as Lin Biao played destabilizing roles in elite struggle. Thus, in a post-Deng succession contest, the military could become drawn into the fray as individual contenders reach out to military leaders for support. As a result, regional forces at various levels might be prompted by their officers to take action against one another.[6] Alternatively, the military leadership might become completely paralyzed, due to an absence of clear directives from above and its own internal debates. In either case, the outcome for the regime would almost certainly be disastrous.

Is it likely that the succession process will produce one or more of the above highly destabilizing scenarios? Despite the many weaknesses of the system outlined above, the most dire domestic outcomes will probably not occur, especially over the short term. To the contrary, strong incentives exist for the formation of a relatively stable cooperative leadership structure after the departure of Deng Xiaoping.[7] First, the weakness of the party structure and the intense social pressures on the regime will probably promote greater, not less, cooperation among the elite. Each member of the successor leadership realizes that a severe power struggle could lead, at worst, to disaster

---

[6]This danger is increased by two fundamental characteristics of the military command and control system: (1) it presents major irregularities in procedure and potential ambiguities in authority relationships; and (2) it permits direct access by the command center in Beijing to individual combat units. These features could enable military and party elders or their associates within the top military leadership to issue direct orders to factional associates among regional forces in a time of extreme crisis.

[7]Such a structure could consist of a genuinely collective leadership or, more likely, a structure in which a single figure was "first among equals," but definitely not a dominant figure with the power of a Deng Xiaoping.

for them all and at best, to direct military intervention in politics (see below for more on the last point).

Second, the few strengths and apparent weaknesses displayed by each of the foremost contenders suggests the basis for a roughly stable balance of power among them. Each controls a major institution and at least one major policy arena, yet none enjoys a clear advantage in critical political attributes that could motivate him to risk a power play. Moreover, none of the four primary contenders *appears* to stand in implacable opposition to any of his colleagues, unlike the situation during the succession to Mao, when the radical Gang of Four clearly squared off against top party veterans.[8]

Third, there is some evidence to suggest that most, if not all, of the remaining elders support the current successor lineup and will seek to preserve it. Reports in the Hong Kong press and private interviews conducted by the author in Beijing suggest that the leading elders have formed an informal shadow government to fulfill this goal.

Fourth, on the policy level, the successor leadership exhibits an unprecedented degree of consensus on many critical issues, especially when compared to the Maoist period. The utopian or ideologically-motivated views of radical Maoists have been thoroughly repudiated, while orthodox Leninist or Stalinist views are in a distinct minority. In their place, a pragmatic, development-oriented approach to policy holds sway, largely eclipsing potential differences over the pace and scope of reform. Thus, a future policy crisis might evoke similar responses from the successor leadership, rather than serve to drive them apart. A cooperative approach to policy issues is also dictated by China's highly fragmented, incremental policymaking process.[9] Moreover, these factors strongly suggest that few incentives will exist for any leader to make sudden shifts in policy direction.

---

[8]Here, of course, a major caveat is presented by potential outside challengers, discussed further below.

[9]Such an policy environment facilitates obstructionist activities by middle level party and government bureaucrats fearful that further reforms will diminish their power, prestige, and perquisites. Under these conditions, politically weak successors will need to cooperate in many issue areas to ensure even a modicum of policy results. This is especially true in the economic arena.

Fifth, and perhaps most important, the military has no apparent reason to reorder the current succession lineup or back a challenge to Jiang Zemin as the "core" of the successor leadership. Indeed, Jiang probably enjoys the personal support of increasingly influential senior officers such as Defense Minister Chi Haotian, a member of the dominant faction within the military leadership. In contrast, none of his potential rivals enjoy close personal ties to military leaders that could be used to elicit support in a future struggle. Moreover, despite his reportedly poor reputation among many military personnel, Jiang Zemin has done much to address the military's institutional concerns during the past five years. Finally, the military leadership as a group wishes to stay out of politics and concentrate instead on professional concerns and the defense modernization effort.[10]

These factors suggest that some form of cooperative leadership structure, probably (but not necessarily) led by Jiang Zemin, will survive for some time after the death of Deng Xiaoping. The greatest danger to this leadership structure in the short term will probably come from prominent outsiders such as Yang Shangkun and perhaps Zhao Ziyang.[11] Some analysts have even speculated that the two former leaders might ally to challenge the successor leadership. Yet senior military and party leaders would have few reasons to support such a potentially destabilizing challenge and several reasons to oppose it. Many senior military leaders, including a large number of retired yet influential military elders, reportedly dislike Yang Shangkun intensely and would resist any attempt by him to regain power. In addition, cautious, conservative military leaders would likely prove very resistant to a Zhao Ziyang-led power bid, given the former party leader's close identification with those opposed to the Tiananmen crackdown and his support for a more radical approach to economic reform.

A cooperative leadership structure will likely face the greatest pressures over the longer term (i.e. one to three years). Strong incentives will remain for any successor to seek advantage over his associates by

---

[10]The most senior members of the active military, Generals Liu Huaqing and Zhang Zhen, reportedly do not harbor political ambitions.

[11]The author finds it very difficult to imagine that an alliance of princelings or a single princeling could garner enough support to launch a serious bid for power.

establishing stronger links to the bureaucracy and expanding his personal network. Moreover, serious policy problems are more likely to emerge over the longer term, placing greater strains on the leadership. Such developments would likely result in a less stable but still workable cooperative leadership structure. Over time, however, this successor leadership will probably become increasingly susceptible to direct and indirect military influence. Individual leaders will be increasingly inclined to cultivate the military for fear that it might intervene in favor of someone else. Moreover, as a group, the successor leadership group will also be motivated to placate the military on key domestic and foreign policy issues in order to keep it focused on professional concerns, not on political intervention. This could eventually lead to de facto military control of the central government. Yet, as noted above, the military would probably only seek to displace the successor leadership if an open succession struggle eventually broke out and threatened to destabilize the regime.

## IMPLICATIONS FOR THE ASIA-PACIFIC REGION

The above leadership succession scenarios pose several implications for China's future regional posture toward Asia.[12] An open, paralyzing succession struggle (probably accompanied by prolonged economic decline or stagnation), destabilizing military involvement, and widespread social unrest, could produce a weak, insecure, and defensive foreign policy, aimed at preventing foreign intervention or complete regime collapse. Major tenets of this approach would likely include:

- The clear identification of Japan or the United States as a major threat to Chinese security

- Greatly increased concerns over challenges to Chinese territory, perhaps leading to major deployments of military forces in the Spratlys

- A more suspicious/hostile stance toward Western-sponsored positions in the United Nations and other international fora

---

[12]The following presentation of alternative Chinese foreign policy approaches is drawn largely from Michael D. Swaine, *China: Domestic Change and Foreign Policy*, RAND, MR-604-OSD, 1995.

- Increasing pressures on Taiwan and Hong Kong

- Greater efforts to reassert central control over foreign economic activities, involving more repressive government policies

Under such a scenario, civilian leaders would encounter increasing pressures to adopt a more assertive, nationalistic foreign policy stance (including the creation or claim of a severe foreign threat to China from Japan or the United States) to ensure more unified military support and divert public attention from the declining domestic situation. This could lead to even greater leadership disarray, however. Under such circumstances, China's resulting external policy stance could involve sudden or sharp confrontations with the West. Such behavior would reflect a highly *defensive* posture, motivated by the widespread belief, held by many Chinese leaders, that a weakened Chinese state invites foreign aggression.

If social unrest spread, the military fractured, and unresolved (and possibly violent) conflicts continued among both civilian and military successor leaderships, the result would likely be:

- A mass exodus of refugees to neighboring states and regions

- Major ethnic unrest along China's Western borders

- The emergence, among many provinces or regions, of highly independent external economic policies

Such a dangerous scenario could draw sub-national conservative and more pro-reform officials into the conflict and even lead, under certain circumstances, to the sporadic use of regional forces in support of contending factions. Such severe instability would be especially likely if no party or military elders remained on the political stage to maintain discipline and unity among younger civilian and military leaders.

The more likely alternative of an unstable cooperative leadership with growing yet indirect levels of military influence would probably produce a less cooperative, more confident Chinese foreign stance, aimed at regional dominance, but not through direct military action. The major tenets of this external policy approach would probably include:

- Development of a growing power projection ability and increased regional economic clout, to intimidate or greatly influence the actions of smaller states, including Korea and the ASEAN countries

- Increased challenges to U.S. interests (e.g., regarding regional or bilateral trade, Taiwan, counter-proliferation, human rights, policy toward Japan and Russia, etc.)

- More concerted attempts to diversify external economic links while developing the domestic market

Under such a scenario, China's current emphasis on rapid civilian-oriented economic growth would largely give way to the nationalist goals of the defense of national sovereignty and territory and the attainment of big power status.  This would likely lead to a foreign policy keyed to Chinese expectations of more local conflicts, increasing pressures for arms competition in the region, heightened challenges to territorial claims, and greater Chinese concerns over Japan's reemergence as a military power, instability in Inner Asia, and alleged U.S. efforts at containment.

Finally, the most likely succession scenario, a relatively stable cooperative leadership with controllable levels of military involvement in politics, would likely mean a continuation of China's current foreign policy, marked by overall caution and pragmatism, a recognition of the ongoing need for a placid regional environment to permit an emphasis on further economic reform, and a balancing of both cooperation and competition with the West.  Central elements of this approach include:

- The search for closer diplomatic relations with potential economic and political rivals of the United States such as Japan, Germany, or India

- The development of common interests with many Third World (and especially Asian) states, in order to raise China's global stature and increase Beijing's bargaining leverage with the United States and Japan, especially on important economic and political issues

- Increased, albeit highly limited, support for multilateral approaches to various Asian security issues, primarily intended to allay fears concerning China's future intentions toward the region while minimizing constraints on Chinese behavior

- Support for the full resumption of official political and military dialogues and exchanges with the United States and its allies, combined with limited concessions on major U.S. concerns such as human rights, arms sales, and trade

- Maintenance of positive relations with the Central Asian republics and major centers of Islamic influence such as Iran, through enhanced trade and investment links, expanding diplomatic ties, and Chinese assistance in critical development areas, including nuclear power

In general, Beijing's diplomatic approach in these and other areas increasingly seeks to draw upon China's growing involvement in the Asian and world economy. Chinese strategy stresses the use of economic appeals and/or leverage to build international support for diplomatic and security objectives and to make major powers aware that opposing core Chinese interests will likely undermine their own economic interests. This suggests a Chinese emphasis on the economic arena as an increasingly important domain of international competition.

Despite the likelihood of such trends, the uncertainties of the impending succession process should not be minimized. The nature of the Chinese leadership system, and the outcome of this process will have important effects on the contours of the post-Deng Xiaoping China, and hence on China's policy options in the region and beyond.

# Chapter Two

# POST-DENG CHINA AND NORTHEAST ASIA: INVITATION TO INSTABILITY?

Jae-Cheol Kim & Hong Pyo Lee

## INTRODUCTION

Interest in China's future after Deng Xiaoping has been growing rapidly in Asia as well as in the West. This can be attributed largely to two major policy considerations. First, China's economic and institutional reforms and its opening to the outside world have already transformed the character of the Chinese system. Both the success and side effects of the Deng era policies are impelling the post-Deng leadership aspirants to determine new measures and next steps in national policy. Second, China has clearly entered a period of transition. Deng Xiaoping, who has been China's paramount leader for more than one and half decades, will soon "go to meet Marx." Rumors of his imminent demise are ever present. According to recent reports, China's media, including *People's Daily* (*Renmin Ribao*), have started preparations for editorials and commentaries that will be published following the leader's death. Given Deng's central role in Chinese politics and external policies over the last 15 years, his death will have a significant impact on China's future.

What will China be like after Deng dies? In particular, will the post-Deng regime be able to consolidate and build upon the accomplishments of the Deng era? Or will Deng's death trigger political turmoil, a leadership power struggle, and even social unrest? What will be the fate of the current policies of reform and economic opening, and how might future developments affect China's international orientation? These are the questions that increasingly draw the attention of scholars, strategists, and policy makers.

China specialists in the West are generally sanguine about China's future. Most appear to believe, albeit to different degrees, that China will continue to pursue its course of economic reform and opening to the outside world. This change in the evaluation of China's future, especially compared to 1989 and 1990 when one communist country after another collapsed, reflects developments in China's domestic situation over the last five years. Despite some arduous problems, the Chinese economy has maintained high growth rates throughout this period, leading to appreciable improvement in people's living standards. This success definitely increases the chance of a successful, minimally disruptive leadership transition.

In addition, in light of the unfolding situation in the former Soviet Union and in East European countries after the sudden collapse of the communist regimes, many Chinese have concluded that the end of the communist regime could be severely detrimental to the interests and well-being of the Chinese people. Remembering the tragedy of the Cultural Revolution, many fear that the sudden collapse of the communist regime would plunge the country into a chaos.[1] Last, but not least, despite the country's extraordinary transformation in the wake of economic reform and the opening to the outside world, the Chinese Communist Party (CCP) still retains a significant capacity to shape future events within China. Chinese society and its associated institutions are still far weaker than those of its counterparts in the Soviet Union and East European countries in their last phase. These differences strongly suggest that the possibility of China experiencing a sudden breakdown of political authority remains relatively slim.

However, it would be imprudent to totally discount the possibility of instability in post-Deng China. It is not yet clear whether Jiang Zemin, Deng's chosen successor, can consolidate his power and authority once Deng dies. Even if Jiang manages to hold on and to maintain the current policies of reform and external opening, it remains to be seen how well he and his colleagues can deal with the challenges and tensions inherent in these policies, such as the increasing demand for political reform and regional and sectoral in-

---

[1]Richard Baum, "Political Stability in Post-Deng China: Problems and Prospects," *Asian Survey*, June 1992, p.493.

equities. Therefore, it is still conceivable that future political developments could jeopardize domestic stability and order, with major implications for China and for East Asia as a whole.

This paper will examine the prospects for instability in China and evaluate the potential impact of instability on Northeast Asia, which is undergoing reconfiguration in the aftermath of the Cold War.[2] We will first examine whether leadership succession after Deng could jeopardize China's internal stability. Next, on the assumption that the leadership succession will trigger political instability, we will discuss the potential impact of such a development on China's neighbors, especially the Republic of Korea (ROK), and on the United States. We will then offer some concluding observations on what Korea and the United States could do to render instability less likely, or to mitigate its negative effects.

## LEADERSHIP SUCCESSION, POWER STRUGGLE, AND THE POTENTIAL FOR POLITICAL TURMOIL

The continued concern about China's future stability is largely derived from the belief that "China still remains essentially a government of men."[3] The focus of external observers is primarily on leaders and their personal relationships, not on institutions. To be sure, building and strengthening China's legal and institutional structures has been a recurring theme in Chinese politics over the past decade or more. Since 1980, when Deng Xiaoping argued in favor of establishing institutions in order to prevent power from concentrating in the hands of a single leader[4], China has attempted to move away from the personality cult of a supreme leader.

---

[2]There has been a flood of articles and books giving substance to the concept of a post-Cold War political order. It is not possible to analyze all these sources, but they clearly suggest the growing breakdown of the Cold War structure in the international system. Northeast Asia has not been immune to many of these political, economic and strategic changes.

[3]Robert A. Scalapino, "China in the Late Leninist Era," *The China Quarterly*, December 1993, p. 959.

[4] See his "On the Reform of the System of Party and State Leadership," *Selected Works of Deng Xiaoping (1975-1982)*, pp.302-325.

The outcome, however, is mixed at best, and China has not yet reached a point where it can function without a single dominant leader, even if the leader's powers are far less pervasive than those of Mao. The nation-wide publicity campaign following the publication of the third volume of *The Selected Works of Deng Xiaoping* in 1993 clearly showed that China still needed to propagate a belief in a dominant leader to sustain pursuit of specific policies. More recent developments suggest that the situation will not change drastically in the near term. The Fourth Plenum of the Fourteenth Central Committee of the Chinese Communist Party in September 1994, for example, emphasized the necessity of concentrating authority in the hands of an individual leader. The "decision" adopted by the Plenum unequivocally states that having *a core* in the central leading body is essential.[5] Although Deng's successor will not be able to monopolize power to the extent that Deng or Mao did, he will continue to exert, at least for the near future, a pivotal and perhaps decisive influence on whether China will be able to maintain its current policies and secure popular allegiance to the regime.

Thus, whether China continues to have stable leadership in the post-Deng era will remain a critical factor in determining China's future political prospects. This consideration could prove critical to shaping the direction of China's future development, especially in the first several years after Deng's death.

The passing of a dominant leader in an authoritarian system unquestionably creates new possibilities for political change. As Valerie Bunce has persuasively argued, succession in a socialist country presents an opportunity for policy innovation.[6] Indeed, many China specialists have documented how leadership succession after the death of Mao helped initiate new policies.[7] Therefore, in principle at least, it is difficult to totally discount the possibility that the post-Deng leadership succession will heighten pressures for further reforms. By gradually opening up the policy-making process to a wider

---

[5]See "CPC Decision on Party Building," *Beijing Review,* October 31-November 6, 1994, pp.7-10.

[6]Valerie Bunce, *Do New Leaders Make a Difference?* (Princeton: Princeton University Press, 1981).

[7]See, for instance, Harry Harding, *China's Second Revolution: Reform After Mao* (Washington D.C.: The Brookings Institution, 1987).

range of viewpoints and institutional forces, the post-Deng leadership may gradually move in the direction of more expansive political reform. Given that the current CCP leadership has stubbornly resisted such reforms, however, it seems very questionable that the post-Deng leadership will soon democratize the Chinese system.

At the same time, leadership succession could create serious dislocation. Many observers view leadership succession in an authoritarian system such as China as a potential source of crisis that threatens political stability. Among other problems, leadership change is generally believed to trigger power struggles among rival factions, which, in turn, may cause drastic political upheaval. If we view the post-Deng leadership succession from this perspective, we can identify several developments that point in this direction.[8]

First, as in its former fellow socialist states, China has failed to undertake adequate provisions for resolving the problem of leadership succession. Neither the Party constitution nor the state constitution have made realistic provisions for orderly succession. The lack of a procedure for succession lays the basis for a power struggle. The death of a top leader who has virtually monopolized power for years, many argue, creates a power vacuum, which, in turn, encourages his lieutenants to strive to build up their own power bases. Under these circumstances, leadership stability decreases. As a result, participants in the power struggle endeavor to gain support from as wide a political constituency as possible. This is why a power struggle in an authoritarian system often causes wider reverberations within and beyond the party, bringing otherwise dormant social contradictions to the fore.

Second, the fact that Jiang Zemin, the officially designated successor of Deng, still lacks independent power and credentials diminishes the possibility of a smooth leadership transition. It is undeniable that Jiang's power base has grown, and now appears to be far stronger than when he first came to power in 1989. When he assumed the position of General Secretary in the aftermath of the Tiananmen incident, he was generally regarded as "the second Hua Guofeng," Mao's

---

[8]This is not to say that political turmoil is inevitable in post-Deng China. But it should be remembered that examining the possible instability in post-Deng China is the major focus of this paper.

designated successor who rapidly lost power following Mao's death. However, Jiang has managed to gradually strengthen his personal power base. For instance, he has consolidated his hold over several crucial areas, including ideology, propaganda, and finance and the economy, by promoting his protégés to positions of central responsibility.

In particular, Jiang has taken extra efforts to ensure the loyalty of the People's Liberation Army (PLA), which is generally expected to play a critical role in the succession process. In an October 1992 military shake-up, he managed to oust the so-called Yang family faction, who were Jiang's arch rivals for control over the military. Since then, he has attempted to bolster his support within the military by promoting new military leaders, visiting military bases, and expanding the military budget.

As the concurrent head of the party, government, and military, Jiang appears to be best placed to succeed Deng as China's top leader. Recent attempts to boost his personal authority further increase the chance of his succession to top leadership. The Fourth Plenum of the Fourteenth Central Committee of the CCP in September 1994, for example, revealed heightened efforts to consolidate Jiang's position as the Party leader. The decision adopted by the Plenum unequivocally endorsed his core position within the third generation collective leadership.[9] As the Hong Kong press observed, Jiang finally received the Party's official recognition and approval as the supreme leader.[10]

After the Plenum, there followed various efforts to smooth the way for the anointed successor. For instance, *biaotai* campaigns in which participants were asked to profess their absolute allegiance to Jiang ensued. Party units, including the Central Committee of the CCP and the Party's Organization Department, have reportedly held numerous gatherings to swear an oath of fealty to Jiang. There are also reports that Jiang has masterminded a series of ideological campaigns among military officers and implemented a thorough scrutiny of

---

[9]"CPC Decision on Party Building," *Beijing Review*, October 31-November 6, 1994, pp.7-10.

[10] See, for instance, *Jing Bao*, November 1994, pp.24-27.

their loyalty, thereby enabling Jiang to consolidate his position in the run-up to the post-Deng era.[11]

However, it is not clear whether Jiang will be able to stand on his own in the political infighting that seems certain to follow Deng's death. The biggest problem for Jiang is that he does not have the credentials or the depth of support enjoyed by Deng. A recent publicity campaign unintentionally revealed that Jiang does not enjoy widely accepted authority. The preparations for the post-Deng era by the third generation Chinese leadership have focused heavily on invoking the personal authority of the dying Deng, not Jiang. For instance, in early 1995, *People's Daily* published a series of commentaries which appealed for the country to unite around Deng's theory of socialism with Chinese characteristics.[12] This clearly demonstrates that Jiang still needs to depend on Deng's authority for ensuring national unity.

Third, given that Jiang does not appear to be strong enough on his own to overcome potential challenges to his power after Deng's death, the ability of the post-Deng leadership to work together will prove crucial, especially during the first years after Deng's death. Many Chinese leaders have concluded that a collective leadership will best help maintain stability in post-Deng China, since no one from the third generation leadership has enough power to impose a personal dictatorship. Indeed, in the communique of the Fourth Plenum of the Fourteenth Central Committee of the CCP, the necessity of upholding and improving collective leadership is no less emphasized than that of maintaining a core within the leadership. The decision clearly states that "all major matters relating to principles and policies, all issues concerning overall interests... should be determined collectively."[13]

China's fate in the post-Deng era will therefore depend substantially on whether the current triumvirate of Jiang Zemin, Li Peng, and Zhu Rongji survives the coming political transition. The triumvirate, in essence, represents the outcome of political compromises among

---

[11] *South China Morning Post*, December 26, 1994, p.6 and January 8, 1995, p.7.

[12] See *People's Daily*, January 16-19, 1995.

[13] "CPC Decision on Party Building," *Beijing Review*, October 31-November 6, 1994, p.9.

different factions within the CCP. Despite various problems inherent in the process of coordinating the interests of the three leaders and their supporters, the scheme has managed to maintain stability over the last couple of years.

Several factors may help the triumvirate survive the impending power struggle. On some major issues, like strengthening central authority and maintaining macro control of the economy, the triumvirate appears to have common interests. More important, the division of labor within this group allows each faction to have a voice on important policies. Indeed, it seems that the three leaders and their factions have achieved a balance of power among them. Therefore, each leader has an incentive to avoid an overt power struggle in which one or more of them may lose their share of power. Moreover, the apprehension that an internecine power struggle could trigger social turmoil encourages individual leaders to restrain their mutual rivalries.[14] These considerations suggest that the leadership will attempt to maintain the status quo, especially in the initial period following Deng's death. These leaders have already begun to stress that there will be no major political overhaul after the death of Deng. Zhu Rongji, for instance, has contended that "the government functions perfectly; there will be no changes."[15] It remains to be seen, however, whether Zhu's declaration reflects confidence or anxiety about the future.

Some structural developments also suggest the possibility that the post-Deng successor regime will uphold current policies for the time being. The foundation of reform has already been largely institutionalized. In addition, the Chinese economy is likely to maintain high growth rates, thereby contributing to a gradual, nondisruptive transition. These factors suggest that the basic policy will not change after the death of Deng: economic reform will continue, regardless of who succeeds Deng. In short, despite inevitable behind-the-scenes jockeying for power, it is likely that there will be a period of relative stability in the post-Deng era.

---

[14] Baum, *op. cit.*, p.493.

[15] *South China Morning Post*, January 20, 1995, p.8.

However, the triumvirate does not appear to have reached an agreement on the long-term direction of China's development. Indeed, controversy and debate about the scope and direction of future reform have prevented the triumvirate from implementing necessary but inevitably painful policies to deal with such arduous problems as rampant corruption, increasing inequality among sectors and regions, mass migration of peasants, inflation, and major losses in state-owned enterprises.

Therefore, the possibility of the triumvirate collapsing in the medium- to long-run cannot be totally discounted. For one, given that each leader prefers different measures for dealing with social and economic problems, the triumvirate could face a serious crisis when and if economic and/or social turbulence occurs. If serious social turmoil erupts (for example, a renewed democracy movement), then there is a possibility that the existing consensus among the three leaders would break down, as was the case in the spring of 1989 when the radical reformers and conservatives split over the issue of how to cope with the democracy movement. The preoccupation with stable power relationships also could challenge the durability of the triumvirate. The Chinese system still needs a dominant leader to ensure its survival. This suggests that change in the distribution of power may be inevitable. Jiang has already begun to promote officials from his previous Shanghai base in an apparent attempt to strengthen his position. Such moves by Jiang could trigger a power struggle as they would alter the power balance among the three leaders.

If a power struggle breaks out, it could trigger political turmoil which, in turn, would jeopardize China's stability. Two forces appear likely to exercise particularly significant influence in determining the direction and outcome of the power struggle. One force is the military. It is almost without question that the military will play a critical role in the power struggle. If the military maintains its unity and is able to act as a single unit, it could exploit its increased importance and enhance its own sectoral interests. However, it is difficult, although not impossible, to imagine that any Chinese military leader himself would emerge as the supreme leader. China's military, unlike in many Third World countries, has been largely passive politically, usually limiting its role to the support of the most powerful leader. The political commissar system has also helped the party ensure its control over the military.[16] There is little evidence to suggest that the situation will drastically change any time soon. Although the relative importance of the military in Chinese politics has increased since the Tiananmen incident,[17] it still lacks the authority to take the initiative in post-Deng succession politics. If the military splinters along regional lines, the intensity of political turmoil would considerably increase to the extent that local military conflict or even all-out strife could occur, thereby plunging the country into total chaos.[18]

Local or provincial forces will exert no less significant influence on the direction of power struggle. After the dissolution of the Soviet state, some observers argued that China would also dissolve into several republics along ethnic divisions and/or economic zones.[19] However, given the absolute dominance of the Han nationality, the possibility of total disintegration of China is slim. Rather, the issue is localism. As the post-Mao reforms allowed more authority to local elites in the management of the economy, provincial governments considerably increased their voice in the formulation of regional policies. This means that the central government's capacity to control the provincial governments has diminished. The center now has to devise a mechanism through which it can retain and reassert its authority. A power struggle at the center, however, will obstruct any attempt to increase the control over local forces. Exploiting political turmoil at the center, leadership at the regional and local levels is likely to demand more autonomy.

---

[16]On the political commissar system, see Cheng Hsiao-shih, *Party-Military Relations in the PRC and Taiwan: Paradoxes of Control* (Boulder: Westview Press, 1990).

[17]For instance, at the Fourteenth Party Congress in October 1992, military representation on the party's Central Committee increased from 16 percent to 21.7 percent. See Joseph Fewsmith, "Reform, Resistance, and the Politics of Succession," in William Joseph ed., *China Briefing, 1994* (Boulder: Westview Press, 1994), p.12.

[18]See Peter Yu Kien-Hong, "Potential Areas of Chinese Regional Military Separatism," *Contemporary Southeast Asia*, 15:4, March 1994, pp.464-498.

[19]See, for example, Gerald Segal, "China's Changing Shape," *Foreign Affairs*, May/June 1994.

## THE RISE OF NATIONALISM IN CHINA AND ITS IMPACT ON NORTHEAST ASIA

Given China's size and military might, it is inevitable that China's future development will have a significant effect on Northeast Asia as a whole. China's rapid economic growth, which has already prompted speculation that by the early next century China's economy will be the world's largest,[20] suggests that China will play an ever more significant role in defining the Northeast Asian regional order. What would be the potential impact of internal upheaval on China's future regional policies?

The most visible impact on regional policy will be the rise of nationalism. Achieving power and wealth as a nation, and thereby maintaining China's national sovereignty and upholding its national dignity, has been the central goal for Chinese leaders over the last century. It was the ultimate goal that the post-Mao reform leadership pursued when it initiated reform and economic opening. The leadership made it clear that reform and opening were to assist the realization of China's greatness. Nationalism has progressively replaced communist ideology as an integrating force. Since the Tiananmen incident in 1989, in an attempt to ensure popular allegiance to the regime and to maintain national unity, the leadership has relied increasingly on nationalist sentiment. For instance, the leadership has repeatedly manipulated the theme of "peaceful evolution," by which it refers to supposed Western (especially American) efforts to subvert communist rule in China.[21]

Succession dynamics are likely to strengthen this trend further. For the third generation leadership, which lacks sufficient independent authority and power resources to guarantee the integrity of China after the death of Deng, nationalism could prove a very useful tool to strengthen their legitimacy. The promotion of nationalist sentiment could help China's leadership to unify a potentially fragmented and

---

[20] See, for instance, *The Economist*, November 28, 1992, pp.3-5.

[21] Especially following the collapse of communism in the former Soviet Union and Eastern Europe, Beijing claimed that Washington was pursuing a "peaceful evolution" strategy aimed at subverting socialism and overthrowing the current leadership in China. See Yang Kai-Huang, "Mainland Chinese Society and the Campaign Against 'Peaceful Evolution'," *Issues and Studies*, June 1992, pp. 26-27.

conflictual group of leadership contenders. It also is useful in securing support from major domestic forces, including the military, which is the ultimate guarantor of stability. Lastly, nationalism can be used as a means to distract popular attention from internal woes.[22] For instance, if the economic situation in China deteriorates, the post-Deng leadership could blame it on foreign interference.

The rise of nationalism in China will definitely limit the ability of a given leader to accommodate external pressures for change. Given that the Chinese are extremely sensitive to any outside interference in their internal affairs, any leader who is accused of yielding to pressure from the outside could be accused of being unpatriotic. As no Chinese leader could hope to consolidate his power if he acquiesces to outside pressure, most are likely to seek a more assertive stance toward the outside world.

This, in turn, portends further strains in the U.S.-China relationship, at least until the question of leadership succession is resolved. While the Sino-American relationship has somewhat recovered from the acute difficulties caused by the Tiananmen fiasco, the relationship is still facing numerous problems.[23] Some of these issues, like human rights and the Taiwan issue, are stubbornly regarded as "internal" by the Chinese, as evidenced by the harsh Chinese reaction to the U.S. issuance of a visa to Taiwan President Lee Teng-hui in June 1995. The Chinese leadership and many intellectuals regard any pressure on such issues from the United States as interference in China's domestic affairs. Therefore, it is extremely unlikely that the new leadership will make any substantial compromises on issues of national sovereignty.

On the contrary, the dynamics of leadership succession could lead the new leadership to acquiesce to or promote behavior that the

---

[22]As one scholar has observed, the doctrine of peaceful evolution hss served as a psychological scapegoat for domestic political purposes, i.e., to call for national unity under the current leadership. See John W. Garver, "Chinese Foreign Policy: The Diplomatic Damage Control," *Current History*, September 1991, p.244.

[23]See Michel Oksenberg, "The China Problem, " *Foreign Affairs*, 70:3 (Summer 1991); Robert G. Sutter, "Tiananmen's Lingering Fallout on Sino-American Relations," *Current History*, September 1991; Robert A. Manning, "Clinton and China: Beyond Human Rights," *Orbis*, 38:2, Spring 1994.

United States finds distasteful.[24] For instance, in an attempt to build up the military's support, the post-Deng leadership may consent to increased arms exports, thereby obstructing American attempts to curtail China's arms sales to some Third World countries, notably Iran. Alternatively, the post-Deng leadership may be unable or unwilling to control economic behavior which the United States regards as a violation of international rules. For instance, the leadership's attempt to ensure support from as many groups as possible may limit its capacity to enforce China's commitment to upholding intellectual property agreements.

In sum, the fact that the uncertainty over China's future comes at a time of increasing strain in the U.S.-China relationship suggests that bilateral rows between the United States and China will continue in the future. Recent disputes over intellectual property rights offer one such example. Moreover, we cannot discount the possibility of a tug-of-war between the United States and China escalating into a serious crisis. This would be the case when and if a leadership aspirant attempts to put in a bid for the support of China's nationalistic forces by openly challenging the United States, thereby provoking American reprisals.

The strain and disputes between America and China will have an unsettling effect on Northeast Asia. First and foremost, it will have an impact on the three-way interrelationship among China, Japan, and the United States, which will largely shape the security environment of the region early in the next century. To be sure, instability in China will pose serious problems for the Sino-Japanese relationship. If nationalism continues to rise in China, the relationship could be further strained. However, the nature and type of problems that Japan may face with China could be different from those of the United States. Therefore, it is highly possible that America and Japan may differ on what needs to be done about China. The differences in the two countries' policies toward China could have destabilizing effects on the regional order, particularly if China tries to exploit such differences.

---

[24]David Bachman, "Domestic Sources of Chinese Foreign Policy," in Samuel S. Kim ed., *China and the World: Chinese Foreign Relations in the Post-Cold War Era* (Boulder: Westview Press, 1994), pp.48-49.

In addition, the long-term implications of the rapid rise of China could pose serious risks to its smaller neighbors, especially if nationalist sentiment continues to grow. Despite China's repeated assurances that it will not pursue hegemony in the region, some of China's neighbors may find its pursuit of wealth and power to be dangerous. China's efforts to improve its military capabilities could have an especially unsettling effect on the regional order.[25] Uncertain about China's long-term strategic intentions, China's neighbors would probably see the need to strengthen their own military capabilities.[26] As such, China's efforts to increase military strength could prompt an arms race in the region.

Any destabilization within China would also have a considerable impact on the Korean peninsula. Following Deng's death, China is very likely to be absorbed in its internal affairs. The pressing need to maintain domestic stability will inevitably limit its capability to influence what happens on the peninsula. Accordingly, the death of Deng is not likely to bring about any immediate change in China's policies toward the peninsula. Given the particular relationship between China and North Korea, however, the direction of change in post-Deng China would have a direct impact on North Korea's future policies. For example, if the death of Deng is followed by severe political, economic and/or social turbulence in China, it may lead North Korea to reevaluate the option of following what is called the Chinese model, a policy change that some believe North Korea is seriously considering as a means to escape its acute economic crisis.[27] Even if it does not totally dissuade North Korea from adopting reform and opening, it will adversely affect the scope, speed, and direction of North Korea's policy change.

---

[25]Military modernization has received high priority over the last several years. This clearly reflects the rising importance of the PLA in Chinese politics.

[26]On this point, see Samuel S. Kim, "China as a Regional Power," *Current History*, September 1992; Andrew Mack and Desmond Bell, "The Military Build-up in the Asian-Pacific Region," *Pacific Review*, 1992; and Michael T. Klare, " Great Arms Race, " *Foreign Affairs*, Summer 1993.

[27]For a succinct discussion on this point, see Barry Gills, "North Korea and the Crisis of Socialism: The Historical Ironies of National Division," *Third World Quarterly*, Vol. 13, No. 1, 1992.

Over the longer term, the possibility of developments in China causing drastic change in its policy toward the Korean peninsula cannot be totally discounted. If hard-line leaders emerge victorious in the power struggle, and if ideological solidarity and security concerns become once again predominant in China's foreign policy, the Sino-North Korean relationship that has recently become strained would have a chance for improvement. It also could arrest the recent trend of continuous improvement between the ROK and China.

Barring a total collapse, however, China is likely to maintain the current policy of pursuing "good" relations with the two Koreas. It is in China's interest to continue helping North Korea to preserve domestic stability, since turbulence in North Korea would have negative repercussions on China's internal stability. At the same time, China can also benefit from burgeoning economic relations with ROK. In short, upholding good relations with the two Koreas allows China to increase its voice and role in future developments on the peninsula.

So far, we have observed that developments in China will have a direct impact on what will happen outside China. However, this observation needs to be qualified. Despite its growing strength, China's regional policy will not be determined solely by internal considerations and developments. China's opening has tremendously increased economic transactions between China and the outside world. The globalization of its economy has already made it subject to the influence of systemic factors. This will clearly limit China's range of choice in its regional policies. China's new leader, whoever he may be, needs international support and extensive and positive interaction with the advanced market economies to maintain economic development. Any successor is very likely to conclude that autarky would only push China toward economic and political crisis.

To summarize, nationalism will clearly grow in the period of leadership transition, as it is useful in maintaining national unity. However, the very goal of Chinese nationalism, accomplishing power and wealth, dictates that China maintain active and probably cooperative interaction with the outside world. Therefore, we see two seemingly contradictory trends—nationalism and internationalism—coexisting in China. The balance between these two trends, which will be decided by the specific circumstances and conditions at a given time, will determine the mix of cooperation and competition in Chinese regional policy.

## CONCLUDING OBSERVATIONS

There is a wide range of opinions on the challenge posed by the emergence of China. Viewing China's rapid rise from a strategic perspective, some observers fear the implications of a highly dynamic China. In particular, some Americans fear that China's rise is a threat to American interests.[28] Others, however, argue that a developing China is preferable to a stagnating one, regardless of some potentially negative consequences that high growth may cause. A stagnating China would pose problems to its neighbors and to the world. For instance, political instability and economic crisis could lead millions of Chinese to attempt to flee the country. Instead of arresting the negative consequences, stagnation is likely to accelerate them. We should therefore expect that a rise in living standards will moderate China's domestic and foreign policies. In other words, a China striving for economic development would be less likely to fall into dangerous political adventurism and expansionism because it needs to maintain a peaceful and stable environment to accomplish economic growth.

It seems inescapable that the outside world will need to come to terms with a prosperous and strong China. Thus, the challenge is to induce China to be a responsible member of the international community fully committed to international rules. If China's development occurs in a manner inconsistent with international norms, its rise will be troublesome for its immediate neighbors, and also for the world as a whole. Of course, it is debatable whether outside forces can decisively influence what happens in China. Both Chinese leaders and intellectuals are very sensitive about outside control and appear to be resolutely resistant to it. Nonetheless, owing largely to the globalization of China's economy, outside forces have a better chance than in the past to influence the direction of developments in China. As the post-Deng Chinese leadership assesses the benefits and disadvantages of reform and opening, policies pursued by

---

[28] See, for example, Ross H. Munro, "Awakening Dragon: The Real Danger in Asia is from China," *Policy Review*, Fall 1992.

outsiders, including the United States and the ROK, will increasingly influence the direction of China's development.

The best means for America and Korea to assist China would be to adopt an engagement policy. For instance, both countries should continue to promote economic exchange, including trade and investment, with China and to encourage China's entrance to the World Trade Organization and other global fora. It seems that this kind of engagement policy will encourage positive trends such as continued economic liberalization and increased international cooperation, which would eventually support a more pragmatic, forward-looking leadership in China. With the rising nationalist sentiment in China, a confrontational policy toward China would not likely bring about its intended results. By the same token, placing pressure on China would provide grist for the Chinese conservatives' mill and undercut the position of reformers, thus making the possibility of a hard-line dictatorship and decreased economic cooperation with the outside world more likely. How others treat China will affect the balance between internationalism and nationalism in post-Deng China, and seems certain to remain a central policy preoccupation for China's neighbors and for the United States for the indefinite future.

# Section II

# Regional Military Capabilities

The second session was devoted to papers by Ashley Tellis and Taehyun Kim. Though the emphasis in the respective analyses was quite different, the two papers proved highly complementary. Tellis's paper focused principally on the development and diffusion of specific classes of military technologies that might have a destabilizing effect on the present distribution of power and the allocation of defense responsibilities within the region. Kim's paper focused primarily on the political factors that are driving future security calculations, and how rapid economic growth (combined with the increased availability of advanced weaponry in the post-Cold War era) is stimulating military acquisitions throughout the region. Researchers from both institutions recognized the clear incentives to maintain the present strategic framework, but there was no consensus on whether a long-term equilibrium was sustainable at either a political or a technological level. In this regard, several participants drew attention to prospective conflicts of interest between the United States and China as a potential long-term destabilizing factor.

But factors that could undermine regional stability were not limited to great power competition. Under conditions of strategic uncertainty, numerous nations are seeking to enhance their strategic autonomy, while also continuing to rely at least partially on existing alliance arrangements. In Tellis's view, this could create growing tensions in defense planning between the United States and various regional allies. For example, an unspoken but widely understood premise in regional security arrangements has been that the United States would retain specific military capabilities that its allies would not. Should these boundaries be breached or eroded, it could stimulate an intraregional arms competition that would undermine (or at least severely complicate) future security collaboration within the region.

There was also a spirited discussion on how to define stability and how best to realize it. In this regard, though some technologies might be seen as being intrinsically destabilizing, it is the political objectives of states that still assumed paramount importance. Thus, security structures could prove robust enough to accommodate the diffusion of specific technologies under some, but not all, circumstances. But East Asia's economic and technological dynamism reinforced the belief that the desire for stability could not be viewed as a means of reinforcing the status quo. The challenge is to find means to reconfigure the security roles and activities of different states that would enable a division of labor appropriate to the capabilities and interests of all regional actors. Kim argued that various forms of multilateral security collaboration had ample potential for ameliorating rivalries within the region, but Tellis asserted that the United States should retain distinctive military capabilities to underscore its continued commitment to a singular regional security role.

It seems clear that the United States and Korea will need to address the possibility of adaptations and adjustments in their alliance ties over the coming decade. The political sustainability of past "alliance bargains" under conditions of rapid economic growth and technological dynamism is clearly a very fruitful avenue for continued exploration in future research.

# Chapter Three

# MILITARY TECHNOLOGY ACQUISITION AND REGIONAL STABILITY IN EAST ASIA[1]

Ashley J. Tellis

## INTRODUCTION

The East Asian region has been one of the great success stories of the postwar period. The many indices testifying to this success include sustained region-wide economic growth, relative order in domestic politics, and social stability at the level of civil society. The region has also witnessed a remarkable absence of active inter-state conflict—an outcome conditioned both by the disciplining effects of global bipolarity and the intimate presence of the United States as friend, ally, and guarantor of regional security.

However, the end of the Cold War has transformed both these pacifying conditions in varying degrees. The loss of bipolarity is irrevocable. As a result, the latent suspicions harbored by the regional states could once again become manifest and, if left unaddressed, could lead to active conflict.[2] The future of the U.S. regional presence is more complicated. While some sort of presence will be maintained well into the policy-relevant future, the United States is widely viewed as a hegemonic power in decline—a state facing the kind of progressive debilitation which will eventually lead to its withdrawal

---

[1] I am deeply grateful to Paul K. Davis, Norman D. Levin, Jonathan D. Pollack, Michael D. Swaine, Charles Wolf, Jr., and all the participants at the workshop for their numerous comments and helpful criticisms.

[2] For an extended analysis of this question, see Aaron L. Friedberg, "Ripe for Rivalry: Prospects for Peace in a Multipolar Asia," *International Security* 18:3 (Winter 1993/94), pp. 5-33.

from the region.[3] Even if this perception is mistaken, the U.S. regional military presence has lost the simple, clear, and well-appreciated *raison d'être* it enjoyed throughout the Cold War. In the absence of a clear threat, the rationale for continued presence becomes difficult to understand and possibly even unpalatable, when understood.

The reason for the continued U.S. military presence in East Asia is best summarized by Jonathan Pollack's metaphor, "holding the ring."[4] This metaphor describes a situation where no regional state has any military capabilities that can seriously harm another, while the only external power possessing such capabilities—the United States—lacks the incentives to use them abusively, because it employs its power to serve larger political and economic interests. A strategy of "holding the ring" also capitalizes on America's geographical distance from East Asia: it casts the United States in the role of a non-threatening but engaged external protector, while it seeks to prevent regional states from acquiring military capabilities which would make this protective task either more compelling or more difficult.

American forces forward deployed in Asia are critical to this strategy for two reasons: "insurance" and "investment."[5] The insurance aspect aims at preventing any single power or consortium of powers from being able to dominate East Asia.[6] In this context, the superior war-fighting capability of American military forces serves as a reminder to others that attempts at hegemonic dominance would be extremely costly and, ultimately, unfruitful. Should a prospective challenger fail to get this message, American forward deployed forces immediately serve a second function: they become the means to bolster the resilience of the regional states, and the instruments

---

[3] This perception, and its consequences for the recent surge of weapons acquisitions in East Asia, is analyzed in some detail in Andrew Mack and Desmond Ball, "The Military Build-up in Asia-Pacific," *The Pacific Review* 5:3 (1992), pp. 203–204.

[4] Jonathan D. Pollack, "The United States in East Asia," in *Asia's International Role in the Post-Cold War Era*, Adelphi Paper 275 (London: IISS, 1993), pp. 69–82.

[5] Ibid, pp. 79 ff.

[6] Jonathan D. Pollack and James A. Winnefeld, *U.S. Strategic Alternatives in a Changing Pacific*, R-3933-USCINCPAC (Santa Monica: RAND, 1990), pp. 6-9.

through which a containment strategy can be operationalized, if necessary.

The investment aspect aims at bearing the costs of region-wide order so that the local states do not fritter away resources in ill conceived attempts to produce security.[7] In the absence of such tangible American protection, every regional state would have to rely on its own capabilities for ensuring its safety. This imperative would inevitably lead to the destruction or appreciable weakening of the East Asian "economic miracle." Without the United States fulfilling its guarantor role, each state would be forced to engage in security competition rather than economic competition. Engaging in the former would retard the processes of wealth production within East Asia and, to the degree that trade produces wealth, it would also diminish American economic growth and prosperity. American forward deployed forces, therefore, obviate the need for local security competition: they create the preconditions for continued prosperity in the region and, by extension, ensure the continued economic well-being of the United States.

Military technology acquisition and stability in East Asia need to be examined in this context. Studies of this subject have traditionally focused on: (1) cataloging the kinds of weapons technologies being acquired in the region; (2) assessing the numbers of new weapons and their effects on local military balances; and, (3) understanding the political and economic motivations beneath the flurry of new military technology acquisitions in East Asia over the last half decade.[8]

This essay, while building upon such research, aims to shift the focus in a different direction. It seeks to identify *which* military technology acquisitions could be most destabilizing when measured against a definition of stability centered on enduring American strategic inter-

---

[7] This argument relies on some minimal version of the "hegemonic stability" theory associated with political realism. See Robert Gilpin, *The Political Economy of International Relations* (Princeton: Princeton University Press, 1987), pp. 85–92, for an elaboration.

[8] See, for example, Mack and Ball, "The Military Build-up in Asia-Pacific," pp. 203–204; Amitav Acharya, "Explaining the Arms Buildup in Southeast Asia, *Asian Defence Journal* 1/93 (January 1993), pp. 66-68; Gerald Segal and David Mussington, "Arming East Asia," *Jane's Intelligence Review* 5:12 (December 1993), pp. 565-566; Desmond Ball, "Arms and Affluence," *International Security* 18:3 (Winter 1993/94), pp. 78--12.

ests in East Asia. The discussion is divided into three parts. The first part will analyze the nature of destabilizing military technology acquisitions and suggest how the concept of "destabilizing" technologies can be understood from a political perspective. The second part will identify the technologies themselves in more detail in order to indicate how their possible acquisition could affect regional stability. The third part will briefly evaluate what the United States and the East Asian states could do to respond to the introduction of such destabilizing military technologies in the region.

The analytical focus of this paper emphasizes technology and not politics. We will not discuss which political changes in East Asia are desirable. Neither will we discuss how specific military technology acquisitions would affect different political contexts. Rather, in aiming to *ascertain* the kinds of military technology acquisitions that would be destabilizing—given certain defined American regional objectives—the paper seeks to pave the way for future research. A longer-term research approach would describe how particular technologies would be problematic in specific operational contexts, taking into account the number of systems present, their anticipated effectiveness, their flexibility of usage, their susceptibility to countermeasures and, finally, how various states might use these technologies in some instances and not others. Such research would require dynamic combat modeling under various strategic assumptions and under several alternative force postures and sizes. Dynamic analysis of this sort, though ultimately very crucial, lies beyond the scope of any single paper, and it cannot be initiated unless certain critical technologies are first identified as problematic. The present article must, therefore, be viewed as a preliminary contribution towards understanding the larger issue of how recent and future military technology acquisitions in East Asia could affect the operational levels of war-fighting and campaign management from an American perspective.

## UNDERSTANDING THE NATURE OF DESTABILIZING MILITARY TECHNOLOGIES

Since the beginning of this century, political leaders have often believed that it is possible to identify intrinsically destabilizing military technologies. This search has been premised on the belief that some military instruments are inherently "aggressive" and, consequently, identifying such instruments made it possible to either limit or outlaw them. If these inherently aggressive technologies could be either limited or outlawed, political stability would be an inevitable consequence. Because this idea had both simplicity and appeal, it quickly became a staple of the various disarmament conferences in the first half of the century.[9] However, the notion of intrinsically destabilizing technologies was riddled with severe conceptual difficulties. Despite the demonstrated inadequacies of this premise, it has persisted at both an analytic and policy level. As recently as 1993, for example, the Congress of the United States instructed the Executive Branch to identify the "types and numbers of advanced conventional weapons" which could be inherently "destabilizing."[10]

The notion that inherently destabilizing weapons exist is an illusion. All weapons can be used with varying degrees of effectiveness for a variety of roles and in support of either defensive or offensive operations.[11] Consequently, their destabilizing potential cannot be identified abstractly, but only within the context of how they affect a state's capacity to execute its preferred strategy. This determination is always contingent: it is a normative judgment with strong prescriptive content and it is *always* determined within the framework of a state's political goals.

The issue of how certain military technology acquisitions could affect stability in East Asia, therefore, needs to be approached in straightforward fashion. A first approximation is as follows: Region-wide stability will be enhanced if no local East Asian state possesses military technologies that could (1) seriously threaten the territorial integrity of another local state; (2) seriously threaten the ability of the United States to defend a local state; and, (3) seriously impede the ability of the United States to either operate within the region or to

---

[9] For a useful early history of this problem, together with an analysis of the various difficulties associated with the concept, see Marion W. Boggs, *Attempts to Define and Limit "Aggressive" Armament in Diplomacy and Strategy* (Columbia: University of Missouri Press, 1941).

[10] U.S. Congress, *Department of Defense Appropriations for FY 1993,* sec. 1607.

[11] For an excellent discussion of this issue, see Stephen Biddle, *The Determinants of Offensiveness and Defensiveness in Conventional Land Warfare* (Ph.D. dissertation, Harvard University, May 1992), pp. 21–56.

reinforce its already existing capabilities in East Asia. *Every* military technology acquired by any regional state will obviously influence these three criteria to some degree. It would be impossible, however, to prevent various East Asian states from acquiring *any* kind of military technology on the grounds that *all* technologies affect the above calculus. In an environment where multiple weapons producers exist, where indigenous production capabilities are not inconsequential, and, where the search for national autonomy is increasingly strong, a strategy of "broad spectrum" technology denial would be both impossible to sustain and, ultimately, self-defeating.[12] Consequently, there is need for a more sensitive definition of which technology acquisitions are treated as significant—relative to the three criteria defined above—and towards which U.S. and allied military planning and counter-proliferation initiatives should be directed.

The U.S. Department of Defense made a concerted effort in the late 1980s to address this issue. In a presentation made to the Senate Committee on Governmental Affairs in 1990, Henry D. Sokolski, then Deputy Assistant Secretary for Nonproliferation Policy, disclosed a broad U.S. policy framework (initially devised by Henry S. Rowen, then Assistant Secretary of Defense for International Security Affairs).[13] The Rowen framework argued that any particular regional military technology acquisition should be deemed destabilizing if: (1) it enabled the possessor to inflict high-leverage strategic harm against the United States or its allies; (2) the United States lacked effective defenses against this capability or if prevailing U.S. defenses were too difficult or cumbersome to employ; and (3) the very acquisition of such capabilities changed the perceived balance of power in the region. These three refining provisos were intended to provide a more sensitive definition of which military technology acquisitions are likely to be destabilizing—understood as making the attainment of U.S. strategic objectives more difficult. Or, as stated by Sokolski, each of these provisos was intended to identify the kinds of

---

[12] See the discission in Michael Moodie, "Beyond Proliferation: The Challenge of Technology Diffusion," *The Washington Quarterly* 18:2, pp. 183–202.

[13] Testimony and Prepared Statement of Henry D. Sokolski, *Proliferation and Regional Security in the 1990s*, U.S. Senate, Committee on Governmental Affairs, 101st Congress, 2nd Session, Oct. 9, 1990, pp. 28–41; 65–88.

technologies which "could enable [other] states to threaten war-winning or victory-denying results against the United States or its friends..."[14] Given the compact nature of these formulations, it is important to elaborate the three provisos further.

The first proviso argues that military technologies which can inflict 'high leverage strategic harm' are of particular concern. The critical phrase is 'high leverage' harm. It should not be understood merely as a proxy for high-technology weaponry. Rather, the phrase is meant to capture the kind of damage that a technology acquisition could inflict on the United States—damage which is either prohibitively costly or simply unacceptable.[15] Shifting the focus from the level of technology *per se* to the kind of *warfighting outputs* that the technology could generate is critical to this concept. It implies that a large variety of military instruments ranging from relatively sophisticated technologies (for example, weapons of mass destruction together with advanced delivery systems) to more primitive capabilities (for example, mine-warfare systems and cheap, accurate, and plentiful sea-based cruise missiles) could be equally problematic, *depending on what they could do to frustrate U.S. military capabilities (or those of our allies) in specific operational contexts.*

The second proviso appears deceptively obvious at first sight but is more complicated upon additional reflection. It asserts that technology acquisitions which lack an effective and usable American countermeasure are to be treated as intrinsically destabilizing. This is because such technology acquisitions—if they were to occur—would be highly exploitative, since they could be used to prosecute certain strategic, operational or tactical objectives with complete immunity from U.S. counteraction. The proliferation of certain kinds of aviation stealth technologies would be the most obvious example in this category. Less obvious, but no less pertinent, examples include advanced diesel-electric submarines and advanced mine warfare systems. These technologies would be problematic because combating such threats in certain operational environments would be

---

[14] Henry Sokolski, "Fighting Proliferation with Intelligence," *Orbis* (Spring 1994), p. 249.

[15] This argument is elaborated at some length in Henry Sokolski, "Nonapocalyptic Proliferation: A New Strategic Threat?" *The Washington Quarterly* 17:2 (Spring 1994), pp. 115–128.

cumbersome, time-consuming, and possibly without any guarantee of complete success, especially in those situations when time is at a premium. Further, prosecuting such operations could result in serious and perhaps unacceptable losses to the U.S. forces.

The third proviso is premised on the Hobbesian insight that "Reputation of power *is* Power; because it draweth with it the adhaerence of those that need protection."[16] It asserts that certain military technologies embody such palpable awe both in the public imagination and in the calculations of policy making elites that their political significance could easily overwhelm their operational merit.[17] As a result, their acquisition by a regional state could cause dramatic shifts in the *perceived* balance of power, thereby precipitating local political realignments that would render attainment of American regional strategic objectives highly problematic. A sudden acquisition of weapons of mass destruction (WMD) together with their associated delivery capabilities is one such example. Similarly, the acquisition of aircraft carriers, advanced nuclear submarines, and dedicated amphibious forces are also unnerving because they signify potential transformations in the ability of their possessors to project power. This, in turn, results in feelings of enhanced vulnerability on the part of others which could lead to temptations on the part of the local states to "bandwagon" with the rising power to the detriment of larger U.S. and allied interests.

These three provisos furnish the basis for a more discriminating judgment about which military technology acquisitions can be considered undermining of stability. The next step is to apply these general principles to identify specific weapons technologies that may be problematic in the context of East Asia, given the requirements of U.S. security strategy in the region.

---

[16] Thomas Hobbes, *Leviathan*, ed. C. B. Macpherson (Harmondsworth: Penguin Books, 1986), Part I, Chapter X, p. 150.

[17] This characteristic captures what Brad Roberts terms "leveraging technologies," which he describes as "technologies creating military capabilities of strategic consequence, which is to say capabilities that operate fundamentally on the perceptions of choice by the leaders of targeted nations." See, Brad Roberts, "From Nonproliferation to Antiproliferation," *International Security* 18:1 (Summer 1993), pp. 148–149.

## IDENTIFYING DESTABILIZING MILITARY TECHNOLOGIES IN THE EAST ASIAN CONTEXT

The discussion thus far has suggested that certain military technology acquisitions can be considered destabilizing to the degree that they impede U.S. regional strategy in East Asia. This strategy, broadly understood, aims to prevent if possible, while checkmating if necessary, any regional state from either threatening another neighboring state or limiting the ability of the United States to operate in defense of the threatened state or within the region at large. The chief instruments through which U.S. regional strategy has been operationalized have been the security relationships with Japan and South Korea and the various lesser agreements with Southeast Asian states for basing, transit, repair, and replenishment rights.

The security relationships between the United States and Japan and the United States and South Korea encompass both nuclear and conventional domains. The United States provides extended deterrence in the form of committing nuclear capable forces as a deterrent to nuclear or WMD intimidation, while also providing significant conventional forces as a symbol of commitment to defending its allies by purely conventional means. The bulk of the conventional defense forces available to the regional commanders, however, are provided by the host country and the division of labor between U.S. and allied forces has generally conformed to the following principle. The military posture of the host country is usually oriented to defending its air, land, and sea space through *reactive* means. In contrast, American military forces take primary responsibility for all initiatory military operations. The United States, with its unparalleled edge in air and naval power, specializes in offensive actions required to eliminate an adversary's coercive capabilities at its source, while the host country's defense forces generally specialize in containing the immediate tactical and operational-level threats on the battlefield. To use a crude distinction, the United States maintains the special capabilities required for fighting "deep," while the allies maintain the general capabilities required for defending "forward." Although such a division of labor cannot be either neat or uniform, the *general* difference in U.S. and allied warfighting orientations has long been clear both to U.S. allies and to the region at large.

The rationale for maintaining such a difference in warfighting orientation has always been obvious. While the United States has encouraged its allies to develop their defensive capabilities, especially though the development of land forces and tactical air power, it has simultaneously sought to prevent these capabilities from becoming so robust as to be threatening to neighboring states. For this reason, the United States traditionally discouraged its allies from acquiring either naval power projection capabilities or strategic air power assets. So long as no allied state possessed such capabilities, their ability to seriously hold any of their neighbors' homelands at risk was minimal. Consequently, they had less to fear from one another and so could concentrate on parrying the one state that did have such threatening strategic capabilities: traditionally, the Soviet Union.

Today, the Soviet Union has ceased to exist. Its military capabilities have atrophied, but the requirements for regional stability—from the perspective of the United States—still remain the same. It is imperative that no state acquire the military technologies capable of threatening the homelands of U.S. allies or the ability of the United States to defend them, while it remains equally important that America's allies not acquire the military technologies which could either threaten one another or, in the limiting case, threaten the United States.

If these technologies are reviewed in terms of the criteria identified previously, the following categories of strategic, force projection and battlespace denial technologies would arguably make the list of potentially destabilizing weapons.

## Strategic Technologies

Strategic technologies essentially consist of weapons of mass destruction together with advanced delivery systems, and new strategic conventional technologies which can inflict significant damage in a wartime situation.

• Weapons of Mass Destruction and Advanced Delivery Systems

Weapons of mass destruction include nuclear, chemical, biological, and radiological weapons, and advanced delivery systems include ballistic and cruise missiles which are difficult to detect, intercept, and destroy. This category of technologies is unambiguously destabilizing because it can be subsumed under all of Rowen's three provisos identified earlier.

WMD and the associated delivery systems represent capabilities that yield high leverage strategic harm: a small number of such weapons can inflict a disproportionate amount of damage, often indiscriminate, in a highly compressed period of time. WMD capabilities thus differ from conventional weapons in that they possess greater destructive efficiency and are relatively more indiscriminate in their destructive effects. Since these destructive effects are, in general, widespread, generalized, and harder to defend against, WMD assets can inflict great strategic harm even if their possessor has only a small number of them.[18] When mated with advanced delivery systems like ballistic and land-attack cruise missiles, they become even more problematic in that the former method of delivery increases the probability of a successful penetration of defenses (if any), while the latter method increases the potential for more accurate attacks on a variety of targets.

The following considerations are pertinent with respect to delivery systems. Ballistic and cruise missiles in fixed silos are easier to detect and monitor routinely and destroy in a crisis; their relative vulnerability is simply a function of their structural hardness, so fixed and immobile delivery systems would be less threatening. Mobile ballistic missiles launchers, however, are a different matter because these systems are often difficult to detect when concealment and deception techniques are used to disguise the launcher's location. The Gulf War demonstrated the great difficulties associated with tracking the whereabouts of primitive mobile missiles like the Iraqi Scuds, even when coalition forces had unquestioned air supremacy. The war also revealed that Ballistic Missile Defense (BMD) technologies are not yet mature enough to ensure successful intercepts routinely—a

---

[18] The nature of various weapons of mass destruction have been usefully described and compared in U.S. Congress, Office of Technology Assessment, *Proliferation of Weapons of Mass Destruction: Assessing the Risks*, OTA-ISC-559 (Washington, DC: USGPO, 1993).

problem that acquires heightened significance when the missile payload involves WMD.[19]

Similar judgments apply in the case of mobile, land based, WMD-equipped, land attack cruise missiles. These systems are difficult to detect when concealment and deception techniques are used to disguise the launcher's location. Parenthetically, submarine launched land-attack cruise missiles would also be very problematic because the sea as an operating medium provides a high degree of concealment and because enforcing transparency through Anti-Submarine Warfare (ASW) campaigns are costly, time consuming, and without any guarantee of complete success. For this reason, the primary weapons carrier—the submarine—is itself a destabilizing weapon in that it can inflict considerable high leverage strategic harm. (This problem will be discussed later when battlespace denial technologies are reviewed.) Thus, acquisitions of submarine launched, WMD-equipped, land-attack cruise missiles would be as destabilizing as acquisitions of mobile land based, WMD-equipped, land attack cruise missiles. However, more reliable technology currently exists to intercept cruise missiles—*if* they are detected after launch. But a failure to detect and intercept could conceivably be more costly if highly accurate modern land attack cruise missiles are able to inflict serious counterforce damage. For these reasons, WMD-equipped advanced delivery systems like mobile ballistic and cruise missiles (especially those fitted with sophisticated on-board terminal guidance systems or those employing sophisticated external systems for reducing targeting inaccuracy) would be highly destabilizing in terms of the criteria outlined earlier.

WMD capabilities are not easily susceptible to traditional forms of defense. The use of WMD by an adversary can arguably be deterred by threats of retaliation, but it has proven difficult to counteract the effects of such weapons once they have been employed. The acquisition of nuclear weapons by states other than the traditional possessors has therefore been viewed with great alarm simply because, in the final analysis, there is no effective antidote to their lethal effects.

---

[19] The debate about counter-ballistic missile operations in the Gulf War has been summarized in Stewart M. Powell, "Scud War, Round Two," *Air Force Magazine* 75:4 (April 1992), pp. 48-53; Stewart M. Powell, "Scud War, Round Three," *Air Force Magazine* 75:10 (October 1992), pp. 32–35.

Chemical and biological weapons in contrast offer greater latitude: their lethal effects *can* be minimized through a variety of immunization and decontamination techniques, although such techniques often impose considerable cost on warfighting efficiency and the desired tempo of military operations. As a result, the acquisition of chemical and biological weapons by others is also highly undesirable and must be viewed as destabilizing.

WMD represent palpable symbols of power: their acquisition by a state can change the perceived balance of power; they can increase the diplomatic and political costs of creating counter-coalitions; and their acquisition by additional states shifts the balance of *relative* power capabilities to the disadvantage of the United States. To date, only China and Russia are known to unambiguously possess WMD in the East Asian region. The United States traditionally relied on its central and in-theater nuclear forces to deter against the use of WMD by these states. The acquisition of such weapons (together with the advanced delivery systems identified previously) by additional states would thus result in a severely complicated security environment. It would encumber U.S. power projection operations; it would result in feelings of increased vulnerability on the part of the other non-possessor states in East Asia; it would devalue U.S. conventional deterrence and warfighting capabilities and would increase the cost of mounting conventional operations against states possessing WMD capabilities; and, it would create increased pressures towards even greater horizontal proliferation in the region at large.

For these reasons, among many others, any attempt by Japan, North Korea or South Korea to acquire and deploy WMD, together with any associated delivery systems, would be destabilizing. It would result in an increased capability on the part of local states to threaten one another; increase the costs and risks of U.S. military operations; and ultimately, subvert the strategy of "holding the ring."

- Strategic Conventional Technologies

Strategic conventional technologies are essentially an umbrella category encompassing both weapons and supporting systems. It includes long range weapons which can exploit advanced external or internal guidance systems to attack critical operations nodes in wartime or in a crisis as well as critical support systems like imaging satellites, Command, Control, Communications and Information (C³I) technologies, and advanced satellite launch vehicles. Mobile ballistic missiles and mobile cruise missiles armed with advanced conventional warheads and exploiting Global Positioning System (GPS)/GLONASS, differential GPS, or some other terminal guidance system, are often the best examples of the first class of technologies. The availability of new sophisticated civilian imagery systems like SPOT and LANDSAT, modern microwave communications systems, and commercial satellite launch technologies are good examples of the latter class of technologies.[20]

The proliferation of these systems is judged destabilizing for at least two reasons: First, they can inflict high leverage harm. Accurate conventional missiles which often are undetectable before launch can interdict certain crucial warfighting nodes and severely impede the pace of military operations. Advanced support systems allow an adversary to exploit information technologies either to checkmate U.S. and allied counter-responses or to attack U.S. and allied interests more efficiently. Second, the acquisition of such systems can signal a perceived change in the balance of power. To be sure, all of the new strategic conventional technologies can be countered at the operational-technical level of combat, but the countermeasures often vary in effectiveness and some can require a substantial amount of time to be effective. For these reasons, the operational effectiveness of new strategic conventional technologies can converge with their symbolic importance to create destabilizing perceptions of changes in the relative balance of power within the region.

Besides these strategic technologies, it is possible to identify a variety of other weapons technology acquisitions which could be destabilizing in that they conform to one or more of Rowen's provisos. In general terms, these conventional technologies can be divided into two generic classes: force projection and battlespace denial technologies. The former category refers to those technologies which enable a state to hold at risk the homeland of a regional neighbor, while the latter refers to those technologies which enable a regional state to impede U.S. power projection operations in defense of its allies or its general operations within and around the theater. Very obviously, technolo-

---

[20] For further discussion see, Sokolski, "Nonapocalyptic Proliferation," pp. 115–128.

gies associated with force projection can be used with remarkable flexibility for battlespace denial, but the reverse relationship does not usually hold true in most instances.

## Force Projection Technologies

Force projection technologies can be defined as those capabilities which enable a state to attack or hold at risk the homeland of a neighboring state in a serious or sustained way. Since force projection requires literally thousands of discrete technologies working synergistically, only the most critical combat end-systems will be identified. The object of the discussion here is not so much to identify which force architectures hold the key to successful force projection but to specify which combat technologies appear to be *both* critical to projection success *and* conform to the Rowen provisos.

• Land Warfare Technologies

Of the three dimensions of projecting force—land, air and sea power—it is appropriate to begin with land power. This combat arm represents the "ultimate" conventional threat: ground forces can threaten a state in a decisive way through their ability to seize, occupy, and hold territory. Ground forces usually take the form of light troops, designed to seize beachheads or bridgeheads in preparation for follow-on forces, and heavy troops, capable of sustained, high-intensity, combat operations over a longer period of time. The former category includes light infantry, marine, airborne and air assault elements, while the latter category involves armored and mechanized forces. All the major East Asian states—China, Japan, North and South Korea—have some such forces, each with varying levels of sophistication and competence.

The best way to analyze which land warfare technologies might be problematic for stability is through an examination of the styles of warfare practiced in the region. At the present time, the ground forces of all the major regional states are incapable of action much beyond attrition warfare. The Chinese People's Liberation Army represents the epitome of such capability. The North and South Korean forces are capable of some limited maneuver warfare: In the North, this is principally a function of its hypothesized invasion plans; and, in the South, this is mainly a function of the American style of warfare overlaid on South Korean forward defense planning. The Japanese ground forces are principally designed as a home defense force which specialize in attrition tactics associated with large-scale perimeter defense.

Since all the major regional ground forces are capable primarily of attrition styles of war, there is at present effective deterrence stability. Attrition warfare is slow and plodding: it does not enable quick and decisive victories and, even in the North Korean case, where the emphasis on maneuver is perhaps more conspicuous, this strategy stands some chance of success only because the relatively small size of the peninsula make limited maneuver capabilities more significant than they would otherwise be. The net result is that each of the regional states have relatively little ability to significantly threaten the homelands of the others through sustained ground action. Two specific factors converge to create this result. First, the East Asian region is a maritime theater: the major states do not share contiguous land borders and therefore problems of reach and access become critical impediments to mounting significant cross-border operations. Second, the ground forces of the major regional states cannot fight large-scale wars of maneuver because their forces lack the technology, doctrine, training, and sustaining capability required to prosecute such operations over significant distances, *even if the problems of reach and access were somehow surmounted.* The Korean case is somewhat of an exception here, but even this anomaly will conform to the rule once reunification takes place.

The inability to prosecute anything much beyond attrition warfare (and that too, only at short distances) makes the regional situation stable at present. As a consequence, no regional state can effectively undertake a quick and decisive, large-scale, theater campaign which threatens the political integrity of its neighbors, and no regional state has the capability to prevent the United States from dominating the battlefield with its maneuver/maneuver-by-fire methods of warfighting. So long as this situation persists, the larger U.S. strategy of holding the ring would be sustainable. But, should one or more regional states acquire the technologies which allow them to prosecute maneuver/maneuver-by-fire methods of warfighting—thereby making quick and decisive battlefield victories a possibility—regional stability would then be threatened.

Technology acquisitions which allow regional states to fight deep battles efficiently through the use of information dominance regimes, would be particularly problematic for U.S. regional strategy. Three core classes of land warfare technologies can be identified in this connection. The first class consists of advanced sensor technologies capable of long-range, all-weather, battlefield target detection and acquisition. These systems range from comparatively simple technologies like the Israeli Pioneer series Unmanned Aerial Vehicles (UAVs) to very sophisticated and complex deep battlefield reconnaissance systems like J-STARS and advanced reconnaissance satellites. These technologies are critical because they enable a field commander to "see" farther and clearer than an adversary, thereby enabling the former to increase his situational awareness while simultaneously denying the latter any advantage accruing from opacity and surprise.

The second class consists of advanced communications networks which are rapid, reliable, and secure, and advanced battlefield fire-management systems, which process, prioritize, and rapidly distribute large volumes of accurate targeting information to the various fire support units on the battlefield. This class of technologies comprises a whole range of systems including communications satellites, information processing centers, and fire management systems like TACFIRE. These technologies are critical because they act as the links between the "eyes" of the force and its combat capabilities; they allow the force as a whole to react in a coordinated way to the evolving threat and they help reduce the complexity of the battlefield to manageable levels.

The third class consists of advanced fire systems like artillery, rockets, tanks, and tactical aviation systems which can deliver a variety of highly lethal, long-range, guided munitions. This class of technologies comprises a wide variety of intelligent munitions, sensor fused weapons, and guided projectiles and bombs which, taken together, enable an increase in lethality orders of magnitude greater than that achievable through employment of "dumb" munitions. They serve to reduce the mass of fires required for attaining certain pre-specified kill ratios even as they simultaneously expand the rate at which an adversary force can be effectively neutralized. These technologies are critical because they allow a battlefield commander to neutralize the adversary with great accuracy and effectiveness throughout the depth of the battlefield and sometimes even before he actually arrives at the Forward Line of one's Own Troops (FLOT).

If such technologies are acquired in sufficient numbers by any regional state—*such that they could effectively transform their present attrition style of warfighting*—this development would be destabilizing according to the provisos described previously. To the degree that they allow a regional state to (1) prosecute information dominant forms of warfighting; (2) execute maneuver/maneuver-by-fire strategies that lead to quick and decisive campaigns; (3) fight effectively in night and adverse weather conditions; and, (4) to disrupt the $C^3I$ systems of the United States or its allies, such capabilities provide the means to inflict high leverage strategic harm. A proliferation of such military capabilities would attenuate the greatest strength of the United States: the ability to circumvent larger numbers and greater distance through innovative applications of military technology, superior doctrine and training, and creative force employment concepts.

However, the diffusion of such technology would not necessarily leave the United States or its allies abjectly vulnerable. This is the one significant difference between the proliferation of WMD and conventional military technologies. Rowen's second proviso may therefore not apply completely in the case of land warfare technologies. But, to the degree that one state acquires such capabilities when others either cannot or do not, it could result in a change in the perceived balance of power. For this phenomenon to occur, however, the regional states would have to be convinced that the possessors of these new technologies could actually use them effectively in combat. This question is difficult to assess because success in land warfare is dependent on the complex interaction of man and material and not simply on the acquisition of several discrete high technology instruments. For this reason, accurate *ex ante* evaluations of ground force capabilities have been difficult to undertake in peacetime. In all likelihood, therefore, even if information-exploiting military technologies for land warfare are acquired by some states in East Asia, the relative inconspicuousness of these technologies and their non-obvious impact on warfighting capability would prevent any dramatic shifts in the perceived balance of power—until it may well be too late. It is this characteristic which make transformations in land warfare so dangerous, thereby warranting careful attention on the part of the United States.

The inability to fight large-scale wars of maneuver effectively constitutes one reason for believing that regional land warfare technology acquisitions do not as yet significantly threaten political stability in East Asia. The other reason for this stability derives from the inability of the major regional states to project power across the maritime divides that separate them one from the other. This latter reason, loosely speaking, constitutes the sufficient condition for regional stability: it suggests that even if some regional states acquire the ability to execute war-winning strategies on the battlefield, this capability will remain relatively unimportant so long as they cannot overcome the separation of political space imposed by geography. But this separation can be overcome by air and naval power, to which we will now turn.

• Air Warfare Technologies

There exist essentially three general kinds of air warfare technologies which, if acquired, would enable regional states to project power over strategic distances and thereby disturb the current stability in the region. Each of these technologies either enables a state to enhance its strategic reach or enables it to maintain that enhanced reach more robustly.

The first kind of "breakthrough" air power technology is long-range transportation and lift capabilities. The acquisition of a dedicated long-range lift capability would enable states to transport troops and materials over long distances, thereby enabling a state to use ground forces to affect strategic outcomes in areas that are relatively far from home. If such dedicated aircraft are in fact able to operate from austere and unprepared airfields close to a battlefront, they become particularly potent instruments of force projection, since they can disgorge troops and equipment much closer to the scene of action. No East Asian state currently has such a fleet of dedicated long-range transports, but both China and Japan have shown interest in the acquisition of such a capability.

By itself, however, long-range transport and lift capability does not a superpower make. For one thing, the ability of aircraft to move significant amounts of heavy weaponry is severely limited.

Consequently, such aircraft are best suited for transporting light forces either to prepare airfields or as part of an airborne operation (designed, for example, to secure an airfield, after which they could be used to move vital supplies in support of the military forces already committed). Airlift capabilities, by themselves, are therefore limited instruments of power projection. But their acquisition by one or more regional states would be destabilizing because: (1) it would symbolize a desire for extended strategic reach, and possibly be a precursor to some greater and more sustainable form of force projection; (2) it would enable its possessors to mount at least some limited projection operations, involving ground troops, with the intent of holding and occupying territory; and (3) it would enable its possessors to sustain military operations in a more concentrated way at a greater distance from home. To the degree that one or more of these objectives are sustainable, regional states will begin to acquire capabilities that are threatening to one another. In the Japanese case, such fears are exacerbated by memories of the past; in the Chinese case, such fears are exacerbated by uncertainties of the future. In any event, they conspire to put increased pressure on the U.S. regional strategy of holding the ring.

The second kind of "breakthrough" air power technology is air-to-air refueling capabilities. Such capabilities would be embodied by a fleet of dedicated refueling tankers which enables states to augment their force projection capabilities in two ways. First, they extend the range of tactical aircraft, thus allowing even relatively short legged combat aircraft to acquire deeper operational reach. Second, they increase the tempo of operations and warfighting efficiency by preempting the need for aircraft to return to base merely to refuel.

Both these considerations are germane in the East Asian region. First, large numbers of advanced tactical aircraft would suddenly acquire greater strategic reach if one or more regional states should possess dedicated tanker capabilities. This extended reach would be particularly useful, given that several of the contested areas of interest to the regional states lie at some distance from their principal air bases. Second, dedicated tanking capability would allow a regional air force to undertake extended combat missions either in the close support or in the air superiority role. No East Asian state currently possesses dedicated tanker assets, but China and Japan have expressed interest in acquiring such aircraft. The Chinese People's Liberation Army Air

Force (PLAAF) is known to have conducted some refueling demonstrations and it is expected that China will have a fleet of dedicated
tankers somewhere early in the next century.[21] For such a capability
to be significant, however, the tanker fleet itself must be significant
in size relative to the rest of the force and the kinds of missions that
the force pursues; it must also be part of a larger transformation in
combat force structure and capabilities, and must be available to
support a large number of aircraft on a routine basis.

The third kind of "breakthrough" air power technology is advanced
combat aircraft, advanced munitions, and a sophisticated employment doctrine. Advanced combat aircraft, including long-range
strike aircraft and interceptors, stealth aircraft, and various specialized combat capabilities like Electronic Counter Measures (ECM),
Suppression of Enemy Air Defenses (SEAD), reconnaissance and
Airborne Warning and Control System (AWACS) platforms, represent
a major transformation in the force projection capability of a state.
This is particularly true today because the availability of advanced
conventional munitions has brought air power closer than ever before to Douhet's concept of the "destruction of nations"[22] from the
air.

When mated to a sophisticated air power doctrine, modern combat
aviation technologies can be extremely effective in destroying both
an adversary's capability and will to fight. Current advanced munitions have helped attenuate considerably the traditional weakness of
air power: the inaccuracy of conventional weaponry which brings in
its trail the need for a large number of aircraft sorties and a huge
amount of expended ordnance to attain a given desired level of
destruction. For this reason, several East Asian states have begun to
invest in advanced combat aircraft and sophisticated munitions. The
Japanese, followed by the South Korean air force, have traditionally
been the principal employers of high quality combat aviation. Today,
the Chinese PLAAF and several Southeast Asian states are seriously

---

[21] For an extended analysis of trends in Chinese airpower development, consult
Kenneth W. Allen, Glenn Krumel, and Jonathan D. Pollack, *China's Air Force Enters the
21st Century*, MR-580-AF (Santa Monica: RAND, 1995), especially Chap. VIII.

[22] This theme, and the traditional limitations thereof, is explored in Edward Warner,
"Douhet, Mitchell, Seversky: Theories of Air Warfare," in Edward Earle Mead (ed.),
*Makers of Modern Strategy* (Princeton: Princeton University Press, 1973), pp. 485-503.

endeavoring to catch up. In the first quarter of the next century, at least a half dozen regional states could be equipped with a comprehensive set of combat aviation technologies including late generation long-range interceptors, attack aircraft, and specialized escorts, all armed with advanced munitions and capable of being employed in highly centralized and well orchestrated theater air campaigns.

While is relatively easy to identify which air warfare technologies would advance the force projection capabilities of a particular state, it is more difficult to assess which of these technologies would be unambiguously destabilizing. It is also difficult to make the case *in the abstract* that long-range transport and lift capabilities, dedicated air-to-air refueling tankers, and advanced conventional combat aircraft represent capabilities which could inflict high leverage strategic harm. Such technologies would certainly make for more capable adversaries, a higher level of combat opposition, and more difficult theater campaigns, but whether they can inflict high leverage strategic harm is difficult to evaluate outside of a specific operational context.

For all its sophistication, the limitations of air power should also be recognized. While the presence of air power transforms previously insular land forces into potent projection instruments, and while air power can provide a projection role independently, its flexibility and ubiquity are often insufficient to overcome its limited sustaining power. Conventional air power can do a great damage in small spasms, but its ability to serve as a sustained source of threat is a function of whether its possessors know how to generate strategic air campaigns and whether secure forward facilities are available to maximize its employment. Whether air power acquisitions in the region constitute capabilities which can inflict high leverage strategic harm turns not on the presence of one or another discrete technology, but on how technologies are integrated into a coherent air power employment regime. For example, if regional states begin to acquire and maintain secure forward bases, such acquisitions would constitute a significant indicator of an effort to think about air power strategically. Such a change would bring present air power acquisitions closer to the level where they can be deemed capable of inflicting significant strategic harm.

However, the acquisition of stealth aircraft by regional states is a different matter. No reliable detection system capable of acquiring and tracking these systems currently exists, and consequently the acquisition of stealth aviation technologies in the region would represent a straightforward example of a technology capable of threatening regional neighbors and imposing a significant (and possibly prohibitive) cost on American warfighting capabilities. Such a technology clearly comports with Rowen's second proviso—the absence of an effective defense—and for this reason alone would be deemed destabilizing.

In addition, most of the air warfare technologies considered thus far would be problematic in that each of them—if acquired in some critical minimum number—would entail significant alterations in the perceived balance of power. Long range transports, dedicated refueling tankers, and advanced long-range combat aircraft armed with advanced guided munitions possessed by China or Japan would signify an augmented capability by these states to affect politico-strategic outcomes far from their borders. The acquisition of such technologies could signify an increase in Chinese and Japanese relative power vis-à-vis each other and vis-à-vis a more distant United States and, consequently, would increase the pressures on holding the ring. But the difficulties of acquiring such capabilities in strategically significant numbers should not be minimized.

• Naval Warfare Technologies

Naval warfare technologies for force projection can help compensate for the limited sustaining capability of air power analyzed above. Three kinds of technologies are critical in this regard.

The first kind of naval warfare technology which would allow states to deploy large amounts of sustainable combat power in close proximity to other maritime neighbors is afloat aviation in the form of aircraft carriers. Aircraft carriers come in many shapes and sizes, and the configuration chosen crucially affects the ability to project power. At the most sophisticated end lie designs like the Nimitz class carriers which displace more than 80,000 tons, carry balanced air wings of about 100 aircraft, and specialize in the full spectrum of combat operations. In the middle lie a variety of carrier designs ranging between 40-75,000 tons, with much smaller air wings (25-40 aircraft) and specializing in one or two specific combat tasks. At the low end are primarily V/STOL designs for ships displacing between 20-30,000 tons, carrying air wings of about 10-25 aircraft and specializing in a single primary mission like ASW or convoy escort.[23]

Irrespective of the precise carrier design, the possessors of carrier aviation acquire increased power for projection operations, though the quality of that power can vary considerably, depending on the size and quality of onboard aviation. At the present time, no East Asian state deploys aircraft carriers of any kind. That is certain to change, however, as the Chinese Navy acquires its first carrier in the early 21st century. During the 1980s, the Japanese Navy discussed the possibility of acquiring some aviation capable ships in order to defend the air and sea lanes a thousand miles from the home islands, but nothing resulted from these discussions. In Southeast Asia, the Thai Navy appears to be the first fleet that could see a small helicopter carrier in service by the end of the century, while further away the Indian Navy, which has always been a consistent believer in carrier aviation, probably will maintain a two carrier component well into the future.

The second kind of "breakthrough" naval warfare technology involves surface action groups consisting of large ocean going vessels specializing in various missions including Anti-Air Warfare (AAW), Anti-Submarine Warfare (ASW), Command, Control and Communications ($C^3$), or fire support. In some circumstances, capable vessels of this sort can substitute for aircraft carriers in the force projection and support role. For example, a ship equipped with long-range surface-to-air missiles, together with its associated sensors and fire control systems, could provide potent air defense cover for either squadrons at sea or for offshore invading forces. Not surprisingly, most East Asian states, including Japan and to a lesser degree, South Korea, have maintained major surface combatants capable of operating with a relative degree of autonomy. Those that did not traditionally maintain such forces, like China, are actively involved in programs designed to catch up. The value of such naval capabilities essentially lies in the fact that they allow its possessor to fulfill two

---

[23] A good survey of the variety of carrier designs and their implications for naval warfare can be found in John Lehman, *Aircraft Carriers: The Real Choices* (Beverly Hills: Sage Publications, 1978).

roles simultaneously: they act as a deterrent against seaborne threats, including amphibious invasion, while concurrently bequeathing some force projection capability, including the ability to "show the flag."

The third kind of "breakthrough" naval warfare technology involves dedicated amphibious forces. The phrase "amphibious forces" is essentially a shorthand for an array of diverse and complex warfighting technologies, which include organic strike aviation, fire support capability, sealift and specialized amphibious vessels, command technologies, and various offshore and beachead mobility systems. Possessing such capabilities in a comprehensive way allows a state to undertake projection operations that pose serious threats to an adversary's homeland. At present, no East Asian state possesses the range of amphibious capabilities required to make independent, high-threat, force projection operations possible. The Chinese Navy has one amphibious division equivalent, but lacks the maritime capabilities required for forcible entry operations. The Japanese and South Korean navies have only token amphibious forces.

The growth of regional naval capabilities will unquestionably increase pressures on the U.S. strategy of holding the ring. Naval warfare technologies, especially amphibious warfare capabilities, will allow regional states to threaten the homelands of their neighbors in a more sustained way than is possible in the absence of such capabilities. This fact, however, must be weighed against other countervailing considerations. Naval warfare technologies are easier to acquire than to use effectively. In particular, employing such instruments against U.S. naval power is almost always likely to be a losing proposition because of the vast difference in comparative advantage. The U.S. Navy has better equipment, training, and doctrine and is designed to fight on and dominate the high seas. For this reason, regional naval technology acquisitions designed for force projection are unlikely to represent weapons which can inflict high leverage strategic harm on the United States *under normal conditions*. They would increase the levels of communicated threat among the regional states, but so long as the potential targeted states are allied with the United States it is unlikely that an ascendant power would be able to hold the homelands of U.S. allies at risk or impede the ability of the United States to defend its allies or operate within the region. In this sense, regional naval warfare projection technologies cannot be counted as significant under Rowen's first and second provisos, which describe weapons capable of inflicting high leverage harm and which lack effective countermeasures.

Regional naval acquisitions, however, would certainly relate to the third proviso: changes in the perceived balance of power. This would apply especially to acquisitions of aircraft carriers and dedicated amphibious capabilities. It is here that potential Chinese or Japanese acquisitions of these capabilities could be destabilizing. It is ironic, however, that naval technologies—though in principle the most serious force projection capabilities—would be the least efficacious instruments of power projection in East Asia because of the combat capabilities of the U.S. Navy. It is only when fears of U.S. withdrawal become real that the new regional naval force projection acquisitions acquire a bite they otherwise lack.

## Battlespace Denial Technologies

While the effect of conventional force projection technologies for stability may be a matter of some debate, no such uncertainty afflicts the battlespace denial technologies identified below.

• Submarines

The proliferation of new attack submarines in the East Asian region would be an issue of great concern. New attack submarines, whether diesel-electric, nuclear, or equipped with air-independent propulsion technologies, would be problematic because their possessors could use them to effect a variety of sea denial strategies.[24] Submarines would be particularly effective for interdicting trade movements and Sea Lines Of Communication (SLOCs). Since the East Asian theater hosts some of the densest seaborne trade patterns in the world, and since trade constitutes the lifeline of all the regional economies, submarines would be particularly capable of threatening the economic well-being of the regional states. Diesel-electric submarines and boats equipped with air independent propulsion systems would be sufficient for *guerre de course* operations. However,

---

[24] James Fitzgerald and John Benedict, "There is a Sub Threat," United States Naval Institute *Proceedings* 116:8 (August 1990), pp. 57–63.

for operations against escorted commerce or against naval forces, advanced, quiet, nuclear submarines would be necessary. Such boats would need advanced on-board sensor systems, connectivity technologies required to operate in tandem with other battlespace denial forces, and sophisticated weapons like anti-ship tactical cruise missiles and wake-homing torpedoes.

Submarines with these capabilities in the hands of all potential U.S. regional adversaries would be clearly and unambiguously destabilizing. Advanced subsurface warfare capabilities thus come closest to meeting all three of Rowen's provisos outlined earlier. Submarines can inflict high leverage strategic harm; they can hold at risk critical surface assets and immensely complicate U.S. power projection operations in the region. They are also difficult to defend against: concentrated ASW operations can counter roving submarine threats, but ASW is a tedious, time consuming business and the desired level of success may not be possible in an operationally relevant time period. Submarines represent high-value assets which can change the perceived balance of power: by being able to impose *relatively* significant costs even on otherwise well-endowed navies, their presence alone often serves to underscore the potential for serious challenges and, to that extent, conveys incipient shifts in the balance of power.

* Mine Warfare Systems

Advanced mine systems can represent destabilizing technologies for reasons similar to that identified for submarines. Unlike submarines, however, mines are highly inflexible instruments. They are effective for the most part only if their intended targets either make physical contact with them or cross their relatively limited sensor range. They can become critical barrier weapons, however, in certain enclosed areas like harbor channels; and, they can function as battlespace shaping devices which serve to channel seaborne traffic into certain predesignated killing zones where targets can be attacked by waiting submarines, aircraft, or surface combatants. While mines can inflict significant strategic harm, their potential effects can be neutralized by mine counter-measures forces. Such mine countermeasure warfare is inherently easier than ASW because of the mine's inability to respond evasively to mine hunting operations. Mines do not enjoy significant visibility either, and so it is hard to make the case that their presence conspicuously alters the perceived balance of power.

But, because they can be laid anonymously and because of their capacity to deny maritime and naval forces free access, they should be treated seriously.

The potentially destabilizing military technologies reviewed in this paper may be summarized in the following way. The regional acquisition of WMD, associated delivery systems, and strategic conventional technologies would be seriously destabilizing because they would significantly undermine the ability of the United States to sustain its regional strategy. They conform to most, if not all, of the Rowen provisos. The acquisition of military technologies which make regional ground forces capable of executing information (maneuver/maneuver-by-fire) warfare possible could be seriously destabilizing, but such acquisitions are unlikely to occur in any significant way in the policy-relevant future. Even if they did occur, changes in the ground combat posture would be of lesser significance so long as they were unaccompanied by changes in the air and naval power projection posture of their possessors. The air power technology transformations in the region could be more destabilizing, because these changes would allow the local ground forces to operate in new areas, thereby increasing the regional perceptions of threat; they will serve as independent instruments of power projection; and, if used effectively, they can impose significant costs on U.S. military operations throughout the region. For similar reasons, any significant transformation in regional naval warfare capabilities is also important, with the key technology of concern being quiet, high endurance submarines armed with advanced sensors and weapons. Disconcertingly for the United States, the most significant changes in the East Asian conventional military posture appears in the area of air power and sea denial technologies—areas which merit careful and continued monitoring and assessment.

## TOWARDS A RESPONSE

There is no "quick fix" to the problems of technology proliferation in East Asia. A variety of responses are nevertheless possible, each of which has lesser or greater utility depending on the kind of technology proliferation in question. It is useful to conceptualize the responses to the problem in two parts: the political and the instrumental, with the political dimension being perhaps the most important.

The political dimension essentially consists of deepening the structures that have brought East Asia its unparalleled stability in the postwar period: the security alliances with the United States. These security alliances essentially guarantee that, no matter what problems of regional technology proliferation ultimately arise, the local allies of the United States will never have to confront them alone. This is particularly important in the case of smaller regional states like Korea and those in Southeast Asia which are disadvantaged by the close proximity of relatively larger and more capable neighbors. Deepening the security relationship with the United States essentially consists of making the asymmetrical responsibilities currently existing within the alliance even more robust. This entails three separate but related ingredients.

First, it means reinforcing the present division of labor. This would allow the United States to provide the offensive capabilities required for local defense, without in any way trying to indigenously substitute or supplant these capabilities in a manner that might be threatening to other neighboring states.

Second, it means discarding the illusory appeal of independence in favor of more robust intra-alliance interdependence. This implies eschewing both the option of independence from the United States and the option of working towards greater regional integration without U.S. participation. Both these alternatives, by eventually resulting in Chinese or Japanese hegemony or Sino-Japanese condominium, will threaten the security and autonomy of the smaller regional states in more ways than are imaginable today.

Third, it means strengthening the triangular relationship among the United States, Japan and Korea. This involves developing a common security strategy to deal with new security threats on the horizon. It involves greater cooperation between the smaller states in the region under the aegis of the United States, with an eye to warding off any potential future challenges from larger regional states along the Asian rimland: China, Russia, and, over the longer term, possibly India.

Besides the political dimension discussed above, the instrumental dimensions of dealing with weapons technology proliferation can take multiple forms.[25]

First, the United States and its regional allies can work towards strengthening the global prohibition regimes currently in place. The most important of these are the Biological Weapons Convention and the Chemical Weapons Convention signed in 1972 and 1993, respectively. Strengthening these regimes would help sustain global monitoring mechanisms, adopt common diplomatic positions when dealing with cheaters, and work to enforce political penalties when they are necessary. Enforcing this regime strictly would be most useful in preventing the deployment of militarily useful quantities of chemical and biological weapons in the region.

Second, the United States and its regional allies can work towards strengthening those global constraining regimes currently in place. The most important such regime is the Nuclear Non-Proliferation Treaty signed in 1970 and renewed in 1995. Strengthening this regime, however, involves more than mere legal extension. Like the efforts connected with the Biological and Chemical Weapons Conventions, it involves contributing to and sustaining monitoring mechanisms, adopting common diplomatic positions when dealing with cheaters, and working to enforce political penalties when such are necessary. Such commitments will help raise the costs of nuclear weapons proliferation while the nuclear weapons states seek more permanent solutions to the larger political problems associated with the future of their own nuclear arsenals.

Third, the United States and its regional allies can work towards developing more robust regimes controlling the transfers of advanced conventional arms or specific weapons technology subsystems. Such regimes would require agreement about what constitutes potentially problematic technology systems (according to the Rowen provisos, for example) and commitments to eschew the sale of such systems.

---

[25] This discussion is based on James A. Schear, "The Diffusion of Advanced Weaponry in the Developing World: Existing Norms, Agreements and Modes of Control," in W. Thomas Wander, Eric H. Arnett, and Paul Bracken, eds., *The Diffusion of Advanced Weaponry: Technologies, Regional Implications, and Responses* (Washington, DC: American Association for the Advancement of Science, 1994), pp. 329–341.

An effective regime would require the creation of a post-COCOM list of strategic technologies; an enforcement mechanism to oversee and regulate the requisite controls; and, perhaps a system of subsidies to compensate those producers who suffer because of forfeited sales of such high technology.[26]

Fourth, the United States and its regional allies can work towards developing a more robust transparency regime which identifies the introduction of specific advanced conventional arms or specific weapons technology subsystems in the region. Admittedly, such a regime would be largely a confidence building measure, and it would have to include all states in the East Asian region and those with weapons systems capable of reaching the region on a routine basis, if it is to be successful. The beneficial effects of such a regime would include: early-warning about potential problems; increasing clarity about intentions; and hopefully, greater self-restraint on the part of the regional states.

Finally, the United States and its regional allies can work towards developing restriction regimes which prohibit the introduction of specific advanced conventional arms or specific weapons technology subsystems in the region. Such a regime would be extremely unpalatable to many states and, consequently, may have to be tagged to larger global restriction regimes like those discussed in connection with the abolition of ballistic missiles.

Undertaking some or all of these responses cooperatively would go a long way towards enhancing stability in the East Asian region.

---

[26] For some excellent recent RAND work in this connection, see Kenneth Watman, Marcy Agmon and Charles Wolf, Jr., *Controlling Conventional Arms Transfers*, MR-369-USDP (Santa Monica: RAND, 1994).

# Chapter Four

# PUTTING MUZZLES ON THE "DRAGONS": MILITARY BUILDUP AND REGIONAL SECURITY IN EAST ASIA[1]

Taehyun Kim

## INTRODUCTION: THE REGION IN PERSPECTIVE

With few exceptions, social scientists are not endowed with the luxury of laboratory experimentation that natural scientists typically enjoy. Comparative political scientists seem to have somewhat better luck. They have units to compare so as to derive theoretical insights and to test hypotheses. International relations theorists are far more poorly endowed. Laboratory experiments are unthinkable, although simulations are possible. Units are not available to compare, since study generally focuses on a single unit—the international system. It is systemic change that motivates theorists to explore new possibilities and test old hypotheses. A typical case occurred in the 1960s when nuclear proliferation among major powers seemed to change the system structure from a bipolar to a multipolar one. The focus of debate concerned the relative stability of bipolar and multipolar systems.[2]

---

[1] In this paper, the East Asian region is defined in geographical terms, consisting of the group of countries ranging from Japan to the East to Myanmar to the West. In the analysis, however, some of the countries are dropped due to their relative insignificance in the context of this paper, and the data problem.

[2] Kenneth N. Waltz, "The Stability of a Bipolar World," *Daedalus* 93 (1964); Waltz, "International Structure, National Force, and the Balance of World Power," *Journal of International Affairs* 21 (1967); Karl W. Deutsch and J. David Singer, "Multipolar Power Systems and International Stability," *World Politics* 16 (April 1964); Richard Rosecrance, "Bipolarity, Multipolarity, and the Future," *Journal of Conflict Resolution* 10 (1966).

Changes in recent years seem even more profound. James Rosenau, for one, argues that such turbulence is unprecedented in three hundred years of international history. This turbulence, Rosenau contends, is characterized by unusual complexity and variability.[3] But this change does not necessarily imply instability or increased risks of conflict between states. There are numerous reasons why we can be optimistic about the world's future. The Cold War is over and disarmament has ensued, albeit selectively. There have been waves of democratization across the world, bringing about substantial improvement of human rights. Central Europe, long seen as the likely main battlefield of another world war, is at peace. The decades-long conflict between the Arabs and Israel is becoming history, and apartheid in South Africa has ended. As the Cold War came to an end and agreements among major powers became easier, the United Nations has also emerged as a significant forum.[4]

Such developments appear to support a theoretical position in the field of international relations—that of neo-liberal institutionalism.[5] Yet neo-liberals have not recorded much success in convincing their neo-realist rivals. John Mearsheimer, for example, in 1990 predicted a "back to the future" environment in Europe. In Mearsheimer's view, the history of modern international politics has been characterized by wars, with the "long peace" since 1945 being more an exception than the rule. Among factors to explain the "long peace," the bipolar structure, which was praised for its stability by Kenneth Waltz, has collapsed along with the balance of power between the superpowers. Even the reduction of nuclear arsenals could become a source of concern, if one subscribes to the proposition that nuclear

---

[3]James N. Rosenau, *Turbulence in World Politics: A Theory of Change and Continuity* (Princeton, NJ: Princeton University Press, 1990), pp. 5, 78.

[4.] Samuel P. Huntington, *The Third Wave: Democratization in the Late Twentieth Century* (Norman: University of Oklahoma Press, 1992); John Mueller, *Retreat from Doomsday: The Obsolescence of Major War* (New York: Basic Books, 1989); Bruce Russett, *Controlling the Sword: The Democratic Governance of National Security* (Cambridge, Mass.: Harvard University Press, 1990); "To Conquer the Past," *Time* (January 3, 1994); James N. Rosenau, *The United Nations in a Turbulent World* (Boulder, Colo.: Lynne Rienner Publishers, 1992).

[5]Robert O. Keohane, "Neo-liberal Institutionalism: A Perspective on World Politics," in his *State Power and International Institutions* (Boulder, Colo.: Westview Press, 1986); see also Joseph S. Nye, Jr., "Neorealism and Neoliberalism," *World Politics* 40 (January 1988).

weapons have made war "unthinkable." History shows that system-wide restructuring has usually been accompanied by major wars, and there is a possibility that ethnic conflicts in Eastern Europe may trigger another war.[6]

From a more evolutionary point of view, however, such pessimism may seem anachronistic. In this latter perspective, current developments may signal the end of "modernity," upon which the pessimistic outlook draws. In modern international politics, sovereign states were sole actors, performing exclusive functions in pursuit of national power and wealth. In post-modern global politics, by contrast, actors are more complex entities with more diverse functions. The sovereignty of nation-states is being challenged by the rise of both supra-national actors such as "region-states" and sub-national actors like ethnic groups with enhanced autonomy. There are other important considerations, such as the environment, technology, information, and communication, that may override the physical security of nations, and more kinds of actors are emerging, typically international organizations, to deal with these new problems.[7]

I will not attempt to evaluate these contending visions. Rather, each claim may contain a partial truth. However, the relative validity of these claims may vary across regions. In this regard, the East Asian region, particularly Northeast Asia, is where trends appear in favor of the pessimists.

First, a major transformation in the power structure of the regional system is underway. The once predominant roles of the two superpowers are diminishing, and those of Japan and China are ascending, both relatively and absolutely. While Russia is struggling with its domestic reform program, the United States suffers from the loss of

---

[6]John J. Mearsheimer, "Back to the Future: Instability in Europe After the Cold War," *International Security* 15 (Summer 1990); John L. Gaddis, "Long Peace: Elements of Stability in the Postwar International System," *International Security* 10 (Spring 1986); Kenneth N. Waltz, *Theory of International Politics* (Reading, Mass.: Addison-Wesley, 1979); Robert Gilpin, *War and Change in World Politics* (Princeton, NJ: Princeton University Press, 1981).

[7]John Gerard Ruggie, "Territoriality and Beyond: Problematizing Modernity in International Relations," *International Organization* 47 (Winter 1993); Young S. Ha, ed., *Post-modern Global Politics* (Seoul: Nanam, 1993) (in Korean). See also Rosenau, *Turbulence in World Politics.*

domestic support for its international commitments. At the same time, however, China is advancing very rapidly in its economic development, and Japan is actively searching for the role of a "normal state."

Secondly, many legacies of the Cold War still remain unresolved. The division of the Korean peninsula is one such example, and the political relationship between China and Taiwan has not progressed very far from earlier days. In addition, the Russo-Japanese conflict over the "northern territories" and historical enmity between Korea and Japan are among the continuing sources of conflict, which were either overshadowed by or dormant during the Cold War. Ironically, these sources of conflict may now again come to the fore, precisely because the Cold War came to an end.[8]

Thirdly, this region is witnessing a disturbing trend towards an arms buildup, contrary to the global trend of disarmament. Military expenditures by the nations in the region are growing and nations are competitively acquiring high-tech weapons. It is another irony that, without an appreciable conversion of military industry to civilian purposes, the military buildup in this region may increase proportionally to the extent of disarmament in other regions.

In the next section, I examine the nature and extent of military buildup by nations in the region, explore its causes, and evaluate its consequences. Then, I suggest what it will take to manage the negative consequences that could ensue from such a buildup.

## THE MILITARY BUILDUP IN EAST ASIA:  TRENDS AND POSSIBLE CAUSES

### Recent Patterns

It has been well documented that the East Asian region is engaged in a "paradoxical" build-up of armaments despite the end of the Cold

---

[8]See, for example, Robert L. Pfaltzgraff, Jr., "A New World Order in Asia?" *The Sejong Review* 2 (October 1993) for a succinct summary of the sources of conflict in the region.

War.[9] In this paper, I briefly examine the trends of military buildup in the region using statistics available in *Military Expenditures and Arms Transfers 1991-1992* released by the U.S. Arms Control and Disarmament Agency in March 1994.[10]

It is clear from Tables 1 and 2 and Figure 1 that the world has undergone a large-scale demilitarization since 1987. World military expenditures decreased by about 4 percent and arms imports by more than 20 percent. Such trends are particularly conspicuous in Europe, the main battlefield of the Cold War. The exceptions include the Middle East, reflecting the region's role as a main locale for "hot" wars in the postwar era. The other exception is East Asia. Military ex-

Table 4.1.

World Military Expenditures and Arms Imports

|  | Military Expenditures | | | | Arms Imports | | | |
|  | World Share | | Real Growth Rate | | World Share | | Real Growth Rate | |
|  | 1981 | 1991 | 81–91 | 87–91 | 1981 | 1991 | 81–91 | 87–91 |
|---|---|---|---|---|---|---|---|---|
| **World** | 100.0 | 100.0 | 0.1 | –3.7 | 100.0 | 100.0 | –6.9 | –21.5 |
| Developed | 79.9 | 76.7 | 0.1 | –5.2 | 21.2 | 24.7 | –5.5 | –19.0 |
| Developing | 20.1 | 23.3 | 0.1 | 2.5 | 78.8 | 75.3 | –7.2 | –21.9 |
| **Region** | | | | | | | | |
| Europe | 54.7 | 47.0 | –1.0 | –6.4 | 19.5 | 16.1 | –7.2 | –24.4 |
| North America | 24.9 | 28.1 | 1.5 | –4.0 | 2.8 | 8.2 | 1.1 | –10.8 |
| East Asia | 9.6 | 11.5 | 1.6 | 2.4 | 9.8 | 14.4 | –3.2 | –20.2 |
| Middle East | 6.4 | 8.5 | –0.9 | 9.3 | 35.9 | 41.4 | –7.7 | –18.6 |
| Africa | 1.5 | 1.5 | –1.1 | –3.1 | 17.5 | 3.5 | –18.4 | –39.1 |
| Latin America | 1.5 | 1.5 | –0.2 | –4.7 | 8.1 | 3.8 | –11.4 | –29.3 |
| South Asia | 0.7 | 1.1 | 4.7 | –0.3 | 4.9 | 11.4 | 4.4 | –14.5 |
| Oceania | 0.6 | 0.8 | 2.0 | 0.4 | 1.3 | 1.0 | –2.9 | –32.5 |

SOURCE: Adapted from *World Military Expenditures and Arms Transfers 1991-1992*, Table (p. 2) and 4 (p. 8).

---

[9]Andrew Mack and Desmond Ball, "The Military Build-up in Asia-Pacific," *Pacific Review* 5 (Summer 1992); see also, Gerald Segal, "Managing New Arms Races in the Asia/Pacific," *The Washington Quarterly* 15(3) (Summer 1992); Michael Klare, "A New Great Arms Race," *Foreign Affairs* 72 (Summer 1992).

[10.]U.S. Arms Control and Disarmament Agency, *World Military Expenditures and Arms Transfers 1991-1992*. The data here cover the period of 1981-1991 and may seem dated. But the overall trend, I believe, remains the same. Throughout this paper, the data source is this volume unless otherwise noted.

Table 4.2.

Military Expenditures in Major Regions, 1981-91

|      | East Asia | | | United States | | | Europe | | | World | |
|------|-----|------|------|-------|-------|------|-------|-------|------|--------|------|
|      | (a) | (b)  | (c)  | (a)   | (b)   | (c)  | (a)   | (b)   | (c)  | (a)    | (b)  |
| 1981 | 101.6 | —    | 9.6  | 253.6 | —     | 24.1 | 576.3 | —     | 54.7 | 1053.4 | —    |
| 1982 | 104.9 | 3.2  | 9.4  | 276.1 | 8.9   | 24.8 | 592.8 | 2.9   | 53.3 | 1112.9 | 5.6  |
| 1983 | 105.4 | 0.5  | 9.2  | 294.4 | 6.6   | 25.6 | 602.7 | 1.7   | 52.4 | 1150.2 | 3.4  |
| 1984 | 105.0 | -0.4 | 9.0  | 306.5 | 4.1   | 26.3 | 606.6 | 0.6   | 52.0 | 1167.2 | 1.5  |
| 1985 | 108.4 | 3.2  | 9.1  | 331.6 | 8.2   | 27.7 | 614.9 | 1.4   | 51.4 | 1196.2 | 2.5  |
| 1986 | 110.0 | 1.5  | 9.1  | 341.3 | 2.9   | 28.2 | 620.1 | 0.8   | 51.3 | 1209.7 | 1.1  |
| 1987 | 110.2 | 0.2  | 9.1  | 339.3 | -0.6  | 27.9 | 632.7 | 2.0   | 52.1 | 1214.6 | 0.4  |
| 1988 | 112.0 | 1.6  | 9.3  | 332.3 | -2.1  | 27.7 | 630.8 | -0.3  | 52.6 | 1200.1 | -1.2 |
| 1989 | 115.3 | 2.9  | 9.9  | 329.9 | -0.7  | 28.4 | 595.8 | -5.5  | 51.3 | 1160.5 | -3.3 |
| 1990 | 120.4 | 4.4  | 10.7 | 318.4 | -3.5  | 28.2 | 548.3 | -8.0  | 48.5 | 1129.6 | -2.7 |
| 1991 | 119.7 | -0.6 | 11.5 | 280.3 | -12.0 | 27.0 | 487.4 | -11.1 | 47.0 | 1038.1 | -8.1 |

NOTES:  (a) military expenditures in billion US$ (1991 constant prices).
(b) annual percentage increase.
(c) percent in world total.

penditures by the East Asian countries increased by 2.4 percent during the period of 1987–1991. As a consequence, East Asia's share of world military expenditure rose from 9.6 percent in 1981 and 9.1 percent in 1986 to 11.5 percent in 1991. It should be compared to the European share, which has declined from 54.7 percent in 1981 to 47.0 percent in 1991.

Arms imports by the East Asian states declined in value during the period of 1981-1991, but at a lesser rate than in other regions. As a consequence, the region's share of arms imports grew from 9.8 percent in 1981 to 14.4 percent in 1991, when the region became the second largest recipient of arms transfers in the developing world. The region is also fast becoming a major arms exporting area, indicating a growing capability to design and produce weaponry.

Within East Asia, Northeast Asia is far more dominant than Southeast Asia. The five Northeast Asian countries together spent about twelve times more than the five Southeast Asian countries combined. Except for North Korea, which has been suffering from a real de-

Table 4.3

Military Expenditures by East Asian Countries, 1981–91

| Year | 1981 | 1982 | 1983 | 1984 | 1985 | 1986 | 1987 | 1988 | 1989 | 1990 | 1991 |
|---|---|---|---|---|---|---|---|---|---|---|---|
| **Northeast Asia** | **90977** | **94080** | **94916** | **94367** | **97217** | **98309** | **98561** | **102354** | **105013** | **110634** | **108588** |
| China | 51220 | 51620 | 50480 | 49580 | 49560 | 48510 | 48970 | 49740 | 49080 | 52330 | 51040 |
| Taiwan | 5490 | 6828 | 7541 | 6909 | 8033 | 8338 | 6543 | 7610 | 8923 | 9426 | 9748 |
| Japan | 20660 | 21890 | 22990 | 23950 | 25210 | 26410 | 27780 | 29110 | 30280 | 31460 | 32560 |
| N. Korea | 6778 | 6607 | 6592 | 6543 | 6563 | 6609 | 6641 | 6622 | 6510 | 6178 | 4660 |
| S. Korea | 6829 | 7135 | 7313 | 7385 | 7851 | 8442 | 8627 | 9272 | 10220 | 11240 | 10580 |
| **Southeast Asia** | **7039** | **7282** | **6778** | **6878** | **7277** | **7505** | **7321** | **7122** | **7565** | **7679** | **8875** |
| Indonesia | 2006 | 2025 | 1806 | 1886 | 1805 | 1903 | 1602 | 1590 | 1635 | 1674 | 1732 |
| Malaysia | 1509 | 1569 | 1398 | 1121 | 1089 | 1243 | 1403 | 910 | 1091 | 1109 | 1651 |
| Philippines | 788 | 729 | 702 | 475 | 485 | 717 | 723 | 878 | 989 | 989 | 947 |
| Singapore | 1058 | 1090 | 998 | 1363 | 1560 | 1461 | 1490 | 1692 | 1749 | 1692 | 2107 |
| Thailand | 1678 | 1869 | 1874 | 2033 | 2338 | 2181 | 2103 | 2052 | 2101 | 2215 | 2438 |

*Unit*: millions of US dollars.

Table 4.4

Growth in Military Expenditures in East Asian Countries, 1981–91

| Year | 1982 | 1983 | 1984 | 1985 | 1986 | 1987 | 1988 | 1989 | 1990 | 1991 |
|---|---|---|---|---|---|---|---|---|---|---|
| **Northeast Asia** | **3.4** | **0.9** | **-0.6** | **3.0** | **1.1** | **0.3** | **3.8** | **2.6** | **5.4** | **-1.8** |
| China | 0.8 | -2.2 | -1.8 | 0.0 | -2.1 | 0.9 | 1.6 | -1.3 | 6.6 | -2.5 |
| Taiwan | 24.4 | 10.4 | -8.4 | 16.3 | 3.8 | -21.5 | 16.3 | 17.3 | 5.6 | 3.4 |
| Japan | 6.0 | 5.0 | 4.2 | 5.3 | 4.8 | 5.2 | 4.8 | 4.0 | 3.9 | 3.5 |
| N. Korea | -2.5 | -0.2 | -0.7 | 0.3 | 0.7 | 0.5 | -0.3 | -1.7 | -5.1 | -24.6 |
| S. Korea | 4.5 | 2.5 | 1.0 | 6.3 | 7.5 | 2.2 | 7.5 | 10.2 | 10.0 | -5.9 |
| **Southeast Asia** | **3.5** | **-6.9** | **1.5** | **5.8** | **3.1** | **-2.5** | **-2.7** | **6.2** | **1.5** | **15.6** |
| Indonesia | 0.9 | -10.8 | 4.4 | -4.3 | 5.4 | -15.8 | -0.7 | 2.8 | 2.4 | 3.5 |
| Malaysia | 4.0 | -10.9 | -19.8 | -2.9 | 14.1 | 12.9 | -35.1 | 19.9 | 1.6 | 48.9 |
| Philippines | -7.5 | -3.7 | -32.3 | 2.1 | 47.8 | 0.8 | 21.4 | 12.6 | 0.0 | -4.2 |
| Singapore | 3.0 | -8.4 | 36.6 | 14.5 | -6.3 | 2.0 | 13.6 | 3.4 | -3.3 | 24.5 |
| Thailand | 11.4 | 0.3 | 8.5 | 15.0 | -6.7 | -3.6 | -2.4 | 2.4 | 5.4 | 10.1 |

*Unit*: annual percentage increase.

crease in national output,[11] the military expenditures of all Northeast Asian countries were increasing. But the increase in regional spending was led by the three market economies (i.e., Japan, South Korea and Taiwan). Most of the Southeast Asian countries recorded real increases in military expenditures, particularly after 1987. The only exception is Indonesia, but it began to increase spending again after 1987. Thailand became the sub-region's largest spender at $2.4 billion in 1991.

The asymmetry between these two sub-regions in terms of military spending is not observed in the case of arms imports. Northeast Asian countries still outspend Southeast Asian countries, but the difference is not as big as in the case of military spending. This is related to the fact that Northeast Asian countries are also arms producers and exporters.

The cross-regional comparison of patterns of military build-up suggests that East Asia is building up arms faster than other regions. Further, the region shows an anomalous pattern of increased military expenditure over time, contrary to the global trend of demilitarization. How can we explain such an anomaly?

## Why Do Nations Arm?

Let us start with the basic question of why nations arm. One of the classic and most succinct answers was provided by Lewis F. Richardson more than half a century ago.[12] In essence, Richardson's model states that nations arm because they need weapons *and* they can afford them. Nations need weapons either because they feel threatened or insecure, or because they have "grievances" regarding the status quo and want to change it, or both. But weapons can be used not only to defend oneself, but to attack or dominate others. This dualism in the usage of weapons drives nations into the dynamic process of a defensive arms race. It is akin to what John Herz calls the security dilemma, a phenomenon in which

---

[11]ACDA assigns 20 percent of the estimated Gross National Product of North Korea as its military expenditure.

[12]Lewis F. Richardson, *Arms and Insecurity* (Chicago: Quadrangle Books, 1960).

## Table 4.5

### Arms Imports by East Asian Countries, 1981-91

| Year | 1981 | 1982 | 1983 | 1984 | 1985 | 1986 | 1987 | 1988 | 1989 | 1990 | 1991 |
|------|------|------|------|------|------|------|------|------|------|------|------|
| **Northeast Asia** | **2881** | **3007** | **2614** | **3025** | **3786** | **3353** | **4676** | **4365** | **3906** | **2605** | **2330** |
| China | 194 | 98 | 135 | 634 | 811 | 699 | 736 | 340 | 271 | 187 | 240 |
| Taiwan | 821 | 984 | 648 | 517 | 717 | 474 | 1531 | 1247 | 570 | 598 | 450 |
| Japan | 970 | 843 | 1047 | 1228 | 1248 | 1002 | 1178 | 935 | 1844 | 1040 | 775 |
| N. Korea | 314 | 478 | 257 | 155 | 474 | 510 | 495 | 1134 | 651 | 208 | 90 |
| S. Korea | 582 | 604 | 527 | 491 | 536 | 668 | 736 | 709 | 570 | 572 | 775 |
| **Southeast Asia** | **1508** | **843** | **1325** | **1371** | **1147** | **814** | **1200** | **1400** | **728** | **655** | **730** |
| Indonesia | 657 | 323 | 216 | 168 | 187 | 182 | 294 | 295 | 163 | 218 | 70 |
| Malaysia | 134 | 141 | 365 | 530 | 586 | 73 | 82 | 34 | 76 | 31 | 30 |
| Philippines | 90 | 84 | 41 | 52 | 37 | 49 | 59 | 68 | 76 | 73 | 80 |
| Singapore | 134 | 70 | 284 | 233 | 150 | 340 | 306 | 408 | 163 | 135 | 120 |
| Thailand | 493 | 225 | 419 | 388 | 187 | 170 | 459 | 595 | 250 | 198 | 430 |

*Unit*: million US dollars.

individual pursuit of security produces collective insecurity.[13] That is, in the context of multi-nation interaction under conditions of international anarchy, one state's acquisition of arms is perceived to threaten others. Weapons acquired by states to defend themselves from those who feel threatened, in turn, threaten the first, spiraling into a dynamic process of arms race. This is the tragic reality of the modern security problematique. The dual usage of weapons may also disguise the aggressive aims of revisionist states. Thus, decision-makers face another dilemma—how to evaluate the intentions of others.[14] This double-layered dilemma explains why the dynamics of arms race and mutual threat has been such a durable feature of international politics.

However, and perhaps fortunately, weapons (especially modern weapons) are also costly. To acquire weapons, nations may have to

---

[13.]John Herz, "Idealist Internationalism and Security Dilemma," *World Politics* 2 (1951).

[14]This is what Jervis made clear by juxtaposing the "deterrence model" and the "spiral model." Buzan calls it the "power and security dilemma." Robert Jervis, *Perception and Misperception in International Politics* (Princeton, NJ: Princeton University Press, 1976), ch. 3; Barry Buzan, *People, States and Fear*, 2nd edition (Boulder, Colo.: Lynne Rienner Publishers, 1991), ch. 8.

give up some other "good". Weapons also function best when they are not used. Even if they are not used, however, they must be replaced as technological progress renders the accumulated stock of old weapons obsolete. Technological change also makes the armament process increasingly costly. For these reasons, the political costs of armament, i.e., the necessity of mobilizing public support for armaments, are particularly burdensome.[15] The other side of the coin is that when nations can afford weapons, the dynamics of mutual threat and insecurity may become unstoppable.

East Asian countries seem to be well equipped for a region-wide arms race. First, they have many reasons to be concerned about their security. The most obvious is "the perception of probable American withdrawal and relative decline," either real or imagined.[16] Many East Asian countries have relied upon the American military presence for their security. To them, the decline of American power is a source of concern. To be sure, U.S. military power is still strong and may be even stronger after the fall of the Soviet Union. But precisely for this reason, combined with America's relative economic decline, the nations in East Asia may worry about the decline in American public support for the defense of overseas "friends" that are not perceived to be as vital to American interests as the European powers.

The prospect of the withdrawal of the American presence in the region leads to another source of concern. The decline or withdrawal of a hegemon creates a power vacuum, which provides an opportunity for potential revisionist powers. The East Asian region is characterized by a huge asymmetry in power among regional states. China and Japan are far more powerful than the rest of the countries in the region. Both of them have underplayed their regional roles, and may have "grievances" with respect to the status quo over the last few decades. The Japanese search for a role as a "normal state," for example, may seem abnormal to the smaller countries in the region. That the region has two, not one, potential hegemons may become a further source of concern, since it increases the possibility of regional rivalry and confrontation.

---

[15]Of course, the political costs of disarmament may be equally burdensome once the military machinery is established.

[16]Mack and Ball, "The Military Build-up in Asia-Pacific," pp. 203-4.

The third source of concern is that the region includes three of the four remaining countries who have not officially foresworn their socialist ideology. Two of them, China and Vietnam, are growing faster than the other socialist countries which have officially given up the socialist mode of production. That fact is again a source of concern. The other Asian socialist country, North Korea, has been suspected of simultaneously vying for supremacy and survival, through the development of nuclear weapons. For many people, that suspicion has not been eliminated.

Secondly, and very important, regional states can afford weapons. The economies of the East Asian "dragons" have been growing faster than those of any other nations in the world. During the period between 1981-1991, the gross world product increased by roughly 27 percent. The developing world outgrew the developed world by the ratio of 45 percent to 23 percent. East Asian countries recorded an astonishing growth of 75 percent. In fact, even though the region recorded real growth in military expenditure during the decade, overall economic output outpaced military expenditures so that the share of military expenditure in GNP dropped from 3.1 percent in 1981 to 2.1 percent in 1991.

Second, there are weapons available to purchase. While overall demand for arms fell sharply due to the end of the Cold War, the supply of weapons did not fall as fast as demand because the conversion of military industry to civilian purpose turned out to be costly and cumbersome. Thus, there is an oversupply of weapons, which has forced the export market to become more competitive, thereby reducing the unit cost of weapons. Further, as the Cold War came to a conclusion, the price factor became more important than political factors, so that the number of weapons to be exchanged may increase without an increase in the value of sales.[17]

## Why Do East Asian "Dragons" Arm — A Regression Analysis

The discussion in the above section suggests two basic reasons why nations in East Asia arm: (1) they feel threatened, either in real terms

---

[17] *World Military Expenditures and Arms Transfers 1991-1992,* pp. 29-34; Segal, "Managing New Arms Race in the Asia/Pacific."

or potentially; and (2) they can afford weapons both because of their economic prosperity and because they are cheaper and more abundant in the post-Cold War world. At the same time, the prospect of the withdrawal of the American presence in the region might also be a precipitating reason why nations in the region feel insecure. It is possible that an arms buildup process generated from this sense of insecurity may spiral upwards due to latent feelings of threat and distrust which could result from the military buildup by neighboring states.

This analysis suggests a set of propositions regarding the determinants of the military buildup by regional states.

*Proposition* 1: Nations in the East Asian region increase their level of military preparedness because of a decline (either potential or real) in the U.S. military commitment to regional security. The cause-effect relationship involved may be two-fold: (1) regional states may feel threatened directly due to the potential withdrawal of their patron or stabilizer; and (2) they may feel threatened because the U.S. withdrawal could allow potential revisionist states to assert themselves within the region.

*Proposition* 2: East Asian countries increase their level of military preparedness, despite world-wide disarmament, because of the fast growth in their economies *and* more abundant and cheaper weapons.

But are such feelings of insecurity real? Or, is the "perception" of the felt insecurity real enough to influence the regional pattern of arms buildup? Relatedly, what about the "derivative" fear of regional states from the potential withdrawal of American power?[18]

As a way to examine these propositions, I pooled the data of armament level by the regional states and ran a regression analysis to examine the extent of such influences. The analysis is largely preliminary in that I have not undertaken a complete and/or exhaustive modeling progression in terms of cause-effect hypotheses and measurement of relevant variables. However, if nations in the region

---

[18]Derivative here means that American withdrawal might cause reassertion by regional hegemons, which in turn becomes a source of concern to other regional states.

have been behaving in a manner that the theory posits, one may expect a discernible pattern to emerge.

First, I posit that the level of armament by regional states is a function of three basic factors. The first is the size of armed forces, or basic maintenance and operational cost of the military establishment. The second is the size of the economy, which is supposed to support the cost of armaments. One might argue that such a relationship is trivial by saying that "larger nations maintain more arms." Such a criticism may be valid *cross-nationally*, but not necessarily in this context, because *over time*, the correspondence of economic performance and military expenditure has worked the other way. The third is the cost of military equipment, i.e., procurement of new weapons. Given that most nations in the region are not yet major arms producers, the value of arms imports may well approximate this pattern.

Thus, the regression equation is as follows:

$$\text{MILEX}^i{}_t = a + b_1\text{AF}^i{}_t + b_2\text{GNP}^i{}_t + b_3\text{AI}^i{}_t + e^i{}_t \qquad (1)$$

where   MILEX means the level of military expenditure,

AF is the size of armed forces,

GNP is the size of economy, in terms of gross national product,

AI is the value of arms imports, and

e is the stochastic disturbances, with superscript $i$ representing actor and subscript $t$ representing time.

I call the equation (1) the basic model, although GNP involves a major hypothesis. The expectation is that while AF and AI variables are functioning as control variables, there will be a positive association between the military expenditure and the size of GNP.

Next, I add the level of military expenditure by the United States to the equation to measure its impact on the level of military expenditures by reegional states. The assumption is that the level of U.S. military expenditure approximates, or at least is perceived by regional states to represent, the U.S. commitment to "internationalism." The expectation is that it is *negatively* associated with the level of military expenditures by regional states. Thus, equation (1) is extended to equation (2).

$$MILEX^i_t = a + b_1AF^i_t + b_2GNP^i_t + b_3A\dot{I}^i_t + b_4USME_t + e^i_t \qquad (2)$$

where $USME_t$ is the level of U.S. military expenditure at time $t$.

In this estimation, logged values are used instead of raw values. The decision to take a (natural) logarithm is made primarily in order to get rid of extreme variability. The regression analysis in fact shows more stable results than raw values. But still, logarithmic transformation has some non-trivial implications. First is that the model becomes non-linear such that:

$$MILEX^i_t = e^a AF^{b1} GNP^{b2} AI^{b3} USME^{b4} e^e \qquad (3)$$

Although I have found no reason why the relationship should be non-linear or log-linear instead of linear, there is also no compelling reason why the relationship should be linear instead of log-linear. Second, the coefficients from a log-linear model have better interpretability—that is, they measure percentage changes in the dependent variable associated with a percentage change in independent variables, or elasticity.

Also in the analysis, I include data of military expenditures for eight East Asian countries during the period of 1981-1991.[19] Finally, I add seven dummy variables for each unit to control possible heteroskedasticity and autocorrelation.[20] Table 6 shows the results of pooled cross-section time series regression.

The column under the heading of "Model 1" represents the estimation results of the basic model of (1). The arms import values turn out not to be a stable predictor of military expenditure of East Asian

---

[19]The eight countries are: Japan, South Korea, Taiwan from Northeast Asia and Indonesia, Malaysia, Philippines, Singapore, and Thailand. China and North Korea are excluded from the analysis because their military expenditures are assumed to follow different processes.

[20]James Stimson, "Regression in Space and Time: A Statistical Essay," *American Journal of Political Science* 29 (1985) for statistical issues involved in pooled cross-section time series regression analysis.

Table 4.6.

Estimation Results for Military Expenditures

| Variables | Model 1 | Model 2 | Model 2' | Model 3 |
|---|---|---|---|---|
| Intercept | 6.140*** | 8.609*** | 8.431*** | 9.219*** |
| | (4.630) | (3.826) | (4.797) | (4.060) |
| Size of Armed Forces | −0.704*** | −0.719*** | −0.683*** | −0.693*** |
| | (3.858) | (3.956) | (3.802) | (3.820) |
| Gross National Product | 0.478*** | 0.515*** | 0.419*** | 0.444*** |
| | (6.954) | (6.990) | (5.666) | (5.085) |
| Arms Imports | 0.030 | 0.032 | 0.045 | 0.044 |
| | (1.012) | (1.086) | (1.497) | (1.445) |
| U.S. Military Expenditures | | −0.222 | | −0.101 |
| | | (1.354) | | (0.552) |
| Soviet Military Expenditures | | | −0.195$^\dagger$ | −0.167 |
| | | | (1.942) | (1.477) |
| F-statistics | $F_{10,77}=629$ | $F_{11,76}=578$ | $F_{11,76}=593$ | $F_{12,75}=539$ |
| $R^2$ | 0.986 | 0.987 | 0.987 | 0.987 |

| *** | Coefficient estimates are statistically significant at $p<0.001$. |
|---|---|
| ** | Coefficient estimates are statistically significant at $p<0.01$. |
| * | Coefficient estimates are statistically significant at $p<0.05$. |
| † | Coefficient estimates are statistically significant at $p<0.10$. |

countries, contrary to the earlier hypothesis. This is perhaps due to the fact that regional states show different patterns of arms imports with each other. Some of them are mainly arms importers and some of them are arms producers as well as importers. In addition, arms import values fluctuate more rapidly over time than military expenditures. Second, the size of armed forces shows *negative* and significant association with military expenditures, contrary to the initial expectation. It is a disturbing, but illuminating finding. One interpretation may be as follows. Cross-nationally, larger nations, which are able to spend more money on armaments, tend to build their military programs more around equipment than personnel; over time, on the other hand, as nations in the region grow economically, they also tend to spend more money on equipment than on personnel. Such a pattern may suggest future directions for the regional military buildup.

Finally, the size of the economy in terms of gross national product has a positive and highly significant impact on the level of military expenditures of regional countries. The pattern holds not only cross-nationally but also over time. This is not a definitive conclusion because no cross-regional comparison is made, but it is obvious that rapid economic growth in regional countries has facilitated the military buildup in the region.

Model 2 includes U.S. military expenditures as a regressor. It also includes Soviet military expenditures as a regressor, instead of U.S. military expenditures, for the purpose of comparison. Model 3 includes both U.S. and Soviet military expenditures as regressors, so as to control for possible confounding effects. As predicted, U.S. defense expenditures have negative impact on the military spending of regional states, but the estimated coefficients are not statistically significant. The Soviet case has the same impact and it is also not statistically significant. So for now, the conclusion is that system level factors do not reveal a consistent effect on the militarization of the region.

These findings suggest that the observed military buildups by East Asian countries may derive from other factors. That is, the reason why the region shows a pattern of militarization, contrary to the global trend of demilitarization (or slower rate of demilitarization than the global trend), may be nothing more than the fact that the region's economies are growing faster than other regions. If so, their strategic calculus has not changed appeciably, suggesting that concerns over their military expenditure are overstated. That is, worrying about their increasing military spending would be just like worrying about their fast growing economies.

Such a conclusion can be supported by an examination of some other data. Table 7 shows the percentage share of the military expenditure to the gross national product over the period of 1981-1991. It reveals three distinct patterns. First, the worldwide percentage share of military expenditure to gross national product has declined steadily during the period. Second, the same pattern is also observed in East Asia, although the region shows an increase in absolute military spending. It confirms the earlier finding that the military buildup in East Asia can be generally attributed to rapid economic growth. Thirdly and rather surprisingly, the region spends much less than the global average on military expenditures, in terms of the

Table 4.7

Share of Military Expenditures in Gross National Product:
A Cross-Regional Comparison

| Year | World | Developed | Developing | East Asia |
|------|-------|-----------|------------|-----------|
| 1981 | 5.4 | 5.3 | 5.7 | 3.1 |
| 1982 | 5.7 | 5.5 | 6.2 | 3.0 |
| 1983 | 5.7 | 5.6 | 6.2 | 2.9 |
| 1984 | 5.6 | 5.5 | 5.9 | 2.7 |
| 1985 | 5.5 | 5.5 | 5.5 | 2.6 |
| 1986 | 5.4 | 5.5 | 5.2 | 2.6 |
| 1987 | 5.3 | 5.4 | 4.8 | 2.4 |
| 1988 | 5.0 | 5.2 | 4.4 | 2.3 |
| 1989 | 4.7 | 4.8 | 4.1 | 2.2 |
| 1990 | 4.5 | 4.5 | 4.5 | 2.2 |
| 1991 | 4.2 | 4.1 | 4.5 | 2.1 |

Table 4.8

Growth of Gross National Product in East Asian Countries, 1982-91

| Year | 1982 | 1983 | 1984 | 1985 | 1986 | 1987 | 1988 | 1989 | 1990 | 1991 |
|------|------|------|------|------|------|------|------|------|------|------|
| **Northeast Asia** | **4.6** | **4.9** | **7.0** | **7.0** | **4.7** | **6.7** | **7.9** | **4.8** | **5.5** | **5.4** |
| China | 8.7 | 10.3 | 14.6 | 12.7 | 8.3 | 11.0 | 11.3 | 4.3 | 5.7 | 7.3 |
| Taiwan | 4.1 | 8.6 | 11.5 | 5.6 | 12.6 | 11.9 | 7.8 | 7.4 | 5.0 | 7.2 |
| Japan | 3.4 | 2.8 | 4.3 | 5.2 | 2.6 | 4.4 | 6.2 | 4.8 | 5.2 | 4.4 |
| North Korea | −2.5 | −0.2 | −0.8 | 0.3 | 0.7 | 0.5 | −0.3 | −1.7 | −5.1 | −24.6 |
| South Korea | 7.2 | 12.6 | 9.3 | 7.0 | 12.9 | 13.0 | 12.4 | 6.8 | 9.3 | 8.3 |
| **Southeast Asia** | **3.8** | **6.7** | **4.0** | **0.2** | **4.3** | **6.5** | **9.3** | **8.9** | **9.2** | **6.3** |
| Indonesia | 2.6 | 8.8 | 6.5 | 2.6 | 6.2 | 4.6 | 6.9 | 7.5 | 6.9 | 6.7 |
| Malaysia | 4.6 | 3.9 | 6.7 | −1.3 | 2.5 | 5.6 | 9.5 | 8.6 | 11.5 | 9.0 |
| Philippines | 2.8 | 1.5 | −8.7 | −7.1 | 4.2 | 5.1 | 7.2 | 5.7 | 3.9 | 0.0 |
| Singapore | 8.0 | 10.7 | 10.9 | 0.0 | 0.7 | 8.3 | 10.2 | 9.6 | 8.9 | 7.9 |
| Thailand | 4.1 | 8.1 | 6.6 | 3.0 | 4.6 | 9.7 | 13.4 | 12.4 | 10.3 | 7.2 |

*Unit*: annual percentage increase.

share of military expenditures in GNP. Table 8 shows the strength and robustness of regional economies.

## PUTTING MUZZLES ON THE "DRAGONS": SOME PRELIMINARY PRESCRIPTIONS

Should it not be a source of concern that East Asian countries are building up their arms for the purpose of regional security and stability? Before answering this question, a few points labeled as sources of concern need to be clarified. One is supply side dynamics. That is, due to the rapid demilitarization elsewhere in the world, there may be an oversupply of weapons in the world market, which puts pressure on the prosperous East Asian economies to modernize their defense establishments. However, this is largely beyond the control of the East Asian countries and beyond the scope of this study. The second issue relates to the direction of change in socialist countries. The biggest concern is China, with its huge size and fast growing economy. But the statistics suggest (see Tables 3 and 4) that China's immediate goal is economic development rather than military buildup. Many observers also believe that China's military power does not yet represent a serious concern.[21]

The third concern is North Korea, whose ambition for nuclear development has become a world-wide source of concern. But the data, and other evidence, suggest that North Korea cannot afford a destabilizing military buildup. An earlier study of mine came to the same conclusion.[22]

The biggest source of regional instability, therefore, may be the dynamics of threat and insecurity which nations inadvertently pose to each other under conditions of international anarchy. That is, even if a regional military buildup is nothing more than the result of autonomous defense planning of regional states with more money to spend and cheaper weapons to purchase, it could still pose serious

---

[21]Gary Klintworth, "Asia-Pacific: More Security, Less Uncertainty, New Opportunities," *Pacific Review* 3 (1992).

[22]Taehyun Kim, "Arms Race in Korean Peninsula: Searching for Patterns," paper presented at the annual convention of Peace Science Society (International) at University of Illinois at Urbana-Champaign, November 1994.

challenge to national leaders in the region, if it turns into a spiraling arms race of mutual threat and insecurity. The logic is so powerful that it should not be easily disregarded.

I believe one of the ways to put muzzles on the fast growing dragons may be by forming a multilateral regional security forum with "cooperative security" as its aim.[23] There is a burgeoning recent literature on the merits of multilateral institutions.[24] A multilateral institution facilitates international cooperation by allowing diffuse reciprocity across nations, and provides a stable forum of dialogue where nations can resolve or manage their differences.[25] Particularly in regions and issues where enmities among nations are acute and nations are concerned about relative gains vis-à-vis cooperating partners, multilateral fora are an ideal environment for encouraging cooperation among nations. Further, multilateral institutions can force nations, which are stubborn and unwilling, to cooperate "defensively."[26]

In fact, there is growing interest in the institutional development of multilateral security cooperation in the region. One approach of primary importance is the ASEAN Regional Forum, which grew out of ASEAN-Post Ministerial Conference. In addition, the Asia Pacific Economic Cooperation (APEC) has enormous potential for two reasons. First, it has evolved around economic cooperation among nations for whom economic interests are the principal bonding forces. Second, it has already been elevated to a summit level conference where comprehensive understandings are possible. Given that there

---

[23]For the concept of cooperative security, see Janne E. Nolan, ed., *Global Engagement: Cooperation and Security in the 21st Century* (Washington, D.C.: Brookings Institution, 1994).

[24]John Gerard Ruggie, ed., *Multilateralism Matters: The Theory and Praxis of an Institutional Form* (New York: Columbia University Press, 1993).

[25]For example, see Ruggie, "Multilateralism: the Anatomy of an Institution," in *Multilateralism Matters*; Robert W. Cox, "Multilateralism and World Order," *Review of International Studies* 18 (1992).

[26] See particularly Duncan Snidal, "International Cooperation Among Relative Gain Maximizers," *International Security Quarterly* 35 (December 1991). For a general survey of literature in this regard and effort to apply it to the security cooperation in the Asia/Pacific, see Taehyun Kim, "New Pacific Community and Regional Security Cooperation," in *New Pacific Community and Korea* (Seoul: The Sejong Institute, 1994).

is growing interest in multilateral security cooperation among regional nations and some forms of institutional arrangements have already been established, it is in the best interests of all the nations to take advantage of their full potential. East Asia is therefore not without options to ameliorate potential rivalries and to keep the tendency toward military buildup in check.

# Section III

# Future International Economic Arrangements and Trends

The third session was devoted to papers prepared by Julia Lowell and Jin-Young Chung. As in the second session, there was a clear complementarity between the two papers, with both highlighting the continued need to integrate geopolitical and geoeconomic analysis. However, regional economic trends do not automatically translate into potential crises or severe disequilibrium. Indeed, most participants agreed that economic regionalism (which could well become a more pronounced factor in the future) does not necessarily pose a threat to the world trading order, and might even contribute to stabilizing relations between the U.S. and Japanese economies (both with global reach) and the smaller regional economies. Seen in this light, regional arrangements such as APEC might well serve as a restraining impulse on U.S. unilateralism directed at the region, as well as a means to induce Japan to permit more meaningful opening of its economy.

At the same time, however, the United States has demonstrated an increased readiness to use trade policy as a means for addressing intractable current accounts deficits with its Asian trading partners. Though predominant attention has focused on the U.S.-Japan relationship, many Korean policymakers see these developments as the precursor to comparable steps designed to open the Korea market. Though Korea has sought to limit the potential risks by diversifying its export strategies within East Asia, these measures have inherent limitations, since economic latecomers such as China and Indonesia will also seek to protect their infant industries. These circumstances, combined with domestic pressures felt within Korea, could prove highly inauspicious for Korea's future position in an increasingly competitive regional trade environment.

These considerations prompted an extensive discussion of the implications of recent changes in U.S. economic policy (i.e., the growing attention to "fair trade" rather than "free trade") and its possible effects on the smaller regional economies. An especially vigorous debate ensued on the possible regional effects should the United States (out of perceived domestic needs) no longer be prepared to absorb the export surpluses of Asian economies that rely on the U.S. market to ensure continued economic growth. This scenario could well prove far more disadvantageous to the interests of various export-oriented rapid developers than the highly visible "hectoring" that frequently dominates headlines and political perceptions on both sides of the Pacific. The prospect of a significant closing of the U.S. market (even if undertaken in order to help "put the U.S. economic house in order"—for example, to help ensure the solvency of the Social Security system) could have a profound effect on regional economies. At the same time, it would be difficult to insulate such prospective economic challenges from broader political and security ties. The discussion highlighted the prospect of major looming domestic adjustments in export-led economies such as Korea that have long assumed an ample and open American market.

Both papers and the conference discussion thus highlighted the critical role that the United States continues to play in shaping the future of global trading arrangements. Despite the extraordinary record of economic growth in the region, the United States still wields principal influence on global trading norms, which in turn shape the options and strategies of other states. This has particular resonance for Korea, which finds itself increasingly buffeted by its much larger economic neighbors. With growing domestic support in the United States for unilateral actions, the necessity of shaping requisite multilateral institutions for the post-GATT era looms as an imperative need on both sides of the Pacific.

Chapter Five

# THE WORLD TRADING SYSTEM IN CRISIS: THE UNITED STATES, EAST ASIA, AND THE 'NO-PATSY' PRINCIPLE

Julia Lowell

## INTRODUCTION

In November 1994, governments around the world breathed a collective sigh of relief when the U.S. Congress voted to ratify agreements reached during the eighth and final round of international trade negotiations organized under the auspices of the General Agreement on Tariffs and Trade (GATT). As a frequent target of unilateral U.S. trade actions in the past, Korea along with other East Asian nations had been especially concerned about the outcome of the November vote.[1] The U.S. ratification of GATT's Uruguay Round agreements signaled a continued American commitment to the idea of a worldwide multilateral trading system, as opposed to bilateral, regional, or even unilateral approaches to trade arrangements. Especially in agreeing to the creation of the World Trade Organization (WTO), a new supranational institution to regulate world trade, the United States reaffirmed its support for multilateral mechanisms to establish trading rules and procedures as well as deal with trade disputes.

East Asian governments have had cause to be concerned about recent American attitudes towards the global trading system in general and towards trade with East Asia in particular. Most observers agree that, since the early 1980s, a worldwide increase in the number of

---

[1]Throughout this paper, "Korea" will be defined to mean "South Korea," while "Taiwan" will be used for "Taiwan, China." "East Asia" consists of the newly industrializing and developing nations of East Asia including China but excluding Japan; "Asia Pacific" is East Asia plus Japan.

national restrictions on both imports and exports has negatively affected growth in global trade. The American response to large U.S. current account deficits beginning in the early 1980s has clearly contributed significantly to the worldwide increase in the use of such trade-reducing measures as "voluntary" export restraints (VERs), antidumping penalties, and countervailing duties on imports. All of these measures have been used against East Asian exporters in the past. Recently, in a new trade policy twist, the U.S. government has also called for the adoption of "voluntary" import expansions (VIEs) by the Japanese government. Although in theory VIEs could promote trade through greater market access, they represent a movement away from the free trade principles espoused by the United States in the past. Korea and other East Asian countries have kept a close and uneasy eye on the progress of U.S.-Japanese talks on market access, wisely fearing that they may be the next to face this new tool of American trade diplomacy.

However, East Asian hopes that the WTO will provide an open, equitable and effective multilateral forum in which to expand export opportunities and work through trade disagreements may be doomed to disappointment. Despite their ratification of the Uruguay Round, none of the larger developed countries seem likely to relinquish sovereignty over their national trade policies in any substantive way. The United States and the European Union (EU) still have a strong propensity for unilateral trade actions, while the non-tariff trade barriers that characterize the Japanese market are likely to be as impervious to attack under the WTO as they were under its GATT predecessor.[2] Furthermore, regional trading blocs that discriminate against non-members have also been left alive and well under the new WTO regime.

For example, less than one month after the WTO opened its doors on January 1, a preliminary investigation by the U.S. Trade Representative (USTR) found the EU guilty of unfair treatment of certain

---

[2]East Asian manufactured exports to Japan have in fact skyrocketed over the past five to ten years, outstripping U.S. or European gains. Nevertheless, Japanese restrictions on imports are significant: for example, Sazanami, Urata, and Kawai estimate that in 1989 nontariff barriers exceeded 400 percent for some products. Yoko Sazanami, Shujiro Urata, and Hiroki Kawai, *Measuring the Costs of Protection in Japan*, Washington, DC: Institute for International Economics, 1994.

agricultural imports.[3]   If the final verdict remains unchanged, the U.S. International Trade Commission will be obligated to impose punitive sanctions on the EU under Section 301 of U.S. trade law. Despite the successful conclusion of the Uruguay Round, therefore, a process that is entirely outside of the multilateral dispute-resolution mechanism authorized by GATT or the WTO appears as popular as ever with U.S. policymakers.[4] The passage of the Uruguay Round also appears to have had little effect on the power of trading blocs.  For example, the EU's newest members are now changing the structure of their duties on outside imports in order to conform to EU standards.[5]   Tariffs on chemicals, plastics, electronics, computer components, precision equipment, and agriculture are all expected to rise, while there will be cuts in some areas such as automobiles and textiles.  Although the EU argues that its expansion fully conforms with GATT regulations because tariff cuts will fully offset any increases, its trading partners remain skeptical.

Korean and other East Asian exporters continue to be highly vulnerable to unilateral trade actions, informal protectionism, and discriminatory trade preferences.  Korean exporters are becoming only too familiar with the Section 301 process, having been frequent targets of allegations of unfair trade practices by American accusers with respect to products ranging from leather shoes to steel bars to color television sets.  Japan has restricted imports of Korean textiles through a VER arrangement, and Korean cement manufacturers are also quite familiar with the less formal means of protectionism practiced in Japan.  And while restrictive local-content legislation makes electronic components producers worry about prospects for further expansion of the EU, textile exporters are even more nervous about

---

[3]The specific issue was preferential treatment of banana imports from the former colonies of Britain and France.  The U.S. claimed that EU policies discriminated against imported bananas from Latin America and Hawaii. The *Economist*, 4 February, 1995.

[4]The recent trade dispute between Washington and Tokyo over market access in Japan, with the United States threatening to impose 100% tariffs on Japanese luxury automobile exports to the United States, vividly captures this continued preference of U.S. policymakers. Although the trade negotiations were able to achieve a last minute settlement that forestalled imposition of the tariffs, the ultimate outcome of the negotiations will likely spur the United States to again employ the threat of unilateral action in future disputes over market access.

[5]The most recent additions to the EU membership are Austria, Finland, and Sweden.

the possible ramifications of the North American Free Trade Agreement (NAFTA) among Canada, Mexico, and the United States. In sum, the Korean government has good reason to mistrust the sincerity of U.S., Japanese and European commitments to the WTO and the multilateral global trading system that it represents.[6]

Of course, East Asian countries themselves are by no means immune to the pressures of domestic protectionism. Infant industry-type arguments have frequently provided the excuse for flagrant violations of the free trade principles of national treatment and non-intervention by governments, even as the perpetrators complain about similar violations by the more advanced industrial countries. Although there has been an overall trend toward economic liberalization throughout much of East Asia, there is still considerable resistance to foreign penetration of certain industries, including financial services and telecommunications. East Asia also has its own history of preferential regional institutions, including the Association of Southeast Asian Nations (ASEAN), which has recently decided to form its own free trade area. Nevertheless, East Asian regional groups have so far been fairly limited in their scope and do not yet pose a significant threat to the principle of non-discrimination described in the most-favored-nation clause of Article 1 of GATT.

This paper looks at some of the challenges to the WTO, and thus to the current global trading system, that could pose a threat to current patterns of East Asian economic growth and prosperity over the next five to ten years. Its major focus is on tensions created by policies adopted in the United States and in Korea. Despite the flourishing of various regional trading arrangements, the greatest obstacle to East Asia's strategy of export-led growth in the future will not derive from political-economic arrangements such as NAFTA or even the EU. Rather, Korea and its East Asian neighbors will be confronted with global macroeconomic trends that, though not inherently political in nature, will tend to empower political constituencies both at home and abroad that favor unilateral, protectionist policy stances. Within the United States, a growing emphasis on reciprocity in trade relations will counterbalance past calculations that focused on the ben-

---

[6]See for example Chulsu Kim, "Super 301 and the World Trading System: A Korean View," in J. Bhagwati and H. Patrick, eds., *Aggressive Unilateralism,* Ann Arbor: The University of Michigan Press, 1990.

efits of free trade.  Within Korea itself, monopolistic local interests as well as cultural traditionalists will resist any form of external pressure to make domestic markets more competitive.  The ultimate crisis scenario would be a breakdown in the multilateral mechanism of the WTO, in the form of a trade war sparked by East Asian unwillingness to accept greater responsibility for maintaining the global trading system, and fed by continued massive savings/investment imbalances in the United States.

The paper is organized into five sections.  Sections two and three consider alternative challenges to the free trade principles of multilateralism and non-discrimination that might culminate in the breakdown of the WTO and the current global trading system.  The likelihood of alternative developments are evaluated and contrasted.  Section four focuses more closely on the costs and benefits of measures designed to end "unfair" trade practices that have been unilaterally imposed by the United States on Korea and other Asia-Pacific nations.  Section five concludes by suggesting possible policies to avoid or minimize the probability of such a crisis.

## The False Threat of Emergent Regionalism

One of the most common fears expressed by supporters of a multilateral, non-discriminatory trading system is that the world is breaking up into regional blocs reminiscent of the economic and political arrangements that blossomed prior to World Wars I and II.[7]  In the worst case scenarios, the separation of Europe, the Americas, and the Asia-Pacific region into hostile trading "fortresses," each dedicated to the restriction and control of access by non-members to their regional markets, would not only endanger the welfare of consumers around the world, but could also engender the worst sort of political as well as economic parochialism.  By restricting the free flow of goods and services between member and non-member countries, regional economic blocs narrow the range of goods available

---

[7]Regional politico-economic arrangements have a long and sometimes inglorious history.  Fairly recent examples include the customs union (Zollverein) centered on Prussia in the 1830s, the Ottowa Agreement of 1932 establishing the imperial system of preferences within the British Commonwealth, and Japan's infamous "Greater East Asian Co-prosperity Sphere" of the 1920s and 1930s.

for consumption and slow economic growth and productivity worldwide by preventing efficient specialization of production. Many policymakers also fear that such blocs could undermine existing multilateral mechanisms for dispute resolution, including the management of issues of global concern such as arms proliferation, public health, and the environment.

For East Asia and Japan, caught between the reality of an expanding and exclusionary regional trading bloc represented by the European Union, and the prospect of another in NAFTA, the long-term prospects for the survival of GATT's most fundamental principle, non-discrimination, may seem quite dim. In fact, the dynamic economies of the Asia-Pacific region are probably correct in asserting that they are the biggest targets of European and American protectionists hiding under the mantle of regionalism. Therefore, the various arrangements now being considered by the countries of the Asia-Pacific region can be seen primarily as defensive maneuvers to counter the perceived threat of exclusion from European and American markets.[8] However, there is some risk that the Asian regional counter-strategy could end up by furthering the very regionalism that they wish to avoid, so the steps up until now have been quite cautious. Most East Asians believe that the best hope for uninterrupted economic growth and prosperity is a successful transition from the multilateral GATT to the multilateral WTO, despite an also widely-shared perception that the Uruguay Round agenda was dominated by the desires of the larger industrialized countries.[9]

There are several reasons why an all-Asian regional trade arrangement would have only limited success, certainly over the next five to ten years and perhaps longer. Although some reasons are political, many are inherently economic. For example, although it is almost a truism that the explosion of trade among the East Asian countries and Japan indicates the rise of a *de facto* new regional economic trading group, the extent to which such a group could be self-sustaining is highly open to question. First, while the share of

---

[8]See for example Bon-Ho Koo, "New World Trading System: A Korean Prospective," in H. Tien and Y. Chu, eds., *The Asian Regional Economy: Growing Linkages, Global Implications,* Taipei: Institute for National Policy Research, 1993.

[9]Lee Hsien Loong, "Future of the World Trading System," *op. cit.*

intraregional trade is indeed rising among the Asian-Pacific countries, much of it can be attributed simply to the rapid economic growth rates of the countries in the region.[10] Just as these countries have increased their share in trade worldwide, so they have increased their trade with each other: growth in intraregional trade does not necessarily imply the development of particular regional preferences.[11] Even so, in 1991 more than half of East Asian exports were still directed outside the region; for Japan the figure was over 70 percent.

Second, while explicit quantitative restrictions have mostly been eliminated throughout the region, most countries still maintain significant tariff as well as non-tariff barriers to foreign imports.[12] The disparity between the policies of the highly protected countries of the region and such notable free-traders as Hong Kong and Singapore suggests that the formation of a unified regional trading structure may be difficult. Certainly ASEAN's 12-year experience with preferential trading arrangements (PTAs) is not encouraging: it has been estimated that PTAs cover less than 5 percent of intra-ASEAN trade.[13] Even under the famous "flying geese" model of Asian integration, with Japan as the technological leader followed by the

---

[10]See for example Peter Petri, "The East Asian Trading Bloc: An Analytical History," in J. Frankel and M. Kahler, eds., *Regionalism and Rivalry: Japan and the U.S. in Pacific Asia*, Chicago: University of Chicago Press, 1993.

[11]However, studies by Frankel, Stein, and Wei indicate that trade patterns among the East Asian countries and Japan are not explained very well by simple factors such as *per capita* GNP and geographic proximity. These results hold both for existing Asian regional groups such as the Association of Southeast Asia Nations (ASEAN) as well as proposed groups such as the East Asian Economic Caucus (EAEC). Jeffrey Frankel, Ernesto Stein, and Shang-Jin Wei, "Continental Trading Blocs: Natural or Supernatural?", National Bureau of Economic Research Working Paper No. 4588, December 1993; and Jeffrey Frankel, Shang-Jin Wei, and Ernesto Stein, "APEC and Other Regional Economic Arrangements in the Pacific," Federal Reserve Bank of San Francisco, Pacific Basin Working Paper Series No. PB94-04, September 1994.

[12]For example, the World Bank calculates that the effective protection rates on manufacturing imports for Indonesia in 1992 and Thailand in 1988 were 52 percent and 51 percent, respectively. Arvind Panagariya, "East Asia and the New Regionalism in World Trade," *World Economy*, London: Basil Blackwell, November 1994.

[13]U.S. International Trade Commission, *East Asia: Regional Economic Integration and Implications for the United States*, USITC Publication No. 2621, Washington, DC: USITC, May 1993. According to Panagariya, *op. cit.*, prospects for AFTA, the ASEAN Free Trade Area established in 1992 (with a 15 year ease-in feature) do not appear considerably more promising than the original PTA.

"Four Dragons" and then the "Four Mini-Dragons," is extremely vulnerable to rapidly increasing competition between leaders and followers. For example, how likely is it that in the next five to ten years Japan and Korea will significantly open their domestic markets to each others' sophisticated consumer electronic goods or automobiles? Would Indonesia welcome Chinese textiles and clothing manufactures?[14]

Perhaps the most important challenge to the notion of an all-Asian trading group is that Japan, the necessary core of such a group, appears to be either unable or unwilling to assume the responsibilities of such a putative role.[15] While Japanese investment in the region is huge, Japanese imports from the region are far smaller and heavily skewed towards raw materials and agricultural products. Japan's manufactured imports from East Asia, although growing quite rapidly, tend to be concentrated in intermediate goods such as parts and components rather than the consumer goods produced in large numbers by many of its East Asian trading partners. Unless the pattern of Japanese imports changed dramatically, rapidly industrializing East Asian countries such as Korea would find it difficult to find markets for their manufactured exports. From Japan's point of view, the East Asian market is still too limited to absorb Japan's huge output of sophisticated and expensive manufactured exports.

But how serious is the challenge posed to East Asia and to the global trading system as a whole by regional economic arrangements? While it would be imprudent to dismiss the possible adverse effects of discriminatory trading blocs, there is no reason to suppose that regionalism *per se* will harm East Asian exporters any more in the next five to ten years than it has in the past. For example, despite "Europe 1992," the world's most exclusionary trading bloc is moving toward a unified market only slowly. It is unlikely that the EU will institute new measures resulting in greater discrimination against outsiders than already exists. The EU has promised to negotiate the terms of accession for its three newest members within the context of

---

[14]A slightly dated but still relevant treatment of these issues is presented in Yung Chul Park, "The Little Dragons and Structural Change in Pacific Asia," *The World Economy,* September 1988.

[15]Japanese membership in any all-Asian economic arrangement also has been actively discouraged by the United States.

the newly created WTO, and the terms will be carefully examined by non-member countries. The United States is fully as anxious as the East Asian countries to ensure that the Europeans do not close export markets further through EU enlargement.

The primary source of anxiety about regionalism for the immediate future, for Korea as well as many of its neighbors, appears to be NAFTA. As described by Bon-Ho Koo, the President of the Korea Development Institute, Koreans are "concerned that the proximity of Mexico to the United States market, together with its lower wages and preferential access, could divert United States imports towards Mexico. The eventual reduction in barriers to trade in the heavily protected industries such as footwear, textiles and garments, auto-parts, and consumer electronics would give Mexico significant advantages over third-country suppliers."[16] It is true that, like the East Asian countries themselves, the Canadian, Mexican, and U.S. economies are becoming more integrated. Some U.S. and Canadian firms have moved or are thinking about moving their manufacturing operations to Mexico in order to take advantage of cheap Mexican labor. Perhaps eventually NAFTA could become a serious regional economic arrangement. But regional economic integration was already taking place well before President Clinton signed the NAFTA agreement into law in December 1993. Prior to NAFTA, Mexico was a beneficiary of the U.S. Generalized System of Preferences, so that U.S. trade barriers against Mexico were already quite low.[17] Furthermore, the Mexican economy still has a long way to go before its industries can seriously challenge those in Korea and Taiwan. As a result of largely uneducated workforces and a weak industrial infrastructure, Mexico's low wages go hand in hand with low productivity. In fact, some American firms that decided to transplant production south of the border during the first excitement of NAFTA's passage have already changed their minds; the recent Mexican financial crisis seems to have caused several others to reconsider.

---

[16]Bon-Ho Koo, *op. cit.*, pp.34–5.

[17]President Reagan announced the "graduation" of Hong Kong, Korea, Singapore, and Taiwan from the USGSP in January 1988 based primarily on their *per capita* GNPs. Approximately between 1984 and 1988, these four countries accounted for over 60 percent of all U.S. imports covered under the GSP program. U.S. International Trade Commission, *Operation of the Trade Agreements Program: 40th Report*, Washington, DC: ITC, 1988.

Most mainstream economists still argue that the true driving force behind NAFTA is political, not economic, and that the economic impact of NAFTA on U.S. trade patterns will probably be small for some time to come. Paul Krugman, for example, titled an often cited article dismissing the economic importance of NAFTA, "The Uncomfortable Truth about NAFTA: It's Foreign Policy, Stupid." [18] Part of the reason is simply that Mexico's economy is so small: Mexico's GDP is less than 4 percent of the U.S. GDP, so that Mexican production can't hope to replace much of the United States' East Asian import bill. While individual Korean export sectors such as footwear and textiles may be forced to respond to a rising Mexican challenge, that challenge is almost certainly much less serious than ones they already face from competitors in their own region of the world. With or without preferential U.S. treatment of imports from Mexico, labor-intensive export sectors of Korea, Taiwan, Hong Kong and Singapore were already under severe assault from producers located in low-wage regional competitors such as China and Indonesia.

Certainly the United States, for all its grumbling, has no wish to cut itself off from the dynamic markets of Asia and the Pacific either as a buyer or a seller. On the demand side, some of the most technically advanced and highest-profile industries—such as the telecommunications and aerospace industries—rely on precision-engineered, high quality, moderately-priced parts and components manufactured in the region, while U.S. consumers have become addicted to East Asian videotape recorders, fax machines and microwave ovens. Mexican-made alternatives are unlikely to appeal. On the supply side, greater access to markets in Japan and East Asia has been a centerpiece of U.S. trade policy since approximately the mid-1970s, and the Mexican market won't provide a good substitute for many years, if ever.

## THE TRIUMPH OF THE 'NO-PATSY' PRINCIPLE: A CRISIS SCENARIO

Over the next five to ten years, a breakdown of the global trading system is most likely to turn on the proper price of a stainless steel

---

[18]Paul Krugman, "The Uncomfortable Truth about NAFTA: It's Foreign Policy, Stupid," *Foreign Affairs,* November/December 1993.

pipe sold by a small private exporter, or on national policies in support of a flagship domestic telecommunications industry, or the foreign market share of a Golden Delicious apple. But no matter what the particulars, the issue under dispute will be mostly symbolic: the true cause of the breakdown will be a quasi-rational calculation, probably by the United States, that the benefits from pursuing the free trade principles of non-discrimination, national treatment, and non-intervention by governments no longer outweigh the costs associated with a fourth principle, hereby called the *no-patsy principle*, which states that trading partners will be unilaterally punished if they appear to have violated any of the first three principles.[19] Despite the rising standards of living in the United States and around the world made possible by the efficient international specialization of production through trade, many Americans no longer believe that the global trading system as embodied by GATT and its WTO replacement is compatible with basic U.S. economic and even security interests.

Central to this judgment is a belief that other countries' violations of the spirit, if not the letter, of the GATT regulations supporting free trade principles are largely responsible for the string of current account deficits run by the United States since 1983. American critics argue that other countries, particularly in East Asia, have taken advantage of the GATT structure to promote rapid increases in their own domestic living standards through export growth. But while the United States has "played by the rules," other countries have consistently violated the principles of governmental non-intervention and national treatment, and even the most fundamental principle of non-discrimination. Through its own passive adherence to free trade principles, the United States has suffered the stagnant growth, declining real wages and rising unemployment connected with persistent current account deficits. Therefore, as the importance of Cold War alliances has declined, a recalculation of costs and benefits has eroded the U.S. government's commitment to the current global

---

[19]From a line in President Ronald Reagan's 1987 State of the Union Message, as cited in Bhagwati and Irwin, "The Return of the Reciprocitarians: U.S. Trade Policy Today," *The World Economy*, London: Basil Blackwell, 1988: "We are always willing to be trade partners, but never trade patsies."

trading system and strengthened its determination to ensure "fair play."

Demands for reciprocity are nothing new in international trade relations. As pointed out by Jagdish Bhagwati and Douglas Irwin, British proponents of fair trade or "reciprocitarians" fought long and hard against "One-sided Free Trade" during the height of United Kingdom's 19th century economic preeminence. They were only able to garner widespread political support, however, with the restructuring of the British economy after World War I.[20] In the United States, accusations of unfair trading practices by foreign partners also have a long history, but American political leaders in the post-World War II economic environment rarely paid much attention. According to free trade doctrine, they had reason for their indifference: a policy of open market access for all imports is in the interest of the importing country regardless of other countries' import policies. Negotiations which require reciprocal concessions are counter-productive, because the concept of a trade concession is itself flawed. The "concessions" in fact benefit the conceder.[21]

Now, however, the reciprocitarians are in the ascendancy in the United States, bolstering popular and appealing arguments for fairness with more sophisticated references to lost American jobs, crises in the international balance of payments, and even eventual U.S. military dependency and decline. Although most economists remain committed free traders, others have developed models emphasizing strategic aspects of trade that suggest trade concessions may indeed be exactly that.[22] These reciprocitarian economists have lent intellectual credibility to the intuitive sense among many Americans that continuing U.S. trade and current account deficits must eventually harm their standard of living. The further implication is that U.S. trade policy has been conspicuously invisible while workers in East Asia and Japan have grown rich behind steep trade barriers.

---

[20]Ibid., p. 112n.

[21] See for example Edmund Dell, "Of Free Trade and Reciprocity," *The World Economy*, London: Basil Blackwell, June 1986.

[22]Paul Krugman, ed., *Strategic Trade Policy and the New International Economics*, Cambridge, MA: The MIT Press, 1986. Krugman himself remains committed to free trade.

American trade policymakers have been anxious to respond to such criticisms by taking a tougher line on trade disputes.

Although the response of U.S. trading partners to unilateral American declarations about what constitutes fairness in trade relations has been unanimously negative, there is a certain irony to the situation with respect to East Asia and Japan. The Asia-Pacific governments, with the notable exception of Hong Kong, have long advocated a strong role for government in trade and industrial policy. Along with the traditional qualities of thrift and hard work, they often credit public targeting of infant industries through subsidies and trade protection for their export-oriented economic dynamism. In addition, largely based on theories of economic mercantilism, flows of goods and services imports into many East Asian economies as well as Japan have in the past been tightly controlled. In contrast, the historical position of the United States has been, at least in theory, that market forces allocate resources most efficiently, leaving little role for government either in promoting rapid economic growth or directing trade patterns. Now, however, the Asia-Pacific region and the United States appear to have almost reversed their positions. The growing momentum for deregulation of the regional economies has been heavily influenced by U.S. pressure, but by pushing VIEs and other government measures to ensure trade reciprocity, the United States is rapidly losing its moral authority as a free trade champion.

Irrespective of the merits of either free or fair trade arguments, the United States will continue to run current account deficits with the rest of the world as long as there is a gap between U.S. domestic savings and investment flows. The most aggressive actions to ensure the free access of American goods and services to foreign markets can in the aggregate do little but push up the value of the dollar, unless steps are taken to reduce the fundamental imbalance. And as investment is key to future output growth, clearly the preferred strategy is for the United States to increase domestic savings: either public or private savings rates must increase in order to make greater resources available for productive investment. According to most economists, the most effective way for U.S. policymakers to increase the national savings rate and thus eliminate persistent current account deficits is to reduce or eliminate persistent large federal budget deficits.

Given the political hazards of deficit reduction, it is likely that many U.S. policymakers will continue incorrectly to advance trade policy, and particularly trade reciprocity, as a remedy for international payments imbalances. With respect to market-opening measures such as VIEs, American exporting as well as import-competing interests will happily concur. What are the likely political and economic risks of such a strategy? Can a U.S. trade policy centered on reciprocity ever achieve free trade goals?

## ASSESSING COSTS AND BENEFITS OF THE 'NO-PATSY' PRINCIPLE

As with virtually all international trade agreements, the original GATT treaty contains provisions that allow the contracting parties to restrict foreign imports under carefully specified circumstances. In general, a GATT-member country may impose restrictions on imports if it can show that domestic producers are threatened with "material" injury due to an import surge.[23] In recent years, both the United States and European Union have increasingly resorted to these provisions in order to impose anti-dumping or countervailing duties on imports that are found to have been priced below market by foreign producers or subsidized by foreign governments. While exporting countries may well complain that the growing popularity of antidumping and countervailing duty provisions represents an abuse of basic free trade principles, these actions still fall within the multilateral framework of the GATT.

However, between 1980 and 1989, almost half of the 774 antidumping and countervailing duty cases processed by the United States ended in the imposition of negotiated export restraints, which lie outside GATT's purview. Against Korea, 26 of 36 cases resulted in the imposition of VERs.[24] Although they are bilaterally "negotiated," as opposed to unilaterally declared, the generally uneven balance of

---

[23]Import restrictions are also allowed in the case of a serious decline in monetary reserves (threat to the balance of payments), or as part of a economic development strategy for low income countries. Bernard Hoekman, "Safeguard Provisions and International Trade in Services," *The World Economy*, January 1993.

[24]J. Michael Finger, "A Rock and a Hard Place: The Two Faces of U.S. Trade Policy Toward Korea," World Bank Policy Research Working Paper No. 1264, March 1994.

political and economic power means that such arrangements tend to be heavily weighted in favor of the larger trading partner.

In contrast, the Section 301 articles of U.S. trade law do not even try to reflect a bilateral or multilateral consensus on appropriate measures to deal with trade disputes. The original Section 301 of the 1974 Trade Act required the U.S. president to identify and redress "unfair" foreign trade practices, with minimal reference to dispute resolution mechanisms authorized under GATT.[25] During its first ten years of existence, Section 301 had little impact on U.S. trade policy because consecutive administrations made very little use of it. However, by 1985 burgeoning U.S. trade deficits had put trade policy at the top of the Congressional agenda, creating frustration with the perceived unwillingness of the President to pursue trade reciprocity. The apparent dominance of other concerns such as foreign policy and national security were blamed for presidential reluctance to take a tough line on trade.

As described by Judith Bello and Alan Holmer, the U.S. Congress amended Section 301 in the 1988 Trade Act by transferring responsibility from the President to the USTR in order to "reduce the likelihood of trade benefits for foreigners being exchanged for non-trade benefits."[26] The amended "Super" 301 mandates U.S. retaliation within a prescribed period in all cases involving violations of trade agreements, export targeting, and wherever it is determined that there exist "unjustifiable practices that burden or restrict U.S. commerce."[27] To avoid U.S. retaliation, the accused country must take measurable action to discontinue the unfair policy or practice, or take steps to eliminate the burden on U.S. producers.

---

[25]According to Bhagwati, "the USTR is not required to act...if the GATT contracting parties have determined, a GATT panel has reported, or a dispute settlement under a trade agreement finds that U.S. trade agreement rights have not been denied or violated." Jagdish Bhagwati, "Aggressive Unilateralism: An Overview," in J. Bhagwati and H. Patrick, eds., *Aggressive Unilateralism,* Ann Arbor: The University of Michigan Press, 1990, p.39.

[26]Judith Bello and Alan Holmer, "The Heart of the 1988 Trade Act: A Legislative History of the Amendments to Section 301," in J. Bhagwati and H. Patrick, eds., *Aggressive Unilateralism,* Ann Arbor: The University of Michigan Press, 1990, pp.50–51.

[27]The one exception to automatic retaliation is if the President determines that it would adversely affect the national economic interest. *Ibid.,* pp.61–2.

Economists have shown that, at least in the short run, the imposition of antidumping penalties or countervailing duties, like any tariff-type restriction on imports, lowers national welfare in the importing country. The VER quota mechanism lowers welfare even further, because foreign producers as opposed to domestic governments collect the monopoly "rent" resulting from the artificial quantity constraint. This then raises the possibility of more serious international political disputes. For example, Kenneth Flamm argues that the VERs imposed on the Japanese semiconductor industry as a result of an antidumping suit in 1986 created a Japanese cartel that collected significant rents on U.S. export sales. American trade policymakers then accused Japanese producers of practicing predatory pricing. The resulting trade dispute with Japan created bad feelings between the two countries that still linger.[28] Another study, focusing on U.S. and European steel import quotas, showed that the restrictions made Korean steel producers better off by $32 million, at the expense of American and European consumers.

However, in certain cases trade actions may increase competition, moving prices closer to free trade levels and thus raising consumer welfare. For example, U.S. antidumping duties imposed on Korean producers of color television sets in 1983 threatened to price Korean televisions out of the competitive U.S. market. In order to equalize domestic and U.S. prices for Korean televisions and so avoid the duties, Korean producers lowered domestic prices by 20 percent within two years. In this instance, U.S. trade actions benefited Korean consumers as well as foreign export interests.[29] U.S. policymakers argue that Section 301 measures, which are designed to open foreign markets to U.S. exports, achieve similar effects.

---

[28]Kenneth Flamm, "Semiconductor Dependency and Strategic Trade Policy," *Brookings Papers on Economic Activity* Microeconomics 1993.

[29]As cited by J. Michael Finger, "A Rock and a Hard Place: The Two Faces of U.S. Trade Policy Toward Korea," World Bank Policy Research Working Paper No. 1264, March 1994. In order for such a price differential to exist, there must have been trade barriers protecting Korean television producers within the domestic market. It is not clear from Finger whether television import barriers in Korea were removed as a result of the U.S. action.

## CONCLUSION

The American use of GATT-legal antidumping and countervailing duty provisions and particularly its use of unilateral Section 301 actions is heartily resented by its trading partners.  Probably in large part as a response to American actions, the EU as well as other countries have also begun to apply antidumping and countervailing duties on selected imports.  Slight changes to the GATT rules covering antidumping and countervailing duties on subsidized exports which were passed as part of the Uruguay Round are unlikely to have much effect on the popularity of their use.

The American insistence on treating trade policy as a tool for reducing trade and current account deficits could make things difficult for East Asian governments, and perhaps especially for Korea.  As U.S. current account deficits stubbornly refuse to respond to negotiated trade agreements reached under the auspices of the WTO, protectionist and reciprocitarian pressures in the United States will continue to mount.  Unilateral demands for U.S. trading partners to take market opening measures will escalate.  Japan will remain the major target of U.S. efforts to even the flow of goods and services across the Pacific, but continuing trade deficits with East Asian nations will also make them a tempting target.

But Korean policymakers will face considerable political pressures of their own to resist further opening of their markets to imports: neither the highly organized Korean labor movement nor the politically powerful *chaebol* are likely to be complacent in the face of increased competition from U.S. goods and services producers.  In addition, the rapid cultural changes that are so often induced by market opening—foreign films, large discount stores, etc.—may be highly unwelcome to certain groups.  Unilateral demands for market opening by the United States are an obvious formula for inciting strong anti-American sentiments among conservative consumers as well as producers hurt by the introduction of a more competitive domestic market.

Korea itself has also run current account deficits quite consistently over the past twenty years or so, and has now amassed a considerable foreign debt.[30]   There appears to be little prospect for greatly increasing exports to Japan or the European Union, and although the economies of Korea's East Asian neighbors are also expanding rapidly, they routinely continue to exclude many of each others' goods as well as most of each others' services.[31]   The U.S. market remains Korea's best bet for obtaining the foreign exchange it needs to service its debts, so that reciprocity will be an important issue for Korean policymakers as well.

A crisis in the global trading system based on aggressive unilateralism, therefore, would arise from political responses to economic determinants.   It could very well be touched off by a dispute between the United States and Korea, or the United States and one of Korea's newly industrializing neighbors.   It would almost certainly involve the United States, because as of yet no other economy is important enough to destroy the current system, and it could expand to include other countries affected by the dispute.   Under the most extreme scenarios, the catastrophic economic impact of a full-blown trade war across the Pacific might well be matched by disastrous political repercussions.   History provides a lesson: the U.S. Smoot-Hawley tariff helped to reduce global trade flows by over 60 percent between 1930 and 1933, setting the stage for the conflagration of World War II.

---

[30]From 1986 to 1989 Korea briefly ran a series of current account surpluses. It slid back into deficit in 1990, and in 1991 the current account deficit reached 3.0 percent of GDP. In 1993, it was estimated to be slightly positive at 0.1 percent of GDP. There is some discrepancy between the U.S. and Korean numbers, but Korean bilateral trade surpluses with the United States also went into deficit by 1991. International monetary Fund, *International Financial Statistics* and Wan-Soon Kim, "Korea-U.S. Trade Relations in the GATT Framework," in I. Chung, ed., *Korea in a Turbulent World,* Seoul: The Sejong Institute, 1992.

[31]Although there has been rapid growth in East Asian intraregional trade, much of it is concentrated in intermediate goods. Final goods produced in the countries of the region still tend to be destined either for domestic markets or for markets in Japan, Europe, and especially the United States.

# Chapter Six

# THE EAGLE, THE GOOSE, AND THE DRAGON: CAGEMATES IN THE ASIA-PACIFIC TRADE ORDER?

Jin-Young Chung

## INTRODUCTION

While a deficit-stricken American eagle hovers over East Asia's fertile markets, the rising sun is ready to fly as a goose leading its flock. At the same time, an awakening dragon has begun to move its limbs in preparation for its flight towards the heavens. Meanwhile, a little tiger, lacking wings, is wandering around trying to find someone who will help him fly. Is the eagle too angry to make friends with any of the others? Is the goose strong enough to stand against the wild eagle? Is the rising-to-the-heavens dragon so powerful that the rest of the world can only wait and see? Or, can they all live together in a common cage called the Asia-Pacific trade order? These are the very fundamental questions when we try to think about the potential for instability and crisis in trade relations in East Asia and the Pacific.

Recently, the world trading system has undergone a fundamental change with the successful conclusion of the Uruguay Round of multilateral trade negotiations. The transition from the General Agreement on Tariffs and Trade (GATT) to the World Trade Organization (WTO) includes the establishment of a powerful international trade organization, broadened and strengthened multilateral trade rules, and an effective dispute settlement mechanism. Though the new system must still be improved, it is certain to have a great impact on the management of national and international trade affairs. In particular, countries and regions will be constrained in their reliance upon discriminatory or protectionist measures. Perhaps the most noteworthy development is that international trade disputes will now be settled through a quasi-judicial process.

Many people believe that this achievement will greatly reduce the dangers of unilateral, bilateral, and regional threats to the multilateral trade system.

However, the future of the WTO is still largely at the mercy of the economic superpowers, especially the United States. If the economic superpowers are very supportive of the operation of the WTO and cooperative in managing international and global economic problems, the new trading system will be very successful, benefiting the superpowers themselves and the whole world. If they disregard or bypass the new multilateral system and are unable to develop an enduring cooperative mechanism for macroeconomic management, however, the foundation of world peace and prosperity could erode very rapidly. In general, the major countries are expected to cooperate for the successful operation of the WTO. The reason is simple: we live in an era where the integration and globalization of the world economy has gone very far and is still proceeding very rapidly, so much so that it is extremely costly and difficult for any country, large or small, not to cooperate in multilateral management. Nevertheless, uncertainties still prevail on the road towards an effective, functioning world trading system.

This conclusion is especially germane in the relationship among the Northeast Asian countries, and in the dealings of these countries with the United States. Relations among these economies contain a great deal of uncertainty, and thus changes in these relationships will have tremendous implications for the Asia-Pacific region as well as the world as a whole. Post-Cold War East Asia awaits the emergence of a new kind of international and intraregional arrangement for the management of bilateral economic interactions, especially among Japan, China, and the United States. The development of these bilateral relationships will shape the economic, political, and military order of the region and the world.

During the Cold War era, the United States provided security and export markets to its East Asian allies. It did so primarily according to its global and regional grand strategies and on the basis of separate bilateral arrangements and negotiations. But the disappearance of its Cold War rival, the Soviet Union, has made America's anti-Soviet containment strategy obsolete. The decline of the American economy relative to the rest of the world, especially in relation to the rapidly growing East Asian economies, together with various domestic economic and social problems, has put heavy constraints on America's international objectives and strategies in general and its foreign economic policy in particular.[1]

In contrast, Japan has risen from the ashes of World War II to become the most competitive, capital-rich economic power in the world. Accordingly, its potential as a regional and global power has prompted serious debate inside and outside Japan.[2] China, the foremost political power in East Asia, is also beginning to rise economically. It has been awakened from decades of Communist dogmatism and has adopted an outward-oriented development strategy. The rapid growth of the Chinese economy, together with its continental-size territory and its huge population comprising a fifth of the world's population, is raising another set of concerns.[3]

The fundamental question facing the United States, Japan, and China is how these three giants can live together in a very competitive world trade environment. It is well known that the United States and Japan have been struggling over bilateral trade imbalances. While China has already emerged as a major trading nation, it is still not a member of the GATT/WTO system. Consequently, the trade relationships between China and its trading partners depend on bi-

---

[1]For a succinct overview about the implications of American decline, see Samuel Huntington, "The U.S.--Decline or Renewal?," *Foreign Affairs*, Vol.67, No.2 (Winter 1988/89).

[2]To list only a few, Chalmers Johnson, "Japan in Search of a 'Normal' Role," *Daedalus*, Vol.121, No.4 (Fall 1992); Ezra Vogel, "Japanese-American Relations After the Cold War," *Daedalus*, Vol.121, No.4 (Fall 1992); Eugene Brown, "Japan's Search for Strategic Vision: The Contemporary Debate," (Strategic Studies Institute, U.S. Army War College, February 1993); Kenneth Pyle, "Where is Japan Headed?: Implications for the Alliance," *NBR Analysis* (National Bureau of Asian Research), Vol.4 No.5 (December 1993); Yoichi Funabashi, *Nihon no Taigaikoso* [Japan's International Vision] (Tokyo: Iwanami, 1993); and Ichiro Ozawa, *Nihon Kaizo Keikaku* [Japan Renovation Plan] (Tokyo: Kodansha, 1993).

[3]As is discussed later in this paper, the future of China and its impact on East Asia and the world involve a host of uncertainties. Some recent publications on this issue include: Nicholas Kristof, "The Rise of China," *Foreign Affairs*, Vol.72, No.5 (November/December 1993); William Overholt, *China: The Next Economic Superpower* (London: Weidenfeld & Nicholson, 1993); Denny Roy, "Hegemon on the Horizon?: China's Threat to East Asian Security," *International Security*, Vol.19, No.1 (Summer 1994); Gerald Segal, "China's Changing Shape," *Foreign Affairs*, Vol.73, No.3 (May/June 1994).

lateral negotiations, which are prone to political intervention. This was the case with the recent trade friction between the United States and China over the protection of intellectual property rights. The Sino-Japanese relationship, on the other hand, has been relatively smooth for the last two decades. However, this vital bilateral relationship has also shown some signs of strain because of the potential conflict and rivalry over their respective spheres of influence in East Asia.

For a middle power in the midst of these three superpowers, South Korea is obviously concerned about future developments in this trilateral context. Koreans fear that if they are forced to choose one of the three, they cannot be sure which side will be the "right choice." For instance, when Koreans witnessed the ratification of the North American Free Trade Agreement, they felt isolated between the U.S.-led American bloc and the Japan-led East Asian bloc.

The emergence and consolidation of two or three separate, exclusionary trading blocs on both sides of the Pacific could be disastrous, not only to South Korea and other countries of the region, but to the whole world. It is therefore imperative to develop a cooperative mechanism which will contain and settle differences and disputes among the three giants. How is this possible? What are some major obstacles to this development? This paper will attempt to tackle these questions.

## THE SETTING

When we think about economic cooperation or conflict among the major Asia-Pacific countries, we need to first examine the environment in which they are situated. Let us delineate several important aspects of the current Asia-Pacific situation.

First, for the last few decades, the most conspicuous phenomenon in the Asia-Pacific region has been the rapid shift in the relative economic size of the major countries, as is shown in the Table 1. The size of the U.S. economy, as a proportion of world output, has fallen from 34.3% in 1965 to 24.2% in 1990. By contrast, the relative sizes of most East Asian economies have grown rapidly during the same period. For instance, the size of the Japanese economy relative to that of the U.S. economy has increased from 13% to 54.5%; the South Korean economy from 0.4% to 4.4%. The size of the major East Asian economies as a whole relative to that of the U.S. economy has increased from 26.7% to 75.5%. Furthermore, if we make an adjustment in measuring the size of the Chinese economy in terms of purchasing power, in 1990 it was equal to 37.6%, instead of 6.7%, of the U.S. economy.[4] In sum, the size of the East Asia economy has become equal to the other two major centers of economic activity in the world.

This change in the distribution of economic capabilities will have important political implications for the regional and global management of international relations. Countries with increased economic capabilities naturally began to develop their own interests, which will be articulated and defended in their relations with other nations. Countries facing economic decline will certainly want to resist this trend by mobilizing political power.

Table 6.1.

East Asia Catching up:  Changes in Relative Economic Size
(% of U.S. GNP, US$)

| Relative GNP | | | | | |
|---|---|---|---|---|---|
| | 1965 | 1990 | | 1965 | 1990 |
| **Northeast Asia** | **23.7** | **69.8** | **North America** | **110.6** | **115.0** |
| Japan | 13.0 | 54.6 | United States | 110.0 | 100.0 |
| Korea | 0.4 | 4.4 | (% of World) | (34.3) | (24.2) |
| China | 9.6 | 6.7 | Canada | 7.5 | 10.6 |
| Hong Kong | 0.3 | 1.2 | Mexico | 3.1 | 4.4 |
| Taiwan | 0.4 | 2.9 | | | |
| **ASEAN** | **3.0** | **5.7** | **EC 12** | **65.7** | **114.1** |

*Source:* World Bank, *World Development Report 1992*, Center for Economic Planning and Development, Republic of China, *Taiwan Statistical Data Book*.

Consequently, the distribution of economic capabilities will inevitably develop into an object of political competition and rivalry. Historically, as Robert Gilpin notes, significant shifts in the distribu-

---

[4]The size of the Chinese economy is much larger if we calculate on the basis of real purchasing power rather than nominal output. According to one estimate, the relative economic size of the Chinese economy in 1992 was as much as 37.6% of the American economy and 88.1% of the Japanese economy. "America and Asia: Treating with Tigers," *The Economist* (April 16, 1994), p.22.

tion of power among major powers has often resulted in war.[5] By now, however, as the possibility of war among the major powers has become almost unthinkable, economic conflicts have to be settled either through political compromise and/or by adjudication according to agreed upon common rules.

Second, the United States has had persistent and large trade deficits in its trade relations with Japan and other East Asian countries. Table 2 shows that the United States has been experiencing trade deficits with Japan and developing East Asian countries, which increased from $2.2 billion in 1970 to $86 billion in 1990. We can also see from Table 2 that, while developing countries in East Asia have had trade surpluses with the United States, they have also had trade deficits with Japan. This means, in part, that they earn dollars from their exports to the United States and spend these dollars to import from Japan.

This imbalance in Pacific trade has been the major source of trade friction between the United States, on the one hand, and Japan and East Asian developing countries on the other. The United States has put strong bilateral pressure on its East Asian trading partners to force them to appreciate their currencies, especially the yen, and to open their domestic markets. Although this bilateral strategy has

### Table 6.2.

### U.S. and Japanese Trade Balances with East Asia
### (Unit: Billion US$)

|       | 1970 Balance with | | | 1980 Balance with | | | 1990 Balance with | | |
|-------|-------|-------|------|--------|--------|------|---------|-------|-------|
|       | World | Japan | DEA  | World  | Japan  | DEA  | World   | Japan | DEA   |
| U.S.  | 0.8   | −1.6  | −0.6 | −36.2  | −12.2  | −5.4 | −123.9  | −44.5 | −41.5 |
| Japan | 0.4   | —     | 1.9  | −10.8  | —      | 2.8  | 52.4    | —     | 22.7  |

*Note*: DEA stands for developing East Asian countries.

Source: IMF, *Direction of Trade Statistics Yearbook*, various issues

---

[5]Gilpin states: "Throughout history the primary means of resolving the disequilibrium between the structure of the international system and the redistribution of power has been war, more particularly, what we call a hegemonic war." Robert Gilpin, *War and Change in World Politics* (Cambridge: Cambridge University Press, 1981), p.197.

worked to bring about significant changes in exchange rates, it has not led to much improvement in the U.S. trade balance. Instead, a rapid economic integration between Japan and the developing countries of East Asia has emerged.

Third, the role of Japan as an absorber of manufactured exports from the developing countries of East Asia has been increasing, but is still quite limited. Table 3 shows that the United States still plays the dominant role as a "demand-side growth pole" for the major East Asian developing countries. As long as this dependence on American markets continues, East Asia's vulnerability to American pressure will remain, and, accordingly, the role of Japan as a regional leader will be limited. But this kind of trade dependence and imbalance cannot remain intact indefinitely. The question is not whether a change will occur, but who is going to adjust its trade patterns, how, and when.

Table 6.3.

**U.S. and Japanese Shares in East Asian Exports of Manufactured Goods (Unit: %)**

|  | 1980 | | 1984 | | 1992 | |
|---|---|---|---|---|---|---|
|  | U.S. | Japan | U.S. | Japan | U.S. | Japan |
| China | 9.0 | 11.0 | 18.9 | 10.8 | 23.7 | 9.7 |
| Taiwan | 38.3 | 7.3 | 53.7 | 6.3 | 35.2 | 8.3 |
| Hong Kong | 34.1 | 2.8 | 46.0 | 3.3 | 28.6 | 4.3 |
| South Korea | 29.0 | 13.3 | 38.6 | 10.1 | 25.1 | 12.8 |
| Singapore | 21.0 | 8.1 | 32.5 | 3.6 | 26.0 | 5.7 |
| Malaysia | 31.7 | 5.7 | 41.3 | 5.9 | 29.1 | 7.5 |
| Thailand | 17.5 | 7.1 | 29.4 | 6.8 | 31.7 | 16.3 |

*Source*: M. Bernard and J. Ravenhill, "Beyond Product Cycles and Flying Geese," *World Politics*, Vol. 47 No. 2 (January 1995), p.205.

Table 6.4.

**Inter- and Intra-Regional Trade of Three Economic Centers, 1990**

|  | N. America | East Asia | EC(EU) |
|---|---|---|---|
| N. America | *34.4* | 23.0 | 20.8 |
| East Asia | 28.9 | *39.4* | 16.3 |
| EC (EU) | 7.9 | 5.6 | *60.6* |

*Note*: The numbers underlined indicate the ratios of intra-regional trade.
Source: IMF, *Direction of Trade Statistics Yearbook*, 1992.

Fourth, while the world seems to be heading towards a tripolar structure centered around the big three--namely, the United States, Japan, and the European Union--the importance of Pacific trade has been growing very rapidly in the last few decades. As a result, the size of Pacific trade now exceeds that of Atlantic trade. Table 4 shows that, for both North America and East Asia, their trade with each other is larger than their trade with the European Union. For each of the three main regions, their intra-regional trade exceeds trade with any of the other regions.

Fifth, the outdated Cold War security arrangement needs to be re-shaped in accordance with new realities in East Asia. The United States-centered bilateral framework, with an American "hub" and Asian "spokes," has lost much of its relevance due to the disappearance of the major common enemy. As Douglas Johnson points out, the anticipated reduction of the American military presence in East Asia has already been "prompting a preliminary jockeying for position among the littoral states of the region as they engage in a major arms buildup."[6] As a result, historical antipathy and rivalry among various regional countries may emerge and replace the U.S.-led alliance system. It is in this context that developments in trade relations among Asia-Pacific countries can have major ramifications for the emerging political and military arrangements in the region.

## MAJOR PLAYERS

How do the major players respond to the changed reality in East Asia? It will be their actions and reactions that will shape the nature of East Asian trade relations. Let us turn to each power's response.

### Hovering Eagle

The 1980s saw the world's richest nation turn into the world's most indebted nation, including a record-breaking trade deficit. This dramatic turnaround was primarily caused by American fiscal and monetary policies during the Reagan era. Huge budget deficits, high in-

---

[6]Douglas Johnson, "Anticipating Instability in the Asia-Pacific region," *Washington Quarterly*, Vol.15, No.3 (Summer 1992), p.103.

terest rates, and an appreciated dollar pulled foreign products and attracted foreign capital into the United States on an unprecedented scale. The United States was able to enjoy the resulting spending spree for a while; since its dollar was the key international currency, the country did not need to worry about its trade deficit as long as foreigners wanted to keep dollars in their pockets. Seen from this perspective, American trade deficits meant that foreign countries were eager to buy dollars with their goods and services. However, this situation can continue only for a limited time.[7]

As foreign holdings of the dollar multiply, its value will decline and its status will be challenged. The United States will then face a very difficult situation.[8] If it allows the continuous erosion of the dollar's value, it will have to accept that the dollar will be supplanted by other currencies or another financial instrument as the key tool of international transactions and reserves. If America wants to maintain the prominent role of the dollar, it has to reduce or even remove its trade deficit by importing less and/or exporting more. In reality, the United States took a mixed strategy of devaluing the dollar by encouraging the appreciation of other major currencies and expanding exports by opening foreign markets. Since the Plaza and Louvre accords in 1985 and 1987 respectively, the United States has allowed rapid depreciation of the dollar (albeit within an unannounced target

---

[7]To a certain extent, America's trade deficit is an important mechanism of providing liquidity to the rest of the world under the dollar standard system of international monetary relations. If the world economy is not provided with a sufficient amount of dollars, an economic slowdown will result. If the dollar is pumped out too much, a confidence problem will arise. This is the so-called "Triffin dilemma." Thus, adequate control on the supply of the dollar is necessary for international monetary stability. However, the United States naturally has a great temptation to maintain its national monetary policy autonomy and to finance its foreign operations by increasing the money supply. To this extent, the tendency towards American trade deficit is built into the dollar-based international monetary system. Therefore, one may argue that the trade imbalance between the U.S. and Japan can only be solved by "a fundamental structural transformation" in their trade-payment relations. See, for instance, Tsuyoshi Kawasaki, "Structural Transformation in the U.S.-Japanese Economic Relationship," in Henry Bienen (ed.), *Power, Economics, and Security: the United States and Japan in Focus* (Boulder: Westview Press, 1992).

[8]The United States is going to face a serious dilemma in its macroeconomic management. In order to maintain the value of the dollar, it has to increase interest rates which, in turn, would cool down economic growth. In order to allow the continuous depreciation of the dollar, it has to accept inflation and a declining living standard.

zone) against its major trading partners. It also put pressure on its trading partners to open their markets. The main target of this strategy, of course, was Japan, along with South Korea, Taiwan, and some Southeast Asian countries.

In 1988, the United States made a major move on the trade policy front by legislating the Omnibus Trade and Competitiveness Act with a new Section 301. The Super 301 requires the United States Trade Representative (USTR) to investigate foreign barriers to trade, establish a priority list of countries with unfair practices, and then set deadlines for their removal through bilateral negotiations and, should this fail, to retaliate.[9] In the following year, the USTR picked Japan, along with India and Brazil, as a "priority" country to be put on the bilateral negotiation table.  In the Spring of 1995, the United States threatened to impose 100% tariffs on Japanese luxury automotive exports, with only a last-minute agreement in Geneva on enhanced U.S. access into the Japanese automotive market forestalling this action.

Although the developing countries of East Asia were not included in the list, this "aggressive unilateralism" made them greatly concerned about American threats; these countries were also fearful of falling prey before the hungry eagle. Americans could do this simply because they had the power and believed that they had the "right" to do so. American power derived from its big domestic markets, on which foreigners were dependent for their exports. Americans believed they were right in exerting such pressure because they were convinced that their markets were more open than those of their trading partners. Since then, the United States has been hovering over its trading partners, especially in East Asia, to get rid of "unfair" trading practices.

The underlying logic for America's aggressive unilateralism has been summarized succinctly by Robert Gilpin:

> [I]n almost all economic sectors the reluctance of Japanese to "buy foreign," the interlocking networks of Japanese firms, and the crucial importance of personal relationships as well as the existence

---

[9]Jagdish Bhagwati, "Aggressive Unilateralism: An Overview," in J. Bhagwati and H. Patrick (eds.), *Aggressive Unilateralism* (New York: Harvester Wheatsheaf, 1990), p.3.

of numerous other informal barriers have constituted formidable obstacles to foreign penetration of the Japanese economy... The distribution system is among the most important restrictions on entry to the market. Many believe that if the Japanese would only behave like Americans or Europeans, the economic conflicts would go away.[10]

Chalmers Johnson also points out that the fundamental cause of the persistent U.S. trade deficit with Japan lies in the very peculiar characteristics of Japanese society. Therefore, the trade imbalance can only be corrected when the United States pursues a very specific, results-oriented strategy. Johnson states: "In my opinion Japan requires narrowly focused, tailor-made, closely monitored, and minutely verified policies—i.e., those based on specific reciprocity rather than the unconditional most-favored-nation status enjoyed by members of GATT." Furthermore, he also recommends that the United States "emulate or match Japan's accomplishments in government-business relationships, industrial policy, and industrial organization" in order to "promote higher-value, higher-tech industries."[11]

This kind of American trade strategy towards its East Asian partners has two serious problems.[12] First, it involves "a unilateral judgment about what is fair and unfair internationally" by making "the United States the judge and jury assessing a foreign country." Thus, this approach will inevitably "bring destructive spirals of mutual retaliation with each country viewing the other as acting unfairly." Second, it violates central tenets of the GATT/WTO-based multilateral trading system, which "will increase the costs of negotiating trade liberalization and will greatly politicize the process."

This new strategy also has clear implications for security arrangements between the United States and East Asian countries. It is expected that the United States calculates the costs and benefits of its

---

[10] Robert Gilpin, *The Political Economy of International Relations*, pp.390-391.

[11] See Chalmers Johnson, "Trade, Revisionism, and the Future of Japanese-American Relations," in Kozo Yamamura (ed.), *Japan's Economic Structure: Should It Change?* (Seattle: Society for Japanese Studies, 1990), pp.133–6.

[12] Helen Milner, "The Political Economy of U.S. Trade Policy: A Study of the Super 301 Provision," in Bhagwati and Patrick (eds.), *Aggressive Unilateralism*, pp.176–7.

military presence in East Asia in terms of its overall gains, including economic benefits. Thus it will certainly use its political and military influence to increase its own economic gains in relations with East Asia. Otherwise, the United States may try to reduce the costs of its military presence simply by withdrawing its military bases or by pushing a burden-sharing arrangement. David Denoon argues that the United States needs to pursue what he calls "real reciprocity" in its relations with East Asian countries:

> If we accept the argument that the United States can no longer afford to let the asymmetries in trade and defense burdens persist, then we must alter the priorities for American policy in the Pacific Basin. Instead of emphasizing such goals as maintaining an open, global trading system and providing a U.S. security umbrella, we must give immediate attention to reducing trade imbalances and a creating a new division of responsibility for the costs of maintaining security.[13]

This point was also made by President Clinton in Seattle in November 1993 when an APEC leadership conference was held: "We do not intend to bear the cost of our military presence in Asia and the burdens of regional leadership only to be shut out of the benefits that stability brings."

In all, America's persistent and huge trade deficit with Japan and the newly industrializing economies in East Asia has been transforming Pacific economic and political relations. America's pursuit of an unilateral aggressive strategy based on specific reciprocity puts strains on its relations with East Asian countries. How can East Asians respond to the pressures and coercion from the other part of the Pacific?

## Leading Goose

Forced by increasing trade tensions with the United States, Japan had to appreciate its currency sharply and open its domestic market. How are Japanese industries coping with declining international

---

[13]David Denoon, *Real Reciprocity: Balancing U.S. Economic and Security Policy in the Pacific Basin* (New York: Council on Foreign Relations, 1993), p.86.

competitiveness in export markets and increasing foreign competition in domestic markets? One way of coping with this adjustment problem has been to increase domestic productivity and efficiency. Another has been to export capital, rather than products, to markets abroad. Still another way has been to relocate production facilities in countries with low production costs. This last method of adjustment has had an enormous impact on economic relations between Japan and East Asian countries since the mid-1980s.

The sharp appreciation of the yen along with increasing trade friction between Japan and its developed trading partners has affected East Asian economic integration in two related ways.[14] First, a sharp increase in Japanese foreign direct investment in East Asian countries has occurred. In order to maintain international competitiveness and lessen trade frictions, Japanese firms have moved their production facilities or parts suppliers to developing countries in East Asia. The result has been massive outflows of Japanese capital into neighboring countries since 1986. For five years from 1986 to 1990, Japanese foreign direct investment in the four newly industrializing economies of East Asia accounted for 67% of cumulative investment for the 40 years period from 1951 on, while ASEAN countries received 42% of the cumulative total during the same period.[15]

Second, the appreciation of the yen and the massive outflow of Japanese capital have brought about a rapid increase in Japanese manufactured imports, especially from East Asian countries. As a result, the proportion of manufactured products of Japan's total imports increased from 31.0% in 1985 to 50.3% in 1990. During the same period, the ratio of manufactured imports from NIEs increased from 57.8% to 73.4%, while for ASEAN it increased from 8.4% to 26.1%.[16] Consequently, intraregional manufactured trade expanded very rapidly. Japan has come to be an important absorber of

---

[14]See Peter Petri, "The East Asian Trading Bloc: An Analytical History," in J. Frankel and M. Kahler (eds.), *Regionalism and Rivalry: Japan and the United States in Pacific Asia* (Chicago: University of Chicago Press, 1993).

[15]Watanabe Toshio, "New Pacific Community- Japanese Perspective," in the Sejong Institute (ed.), *The Idea of a New Pacific Community and Korea* (Seoul: The Sejong Institute, 1994), p.298.

[16]Ibid., p.296.

manufactured exports from East Asian countries, contributing to the growth and integration of East Asian economies.

Does this trend mean that Japan is leading its East Asian neighbors into a competitive regional bloc against North America and the European Union? As we have just discussed, the role of Japan in East Asia has increased a great deal since the mid-1980s as an important demand-pole of manufactured exports as well as the major supplier of capital and technology. This market-led integration has been supported by Japan's East Asia-oriented aid policies. According to one estimate, almost 70% of Japanese aid goes to Asia, especially to Southeast Asia and China. As a result, Japan has replaced the United States as the major provider of official development aid to East Asia. For instance, by the end of the 1980s, two-thirds of the Development Assistance Committee(DAC) aid to ASEAN came from Japan, while the U.S. share dropped below 10%.[17]

In spite of this discernible trend towards East Asian economic integration, the possibility of consolidating Japan-led regionalism seems quite low. This is primarily because Japan is not willing to replace the United States as the major absorber of East Asia's manufactured exports. The trade patterns of East Asian countries are still predominantly characterized by their dependence upon the United States for export markets and upon Japan as the source of technology and parts. As Takatoshi Ito points out, "it is too soon to expect intraregional trade to dominate U.S. trade with Asian countries (including Japan)... The Pacific Asian intraregional trade is not an alternative to Asian-North American trade, unless North American and European markets become closed against Asian products."[18]

Second, Japan's position as a prominent regional leader can be easily checked by the presence of another giant in East Asia: China.[19] The sheer size of mainland China naturally makes it the single most important political power and a potential economic giant in East Asia. It

---

[17]Shafiqul Islam, "Foreign Aid and Burdensharing: Is Japan Free Riding to a Coprosperity Sphere in Pacific Asia," in Frankel and Kahler (eds.), *Regionalism and Rivalry*, pp.334–338.

[18]Takatoshi Ito, "U.S. Political Pressure and Economic Liberalization in East Asia," in J. Frankel and M. Kahler (eds.), *Regionalism and Rivalry*, p.415.

[19] See, for instance, Denny Roy, "Hegemon on the Horizon."

is therefore unthinkable that Japan can lead East Asia without the cooperation and support of China. Even with regard to Southeast Asia, Japanese influence can be countered by the Chinese ethnic connection in the local business community.

Moreover, the potential for Japanese leadership in East Asia has been constrained both domestically and internationally.[20] In order to play a leadership role in and for East Asia, Japan has to resolve historical issues with its neighbors and make the structural reforms necessary for the absorption of Asian exports in order to balance the regional trade relationship. Chalmers Johnson makes this point: "Whatever Japan does, it is constrained by the legacy of the past and by the fact that its leadership in Asia means making some domestic sacrifices, something its people and political system are perhaps unprepared to do."[21] Consequently, Japan's role in East Asia has been generally limited to that of a junior alliance partner with the United States.[22]

However, it is not totally unthinkable that East Asians will form a regional bloc following the models of the EU or NAFTA. If U.S. trade pressures on Japan and other East Asian countries continue and if European and North American markets increasingly close, East Asians will have little choice but to consolidate their own bloc. Malaysia's Prime Minister Mahathir has already proposed such an arrangement in his plan for East Asian Economic Caucus (EAEC). So far, however, Mahathir's proposal has not received a positive official response from major East Asian countries. But it is possible that Japan, China, and Korea will ultimately accept the proposal as a means of responding to and providing leverage against European and American discriminatory blocs.[23]

---

[20]Kent Calder's conception of Japan as a "reactive state" catches the essence of these limitations. See K. Calder, "Japanese Foreign Economic Policy Formation: Explaining the Reactive State," *World Politics*, Vol.40, No.4 (July 1988).

[21]Chalmers Johnson, "Japan in Search of a 'Normal' Role," p.22.

[22]See, for instance, Charles Morrison, "Japan and the ASEAN Countries: The Evolution of Japan's Regional Role," in T. Inoguchi and D. Okimoto, (eds.) *The Political Economy of Japan, Vol.2 The Changing International Context* (Stanford: Stanford University Press, 1988).

[23]See the special reports on Mahathir's proposal in *Far Eastern Economic Review* (July 25, 1991).

## Awakening Dragon

Mainland China, which is already a political giant in East Asia, has been gaining economic might rapidly as well. Since the late 1970s, it has begun to follow the growth path of its East Asian neighbors by abandoning the Maoist development strategy and reforming its Communist economic system. Under the leadership of Mao Zedong, China closed its doors to the outside in the pursuit of an autarkic economic system. As it feared an invasion of foreign influence through coastal areas, it not only forbade coastal cities from having contact with foreign countries, but also shifted the focus of investment inland to the mountainous regions, remote from the coastal zone and away from existing cities.[24] Thus, the turn to the "open door policy" was a complete reorientation of Chinese developmental and international strategy, as John Fincher points out:

> The Chinese policy of `opening to the outside' adopted in December 1978 followed a decision that national defense did not require continued attempts by the State to interfere with the natural concentration of growth in Coastal China... Since 1979 every effort has been made to encourage self-sustaining growth wherever it appears.[25]

Since the late 1970s China has achieved tremendous economic success. Between 1979 and 1992, the average yearly growth rate was 9.0%. After 1992, the Chinese economy has grown by more than 12% every year. This achievement was largely supported by the rapid expansion of trade. Chinese exports increased from $13.7 billion in 1979 to $27.4 billion in 1985, to $62.1 billion in 1990, and to $85.0 billion in 1992. Recently, foreign direct investment in China has also

---

[24]There is an estimate of resource transfer from coastal to inland areas during the Mao Zedong era: "From Liberation to the late 1970s, at least three-fifths of China's investment funds were diverted away from coastal China to inland and frontier areas under a policy which grew ever stronger even though most such funds were generated in the coastal zone." John Fincher, "Rural Bias and the Renaissance of Coastal China," in G. Linge and D. Forbes (eds.), *China's Spatial Economy* (Hong Kong: Oxford University Press, 1990), pp.41–2.

[25]Ibid., p.42.

been increasing very rapidly: $6.6 billion in 1990, $12.0 billion in 1991, and $58.1 billion in 1992.[26]

If we look at the geographical pattern of Chinese economic growth, we can identify an important characteristic, which has enormous economic and political implications for East Asia: the emergence of the so-called "subregional economic zones"(SREZs) in Chinese coastal regions. The SREZ is a special type of economic cooperation across national borders. It is different from international and inter-governmental economic cooperation in that it does not involve the entire national economy, but only the border areas and provinces of neighboring countries. Therefore, national governments are not usually the main actors in subregional economic cooperation. Instead, local governments and the private sector are the principal agents of cooperation.

The shape and location of SREZs along the Chinese borders were greatly influenced by the Chinese open-door policy. In 1979, the central government designated four Special Economic Zones (SEZs) in Guangdong and Fujian provinces. As they were located in distant provinces, it was politically less dangerous to carry out the prelimi-nary reform experiments. After the initial success of four SEZs, four-teen coastal urban areas and Hainan Island were designated as "open cities" in April 1984 and further openings have followed since then. SREZs emerged around these SEZs and open cities.

The most important one of them is the "Greater South China Economic Zone" which includes Guangdong and Fujian provinces, Hong Kong, and Taiwan. It has succeeded by combining South China's abundant labor and land with Taiwan's and Hong Kong's abundant capital and technology. The "Baht Economic Zone" in-cludes China's Yunnan Province, northern Vietnam, Laos, Cambodia, and Northeast Thailand. The "Yellow Sea Economic Zone" has been emerging by linking China's Bohai Gulf area with South Korea's western coastal areas. The Japan Sea Economic Zone links Northeast China with the Russian Far East, North Korea, South

---

[26]The data are from the State Statistical Bureau of the People's Republic of China, *China Statistical Yearbook 1993*. However, these data reflect investment com-mitments, rather than actual levels of investment; the true amounts of foreign investment are much lower than these amounts.

Korea's east coast, and "inner" Japan. The Tumen River Area zone, whose development plan has emerged under the auspices of the United Nations Development Program, includes Northeast China, North Korea, South Korea, Mongolia, and the Russian Far East.[27]

Considering the state of international relations in Northeast Asia, it is easy to see that subregional economic cooperation is not only feasible but also an efficient form of cooperation. Countries in the region still cannot enter into full-fledged intergovernmental cooperation. However, there is an increasing need for regional cooperation to survive and prosper in an era of globalization and regionalism. As Yue-man Yeung notes, SREZs are "more flexible and effective" than are intergovernmental regional frameworks in Northeast Asia. The reason for this is simple: as SREZs do not require nationwide institutional arrangements, but the involvement of only contiguous parts of countries, they can be "established at a relatively lower cost and within a shorter time [thus] minimizing political and economic risks to the countries."[28]

As coastal SREZs have achieved considerable economic success, the Chinese central government has been trying to transplant this pattern into the interior. Especially with strategic issues declining in importance, China has opened up border trade routes with its neighboring countries in the North and the West. As a result, interior border provinces such as Xinjiang, Heilongjiang, and the Uighur Autonomous Region, have benefitted from rapidly growing border trade, which tripled from $3.7 billion in 1986 to $11.8 billion in 1993.[29]

---

[27]Chia Siow Yeu and Lee Tsao Yuan, "Subregional Economic Zones: A New Motive Force in Asia-Pacific Development," in C. Fred Bergsten and Marcus Noland (eds.), *Pacific Dynamism and the International Economic System* (Washington, D.C.: Institute for International Economics, 1993); Yue-man Yeung, "Emerging Natural Economic Areas Surrounding China and their Implications for the Asia-Pacific Region." Paper presented at the Conference on Economic Cooperation in the Asia-Pacific Community, organized by the Institute of East and West Studies, Yonsei University, November 11–12, 1993).

[28]Yeu-man Yeung, "Emerging Natural Economic Areas Surrounding China and Their Implications for the Asia-Pacific Region," p.18.

[29]Frederick Crook, "Trade on the Edges," *The China Business Review* (January-February 1995).

Another important factor in Chinese economic achievement has been the role of some 55 million overseas Chinese. It has been reported that about 80% of the foreign capital flowing into China comes from overseas Chinese.[30] While Americans and Japanese are still hesitant to make big investments in the uncertain future of China, overseas Chinese entrepreneurs with huge capital resources can take advantage of their private connections to make major deals. They stand a better chance of succeeding, since they possess the critical political connections and practical information essential for doing business in China.

Now that mainland China has succeeded in achieving rapid economic growth and has deepened its economic integration with Hong Kong, Taiwan, and overseas Chinese, there has been increasing discussion about the emergence of a "Greater China."[31] Is it possible? If the politically divided Chinese states and the overseas Chinese can create an economic and/or political unit, it would certainly be an enormous force in the global economy. Until now, a rapid increase in trade among the three Chinese states has been the most conspicuous aspect of "Greater China." The trade between Hong Kong and mainland China grew from $5.7 billion in 1980 to more than $80 billion in 1992. During the same period, mainland China's trade with Taiwan increased from around $300 million to $7.4 billion. The trade between Taiwan and Hong Kong rose from $2 billion in 1980 to $17 billion in 1992. As a result, each of the three Chinese economies has become an important trading partner for the other two.

An increase in cross-investment among the three is also conspicuous. Taiwan has invested a cumulative total of $6.7 billion in mainland China and another $2 billion in Hong Kong. Hong Kong has invested $10 billion in mainland China and a further $1.2 billion in Taiwan. Mainland China has invested a total of $20 billion in Hong Kong. If we add up these numbers, cross-investment within these three parts of "Greater China" is almost $40 billion.[32] This figure in-

---

[30]Louis Kraar, "The New Power in Asia," *Fortune* (October 31, 1994), p.40.

[31] *The China Quarterly* focused on this topic in a special issue (No.136, December 1993).

[32]Trade and investment figures are from Harry Harding, "The Concept of 'Greater China': Themes, Variations and Reservations," *The China Quarterly*, No.136 (December 1993), p.664.

creases further if we take into account investment by overseas Chinese. Moreover, it has been estimated that overseas Chinese control some $2 trillion in liquid assets worldwide and dominate trade and investment in every East Asian country except Korea and Japan.[33]

Can the process towards the creation of "Greater China" continue? This question is intimately related with another question concerning the future of Chinese economic and political development: Can China sustain rapid economic growth while maintaining political stability and territorial integrity? As Chinese economic growth has been concentrated in the southern coastal areas, the gap between the coast and the interior, as well as between the South and the North, has been increasing. The difference in economic achievement among regions within mainland China will certainly have great economic, social and political implications.[34] How long can China allow this regional disparity to continue? Moreover, can China carry out continuous reforms in the various aspects of its society in general, including in the political system, in order to sustain rapid growth? The vision of a "Greater China" depends upon the resolution of these questions.

## And A Little Tiger

Surrounded by the world's major powers and constrained by national division, South Korea seems cornered in an impossibly difficult situation. Can it continue to survive and prosper in a rapidly changing international environment? The country has achieved remarkable economic development over the past three decades. In 1962, South Korea's per capita GNP was $87, with foreign trade totaling less than $500 million. In 1992, per capita income had increased

---

[33]See Louis Kraar, "The Overseas Chinese," and John Kao, "The Worldwide Web of Chinese Business," *Harvard Business Review* (March-April, 1993).

[34]Gerald Segal has recently argued that China's economic success through provincial and local autonomy has already reduced and would continue to constrain Beijing's discretionary power. In consequence, China's center is going to experience "a continuing devolution of power." He states: "'Greater China' takes on the economic meaning of closer relations with the mainland, but the political meaning of greater fragmentation of China." Gerald Segal, "China's Changing Shape: The Muddle Kingdom?," *Foreign Affairs*, Vol.73, No.3 (May/June 1994), p.49.

to $6,790 and trade had grown to $160 billion. Korea is now one of the world's major trading nations, accounting for 2% of world trade.

As a consequence of Korea's rapid trade expansion, the country has met with various trade restrictions from developed countries. As Table 5 shows, Korea has suffered most frequently from dumping charges by Australia, the European Union, the United States, and Canada during the period from 1980-92. It has also suffered from safeguard measures and charges of intellectual property rights violations.

An immediate consequence of this frequent trade friction with the developed countries has been increasing restraints placed on Korea's exports. For instance, the ratio of Korea's exports to developed

### Table 6.5.

### Trade Actions Against Korean Exports by Five Developed Countries, 1980-92

|  | U.S. | EC | Japan | Canada | Australia | Total |
|---|---|---|---|---|---|---|
| Safeguards | 14(3) | 1(1) | 2(2) | 1(0) | 13(13) | 31(19) |
| Antidumping | 23(11) | 24(10) | 2(2) | 23(15) | 55(22) | 127(60) |
| Countervailing Duties | 7(2) | 0 | 0 | 0 | 1(0) | 8(2) |
| Intellectual Property Rights | 21(3) | 0 | 1(0) | 0 | 0 | 22(3) |
| Total | 65(19) | 25(11) | 5(4) | 24(15) | 69(35) | 188(84) |

Source: Korea Foreign Trade Association, *Summary of Import Restrictions by Major Industrial Countries*, 1993.

### Table 6.6.

### South Korea's Major Trading Partners
### (Unit: Billion US$)

|  | United States | | Japan | | EC | | China | | Taiwan+H.K. | | ASEAN | |
|---|---|---|---|---|---|---|---|---|---|---|---|---|
|  | Export | Import | Export | Import | Export | Import | Export | Import | Export | Import | Export | Import |
| 1981 | 5.7 | 6.1 | 3.4 | 6.4 | 2.8 | 2.0 | 0.0 | 0.1 | | | | |
| 1985 | 10.8 | 6.5 | 4.5 | 7.6 | 3.3 | 3.1 | 0.0 | 0.5 | | | | |
| 1990 | 19.4 | 17.0 | 12.7 | 18.6 | 8.9 | 8.4 | 0.6 | 2.3 | 5.0 | 2.1 | 4.6 | 4.5 |
| 1991 | 18.6 | 18.9 | 12.4 | 21.1 | 9.7 | 9.9 | 1.0 | 3.4 | 6.4 | 2.3 | 6.4 | 5.5 |
| 1992 | 18.1 | 18.3 | 11.6 | 19.5 | 9.2 | 9.6 | 2.7 | 3.7 | 8.2 | 2.1 | 7.3 | 6.5 |
| 1993 | 18.1 | 17.9 | 11.6 | 20.1 | 9.4 | 10.2 | 5.2 | 3.9 | 8.7 | 2.3 | 8.4 | 6.6 |

*Note*: The data for ASEAN include only Singapore, Malaysia, Thailand, and Indonesia

*Source*: Ministry of Trade and Industry, *Export-Import Statistics*. Bank of Korea, *Monthly Statistics*.

countries under non-tariff barriers was 22% in 1988 and 15% in 1992. This has been reflected in stagnating and even declining exports to developed countries. As we can see in Table 6, Korea's major export markets have been the United States, Japan, and the European Union. However, in the 1990s, Korea's export performance in all three major markets has declined sharply. By contrast, Korea's exports to developing East Asian markets have been increasing very rapidly. In the case of exports to China, the total has grown from almost nothing in the early 1980s to $0.6 billion in 1990, to $5.2 billion in 1993, and, reportedly, to $7.3 billion in 1994.[35] During the four year period from 1990 to 1993, Korea's exports to Taiwan and Hong Kong have also increased very rapidly from $5.0 billion to $8.7 billion, while its exports to ASEAN countries rose from $4.6 billion to $8.4 billion. This trend tells us that the "three Chinas" and the ASEAN countries as a group have surpassed the United States as the largest export market for Korea. Moreover, Korea has an overall trade surplus with developing East Asian markets. Thus, Korea now has a great stake in East Asian economic growth.

### Can They Live Together?

Based upon this review of the East Asian setting and the major players' actions and reactions to each other, can we expect cooperation in building a new trade order in the Asia-Pacific region? We can easily identify several important needs for the development of a pan-Pacific trading system.

First, the existence of a high degree of interdependence among the Asia-Pacific countries underscores the need for a regional framework to manage trade relations. It is true that the establishment of the World Trade Organization will help to settle trade disputes among member nations. However, the global multilateral regime can suffer from free rider problems and, therefore, has some clear limitations in terms of market-opening and enforcement of international trade rules. In this regard, bilateral and regional negotiations can contribute to the expansion and management of the world trading system.

---

[35]*Chosun Ilbo*, February 17, 1995.

Second, the bilateral relationships among the three key players in East Asia have to be contained within some multilateral mechanisms at both the regional and the global levels. The relationships among the United States, Japan, and China are too important for the whole world, as well as for the region, to leave the settlement of trade disputes to these three actors alone. Third, the need for organizing Asia-Pacific trade relations reflects developments in other regions of the globe, especially Europe. In the Asia-Pacific region, there are some competing conceptions for organizing regional countries. In East Asia, ASEAN countries have established their own free trade area (AFTA). At the same time, the Malaysian proposal for creating an "Asians only" club, EAEC, is still alive. In North America, the United States has led the establishment of NAFTA and is trying to expand this agreement to include South America.

However, as demonstrated in Table 7, these three regional groupings have clear limitations due to relatively small intra-regional trade volume and ratios, compared with those of the European Union. We have noted that intra-regional trade in East Asia has been increasing. But its ratio relative to the region's total trade is still very small. So is that of NAFTA. However, if we put East Asia and North America together in a common regional framework, i.e. APEC, both the volume and size of the intra-regional trade ratio would increase to levels comparable to those of the European Union. This simple

**Table 6.7.**

**Intra-Regional Trade Volume and Export and Import Ratios
by Economic Region, 1991
($ billion , %)**

|         | Export Volume | Export Ratio | Import Volume | Import Ratio |
|---------|--------------:|-------------:|--------------:|-------------:|
| AFTA    | 32.8          | 20.3         | 29.0          | 16.0         |
| EAEC    | 330.1         | 41.4         | 332.7         | 46.1         |
| NAFTA   | 245.5         | 41.8         | 236.4         | 34.9         |
| APEC    | 906.9         | 64.9         | 906.1         | 64.7         |
| EC(EU)  | 845.7         | 61.8         | 838.4         | 57.6         |

*Note:* The data for APEC and EC(EU) include only those of 15 and 12 members, respectively, as of 1991.

*Source:* IMF, *Direction of Trade Statistics Yearbook 1992.*

comparison tells us that, while EAEC and NAFTA can compete with each other, they cannot compete separately with the EC (EU) for global leadership. This is one of the main reasons why North America and East Asia should join forces through the development of APEC in the face of the European challenge.

But there are continuing major obstacles to Asia-Pacific trade cooperation. First, the region has been characterized by a persistent North-South cleavage and the attendant fear of great power domination over developing countries. While this situation has become less serious, it is still unfavorable to the emergence of region-wide cooperation. The reason is simple: "The developed economies in this region were skeptical of the cooperative attitude of the developing economies, while the developing economies worried about the fair distribution of benefits resulting from cooperation."[36] As a result, bilateralism has been the predominant mode of interaction. Both developed and developing countries in the region want to maintain whatever bargaining advantages they have while trying to avoid succumbing to external pressures through regional multilateral institutions.

Second, in parallel with the North-South cleavage, the East-West conflict also continues to be strong in the Asia-Pacific region. It has been noted that there are significant differences in business practices, legal and institutional settings, and the roles of social networks and personal relationships among countries in the region. This diversity in the social and cultural compositions within the region, especially between North America and East Asia, can certainly hinder the development and operation of international and regional institutions.[37]

Third, the region still lacks leadership. Efforts to construct institutions for the Asia-Pacific region began after the decline of American influence in the region and the rise of Japan's economic power. Thus,

---

[36]Jae-Bong Ro, "Trade Liberalization in the Asia-Pacific Region," p.8. (Paper presented at the 3rd APEC Trade Promotion Seminar, Korean Institute for Industrial Economics and Trade, October 26-28, 1993).

[37]For a general picture of cultural diversity in the Asia-Pacific region, see Sung-chick Hong, "Cultural Variables of Asia-Pacific Community," in Sung-Joo Han, ed. *Community-Building in the Pacific Region: Issues and Opportunities* (Seoul: Asiatic Studies Center, Korea University, 1981).

defining the respective roles of the United States and Japan in the region has become contentious. The United States has viewed Asia-Pacific regional organizations with mixed motives: to devolve more international responsibility onto Japan while not allowing Japan to become a regional hegemon. Japan, on the other hand, has seen regional organizations as a means of promoting its international role while avoiding the assumption of a visible leadership role. Thus, the United States and Japan reveal an unwillingness to lead regional cooperation.[38] As one scholar argues: "Until U.S.-Japan differences are resolved to a degree at least sufficient to avert collision, it is unrealistic to expect much by way of institutionalized regional cooperation."[39]

The Chinese factor is also important with regard to the leadership problem. China's economic and political systems are still quite different from those of the other major countries in the region. As a result, China's entrance into the WTO will present a problem to most of that body's members, including the East Asian countries. In practical terms, however, China should be allowed to enter into the WTO because of its status as a major trading nation.[40] But a critical question persists: On what terms is China going to be allowed to join the WTO? In this regard, China has yet to approach what its major trading partners, especially the United States, want. The United States

---

[38]The governments that have demonstrated at least sporadic enthusiasm for organizing the Asia-Pacific have been Japan and Australia. Japanese interest in Asia-Pacific regional organizations has been to find "a role between, on one hand, global organizations that appeared dominated by Europe and the United States and, on the other, specifically Asian organizations that might recall imperial structures such as the Co-Prosperity Sphere." Australia has also found its interest in organizing the Asia-Pacific because it could provide the country "an escape from sticky bilateral ties - the overwhelming economic presence of Japan- and a means to adjust to a new niche in the international economy, as ties to Britain and the Commonwealth faded." Miles Kahler, "Organizing the Pacific," p.335.

[39]David Rapkin, "Economic and Security Regimes in the Asia Pacific: Prospects for Progress," (Paper presented at the Conference on Economic and Security Cooperation in the Asia-Pacific: Agenda for the 1990s, Canberra, Australia, July 28–30, 1993), pp.2–3.

[40]China has shown interest in joining the GATT since the early 1980s. In 1986, it submitted its formal application to GATT. Since then, the GATT's Working Party has studied Chinese trading system and negotiations have been going on over the rights and obligations for China. See Morio Matsumoto, "China's Industrial Policy and Participation in the GATT," *JETRO China Newsletter*, No.113 (September-October, 1994).

also has to rethink what and how much it wants to obtain from the negotiations over Chinese entrance into the WTO. In any case, the two powers have to find a way out of constant political difficulties resulting from the annual review of the American provision of MFN status to China.

In addition, potential Sino-Japanese competition in East Asia lies in the way of Asia-Pacific cooperation. China, East Asia's foremost political power, is now gaining economic might. Japan, an economic superpower, is searching for an increased political role commensurate with its economic power. As both of these trends develop, the rivalry between the two may intensify. As one journalist puts it, "Greater China and Greater Japan are increasingly rubbing up against each other along their outer boundaries."[41] Consequently, Southeast Asia, for instance, may become the front line in an economic struggle between Beijing and Tokyo to establish their respective spheres of influence.

Given the above-mentioned need for and obstacles to Asia-Pacific trade cooperation, the development of a regional trading order will follow a tortuous path. The long process towards the establishment of APEC and its subsequent development testify to this. Before the official establishment of APEC in 1989, there had been numerous proposals for and attempts at the establishment of pan-Pacific organizations.[42] These attempts included a Japanese proposal for a Pacific Area Free Trade Association (PAFTA) in 1965, proposals for a Pacific Trade and Development (PAFTAD) Conference and a Pacific Basic Economic Council (PBEC) in the late 1960s, the establishment of the Pacific Economic Cooperation Conference (PECC), and a proposal for the Organization for Pacific Trade and Development (OPTAD) in 1980.

---

[41]Bill Powell, "Asia's Power Struggle," *Newsweek* (November 15, 1993), p.13.

[42]Among the surveys of chronological developments of Asia-Pacific regionalism, the author is indebted to Stuart Harris, "Varieties of Pacific Economic cooperation"; Miles Kahler, "Organizing the Pacific" in R. Scalapino et al., eds., *Pacific- Asian Economic Policies and Regional Interdependence* (Berkeley: Institute of East Asian Studies, University of California, 1988); and Chungsoo Kim, "Regional Economic Cooperation Bodies in the Asia-pacific: Working Mechanism and Linkages," in Jang-Won Suh and Jae-Bong Ro, eds., *Asia-Pacific Economic Cooperation.*

Though limited in success, these proposals constituted precedents for Asia-Pacific organizational efforts and laid the foundation for the inauguration of the APEC process. However, the negotiations over the establishment of the APEC as an intergovernmental forum were heavily influenced by power and interest considerations of certain countries. Until the early 1980s, the United States paid very little attention to organizing Pacific relations, since it was concerned about the subsequent loss of its autonomy and influence within a regional framework. Small states worried about their institutionalized subordination to big powers. Only middle powers like Japan and Australia, at that time, were enthusiastic about organizing regional trade relations.

This situation, however, began to change with the shift in Pacific power structures. The United States became concerned about the erosion of its power in its bilateral relations with East Asian countries and perceived the need for a regional framework in order to maintain its influence through such an institutionalized process. East Asian countries were concerned about increased U.S. bilateral pressures and needed a regional mechanism to contain U.S. influence. Small states in East Asia sought to balance U.S. and Japanese influence and avoid predominance by either of them. Thus, a compromise solution emerged: the establishment of a weak intergovernmental forum named the Asia-Pacific Economic Cooperation. Donald Crone comments: "Despite widespread reluctance, a new organization became strategically rational for all."[43]

At the third APEC meeting in Seoul in 1991, membership increased from 12 to 15 with the participation of the "three Chinas"—China, Taiwan, and Hong Kong. It expanded once again to 18 at the 1993 Seattle meeting with the inclusion of Mexico, Chile, and Papua New Guinea. Ten working groups were established, while, at the Bangkok meeting, decisions were made to establish a permanent, though small, secretariat in Singapore and to set up an advisory panel, dubbed the Eminent Persons Group.

The Seattle meeting in 1993 was a turning point in the development of APEC. First of all, it was an historical event, since it was the first

---

[43]Donald Crone, "Does Hegemony Matter?: The Regionalization of the Pacific Political Economy," *World Politics*, Vol.45 No.4 (July 1993), p.522.

time that nine heads of state out of twelve Asia-Pacific countries met in a single forum. Second, the vision for APEC was discussed and agreed upon in principle: APEC would be made into an economic community for the region. In this regard, President Clinton emphasized that Asia and North America should not be divided into two separate competing regions: "We've agreed that the Asia-Pacific region should be a united one, not divided." Third, such regional cooperative organs as the Committee on Trade and Investment (CTI) and the Pacific Business Forum, and a program to boost cooperation in technology education were established.

These achievements at Seattle became the basis of the "Bogor declaration," which set a timetable for developing free trade within the region. At the 1994 APEC summit at Bogor, Indonesia, leaders agreed that the industrialized economies within the region would achieve free trade by 2010 and the developing economies would follow suit by 2020.[44] This is seemingly a modest achievement. However, the very fact that a target date for free trade was established is important, for it means that the APEC forum has begun to function as a negotiating mechanism.

Still, it is not certain that APEC will develop as an effective regional organization for free trade covering both East Asia and North America. We know that there are many uncertainties and obstacles which lie before APEC. However, the Asia-Pacific region is in need of a common regional framework which functions effectively for the management of interdependent trade relations. It is under such an institutionalized regional framework along with the strengthened global multilateral regime that the three giants in the Asia-Pacific region will hopefully live and prosper together.

## CONCLUSION

In East Asia and the Pacific, we can easily identify several potential sources of serious conflict among the major powers. In trade relations, the U.S.-Japan trade imbalance continues; U.S. trade pressures on East Asian countries may intensify; Chinese economic reform

---

[44]See "APEC: Charting the Future," *Far Eastern Economic Review* (November 24, 1994).

may falter; NAFTA and the prospective EAEC may collide; and a Japan-led Flying Geese and an Awakening Dragon's Greater China may find themselves on a collision course. Each of these sources of conflict has the potential to disrupt global security and economic relations, as well as those of East Asian countries. Thus, they should be managed carefully, not only through bilateral negotiations, but also through strengthened regional and global mechanisms.

For an orderly management of East Asian trade relations, three tasks, one for each giant, must be undertaken. First, America's "aggressive unilateralism" should be checked through the WTO, the consolidation of APEC, and, if necessary, a deepening of cooperation among East Asian countries. Americans tend to behave like a "predatory hegemon" in order to hammer out access to foreign markets. This approach can only serve to increase trade tensions and political disputes with its trading partners, and this is inimical to the multilateral trading system.

Second, Japan's huge trade surplus has to be reduced. Japan's trade surplus has been the cause of many serious problems in the world trading system. Japan has to import more and export less. In order to bring about this change, Japanese domestic economic and social systems must be transformed into a more consumer- and import-oriented society. Japan also must increase its international economic role by providing more economic aid to developing countries and by contributing more to the stability of international monetary relations.

Third, China has to join the WTO by carrying out rapid and fundamental economic reforms. As the world's eleventh largest trading nation, China has to assume its obligations to maintain and improve the liberal world trading system.

As a way of achieving these three tasks, we have suggested the consolidation of APEC as a regional framework for the management and negotiation of trade relations. APEC has already moved in this direction by adopting a timetable for the establishment of a free trade area at the Bogor meeting in 1994. However, the program should be specified and institutionalized through further negotiations in the coming years. If APEC develops into an effective regional trade mechanism, it will be able to function as a channel for addressing

American demands for market openings, putting legitimate external pressure on Japan, and pushing Chinese market reforms. Thus, through such development APEC will be able to pacify Asia-Pacific trade relations by soothing the angry eagle, by reasoning with the stubborn goose, and by urging the tardy dragon.

# Section IV

# The Future of the U.S.-Korean Alliance

The fourth session was devoted to a discussion of papers by Norman Levin and Hyun-Dong Kim. (The discussion was much enhanced by the participation of Donald Gregg, former U.S. Ambassador to Korea and currently Chairman of the Korea Society.) The two papers, though applying a somewhat different method of analysis, highlighted the possibilities of major potential divergence in the workings of the security relationship. This possible divergence was both near term and over the mid to longer term. Although not all scenarios were judged of equal likelihood, several participants foresaw the possibility of significant future changes in the pattern of U.S. forward deployments in the region, which would then recalibrate estimates of the durability of security commitments between the two countries. Such a trend, these participants asserted, was likely to grow even more pronounced should North Korea no longer represent a major political and military threat to the ROK, or should unification take place.

Under these circumstances, an alternative rationale for the security role of the United States was deemed a critical need if Korea and the United States were to sustain close security collaboration in the future. But there was also support for more vigorous exploration of future political and security linkages between Korea and Japan. As one participant observed, a severe deterioration in the regional security setting was far more likely to result from a conflict of interest between China and Japan, rather than because of any presumed Japanese designs on Korea. Numerous institutional and strategic adaptations could be pursued much more vigorously in a reconfigured peninsular environment: many of the long-established verities in U.S. policy would seem increasingly anachronistic in such a context.

However, as one Sejong participant observed, the U.S.-Korea alliance also needed to be viewed through the prism of Korea domestic politics.  Many in Korea continue to see their country surrounded by much more powerful states that could potentially threaten Korean interests; on this basis, several Sejong participants noted, U.S. forces remain a crucial stabilizing factor in the minds of many Koreans.  As others observed, however, this fact alone could not guarantee the sustainability of present alliance arrangements, especially should the peninsular setting undergo major change.  Thus, there seems a potential contradiction between the insistence of many Koreans on an enhanced voice and role in the alliance, while simultaneously expressing increased concern that the United States would no longer assume a primary position in ensuring Korea's security.  There was widespread agreement among the conferees, therefore, that both countries needed to explore much more vigorously how to pursue shared (and less asymmetrical) security interests in the future, lest either or both states sharply devalue the importance attached to the bilateral alliance.

# Chapter Seven

# FUTURE DEVELOPMENTS ON THE KOREAN PENINSULA AND THE U.S.-ROK ALLIANCE

Norman D. Levin

## INTRODUCTION

The history of the U.S.-ROK security alliance, like the post-war history of East Asia more broadly, is one of extraordinary success. Virtually all of the major security objectives of the two allies have been either achieved or significantly furthered: Communist expansion—the principal concern which brought the two countries together in a formal security alliance—has been stopped, in East Asia as in the world at large; deterrence of major renewed North Korean aggression has been maintained; South Korea has grown strong, stable, and significantly more self-reliant (as reflected in the formal move by the United States to a "supporting" rather than "leading" role in the alliance); close bilateral security ties have helped build regional stability; market-oriented economies have flourished, *especially* in East Asia; and democratic values and practices have spread, not least in South Korea itself. Beyond this, the security alliance has facilitated Korea's integration into the international community, while helping "anchor" the United States in the region and providing a basis for broad cooperative efforts among U.S. regional allies. While South Korea's paramount objective of unification remains to be achieved, the U.S.-ROK alliance has helped definitively shift the North-South political-economic balance on the peninsula and make unification less a question of "whether" than of "when" and "in what manner."

However, there are still many uncertainties associated with potential developments on the Korean peninsula. Some of these are spillovers from the seismic global changes of the past half decade and encompass such weighty questions as Russia's future and its implications for the peninsula and for the future of the U.S. presence and military role in the region. Others, including a host of questions associated with the future of North Korea, are more a function of indigenous trends on the peninsula, albeit ones that are often exacerbated by broader regional and global developments. The question is how to think about these uncertainties in a way that elucidates rather than obscures the important challenges facing the U.S.-ROK alliance as the two countries approach the end of the 20th century.

This paper is intended as an initial step in this direction. It first seeks to define the critical assumptions that have underpinned the U.S.-ROK security alliance in the past and whose invalidation would trigger major negative effects on the bilateral partnership. It then identifies various potential developments and sets of events that could bring these critical assumptions into question. The paper concludes with a notional assessment of the prospects for these developments and broad policy guidelines that might help diminish their likelihood or potential negative impact.

Two prefatory comments should be emphasized. First, this paper is about *challenges*—specifically, about those kinds of developments that could, if they transpired, have a *major negative effect* on the U.S.-ROK security alliance. While there are many developments that could have a positive effect and represent opportunities for the alliance, this paper does not address them. Second, the purpose of the paper is as much heuristic as analytical. It is designed to illustrate a *way of thinking* about the future, one that believes that alliances—like other products of national planning—are built on assumptions, that the ground is shifting under these assumptions, and that continuing to base policy on unexamined assumptions is an increasingly risky endeavor.

## CRITICAL ASSUMPTIONS UNDERLYING THE U.S.-ROK SECURITY ALLIANCE

Unlike potential developments in China, Japan, or elsewhere in the region that might adversely affect the U.S.-ROK alliance, it is easy to identify the major source of worry on the Korean peninsula: renewed military conflict. It is also easy to identify potential developments that might trigger such a conflict, and a plethora of scenarios have been generated over the years in countless studies and political-military games that could lead to such a development. It is not our intention to repeat such exercises. While the next section does address several potential developments that could precipitate major military conflict, the focus of this paper is on developments that could have negative effects on the larger U.S.-ROK security alliance, partly because they are less well-understood and partly because—in an era of great uncertainty—they are more interesting.

These developments themselves, however, cover a wide range of potential events. In order to separate those that really matter from those that are simply interesting, it is first necessary to identify the critical assumptions underlying the U.S.-ROK security alliance whose confirmation or invalidation by one or more of these potential developments could have major effects on military plans or national security policies. The following five candidate assumptions, which are drawn from a review of the history of the Korean-American alliance, are put forward for purposes of discussion.

**Critical Assumption #1: There is a threat from North Korea.**

This, of course, is the bedrock assumption underlying the U.S.-ROK alliance and is codified in both the Mutual Defense Treaty and countless joint planning and operational documents. The assumption reflects the view that the possibility of renewed military attack or adventurism by North Korea remains real, a view reinforced by Pyongyang's track record of radicalism and risk taking, its continuing military buildup and forward deployed forces, and its mounting political and economic difficulties. Both the United States and the ROK are right to worry about how economic deterioration in the North could fuel political strife in Pyongyang and perhaps prompt a desperate attempt by North Korea to bring the peninsula under its control before the north itself "goes under." Both are also right to worry about a range of other scenarios involving developments in the north, the ultimate outcome of which would be large-scale military conflict. As long as such possibilities exist, the alliance must remain predicated on the assumption of a threat from North Korea.

But this assumption is somewhat unique among the five candidates in that "negative effects" might be generated by *either* its confirmation or invalidation. Any development that precipitated a major military conflict would obviously have negative effects on the U.S.-ROK alliance, although it might also have the salutary effects of reinforcing alliance cohesion and—ultimately—achieving unification on South Korean terms. It also would confirm the correctness of the central assumption underlying the security partnership. But other developments are possible that would *invalidate* this central assumption, while adversely affecting the security alliance. Indeed, so central has the assumption of a "threat from the north" been to the alliance that little attention has been paid to potential negative consequences of its invalidation. As we have seen in the impact on NATO of the Cold War's end, such effects can be substantial, if wholly different from the kinds of "negative effects" of traditional concern to security planning within the alliance.

The next section begins by identifying some of the major developments that could precipitate a military conflict and hence confirm the assumption of a threat from North Korea. It also identifies some of the major developments that might invalidate this first critical assumption.

## Critical Assumption #2: The U.S. and ROK can together handle the threat from North Korea.

Only slightly less important to the bilateral security alliance has been the assumption that continued forward-deployed U.S. and South Korean forces can successfully deter North Korea from military attack and that, should deterrence fail, ROK ground forces and U.S. air and naval power, supplemented by large-scale U.S. reinforcements (including ground forces), can defeat any such North Korean aggression at an acceptable cost. This assumption is embedded in national strategy and military planning documents and is central to current force deployments and joint operational planning. In the past, the principal challenge to the presumed validity of this assumption was linked to U.S. global strategic requirements and uncertainties about U.S. capabilities likely to be available for Korea in a "global" war. Today, this traditional challenge has been joined by concerns about other actual or potential developments in both Koreas, as well as in the United States.

**Critical Assumption #3: No political, economic, or military/technological development will enable North Korea to negate this U.S.-ROK capability.**

This assumption is largely unspoken. It rests on the overwhelming economic and technological superiority of the United States and the ROK over the north and, perhaps, North Korea's international isolation. The major uncertainty about this assumption in the past related to potential Chinese intervention in any military conflict in Korea. Although this uncertainty remains today, the effects of other potential developments have risen in importance.

**Critical Assumption #4: Public support will be sufficient in both the United States and the ROK to support a close security relationship.**

This assumption is also largely unspoken. By some calculations, it may represent less an "assumption" than a "prerequisite" for a healthy alliance. Lest it be taken for granted, however, it is worth recalling the negative effects on the alliance in the 1960s generated by public opposition in the United States to military rule in South Korea, or by waning public support in the 1970s for a continued American military presence in Korea given indications of serious human rights violations. Democratization in South Korea has diminished the salience of such issues today. But ongoing trends raise a number of different potential developments that could invalidate this assumption and impinge adversely on the U.S.-ROK security alliance.

**Critical Assumption #5: Shared U.S.-ROK interests will outweigh potential policy divergencies.**

In the past, this assumption—spoken or unspoken—seemed reasonable, given the overarching Communist threat. A shared fear of renewed North Korean aggression, and broader opposition to Communist expansion, provided the glue that cemented the security alliance and the means for surmounting frictions in other parts of the bilateral relationship. If potential developments were to undermine this assumption, the U.S.-ROK security alliance would not be unique in having to deal with their negative consequences.

## Potential Developments Adversely Affecting the U.S.-ROK Alliance

Potential developments on the Korean Peninsula that could adversely affect the security alliance—including developments in the United States that have direct implications for Korea—are both numerous and wide-ranging. For the purposes of this paper, a potential development is included only if it would affect one or more of the critical assumptions identified in the preceding section. Evaluating each of these developments and identifying possible countermeasures will be left for the concluding section.

**Critical Assumption #1: There is a threat from North Korea.**

Among the developments that meet this criterion and would have negative effects relating to the first assumption, five stand out. These are listed below, along with brief "thumb-nail" scenarios outlining a plausible sequence of events that could precipitate the potential development.[1] Most of the developments grow out of North Korea's domestic difficulties—especially a deteriorating economic situation that may be even worse than most observers already posit—which would pose increasingly unpleasant choices for North Korean leaders. The first three developments would confirm the candidate assumption; the last two would involve its invalidation.

- North Korea launches a last ditch, "desperation" attack on the ROK to bring the peninsula under North Korean control before the north itself collapses.

Scenario: The North Korean economy continues to deteriorate, spurred by intensified energy shortages, shortage of hard currency reserves, and an inability to implement meaningful economic reforms. Already intense political strife is exacerbated by strident military opposition to cutbacks in defense spending, reductions in conventional forces, and the opening of North Korea to extensive South Korean economic involvement—all measures proposed by leading

---

[1]It is important to stress that these "scenarios" are meant to be illustrative rather than predictive. They suggest a *plausible set or sequence of events* by which the main development identified might occur. The validity of the potential development itself rests on the extent to which it is a credible possibility given ongoing trends, not on full validation of each or any given element of the respective scenarios.

"technocrats" as the only way to prevent a free-fall in the North Korean economy. Faced with the prospect of military cutbacks and South Korean penetration, the North Korean army launches a massive invasion of the ROK, possibly taking advantage of political weakness in Seoul, declining discipline and morale in the South Korean army, significant opposition in South Korea to U.S. pressure on North Korea's nuclear program, and (conceivably) improved DPRK-PRC relations in the wake of heightened U.S.-PRC tensions. Negative effects on the U.S.-ROK security alliance include major human and financial costs and retardation of progress on the U.S. and ROK domestic policy agendas.

- North Korea initiates a limited military provocation.

Scenario: As Pyongyang continues to stall implementation of the nuclear agreement and resorts to renewed brinkmanship to secure additional benefits, pressure mounts in the United States for increased international pressure on North Korea. U.S. officials seek South Korean approval for stepped-up defensive measures in response to North Korean threats of retaliation to any such pressures. Public opinion is split in South Korea, with strong pockets of opposition to U.S. pressure. Fabricating a military incident at the DMZ, North Korea "retaliates" by firing a single artillery round into a town in northeastern South Korea. Pyongyang warns that Seoul will be turned into a "flaming hell" if the U.S. continues its "flagrant aggression," demonstrating a calibrated effort to fan the fear of war in South Korea. Such a development would risk full-scale military conflict on the peninsula with all its attendant consequences. It also would weaken public support in South Korea for required defensive measures, intensify discord between Washington and Seoul, and undermine the push for increased international pressures on North Korea.

- North Korea threatens to suspend the nuclear agreement.

Scenario: After many delays over the source of light water reactors and new demands for additional Western concessions, including significantly increased economic assistance and a permanent cancellation of U.S.-ROK military exercises, North Korea walks out of talks with the United States over implementation of the nuclear agreement. Government spokesmen rail against American "insincerity" and threaten to suspend the agreement and end its nuclear "freeze" if its "reasonable" demands are not met. Pressure mounts in the United States to seek international sanctions against Pyongyang and take immediate measures to bolster U.S. defenses in South Korea. China and Russia both urge dialogue and negotiation. Significantly heightened tensions and the possibility of military conflict on the peninsula once again confront U.S.-ROK defense planners. Additional negative effects include possible splits between the two allies over how to respond to North Korea's demands and potential further constraints on joint U.S.-ROK measures to defend South Korea.

• North Korea officially adopts a policy of "peaceful co-existence."

Scenario: "Technocrats" in Pyongyang appear to gain at least temporary control over North Korean policy as the regime moves to end North Korea's economic decline and international isolation. Several senior army leaders are removed and North Korean media rail against "flunkeyists" (presumably in the Party and bureaucracy) who "only feign confidence" in the superiority of North Korea's "unique, *chu'che*-based" system. North Korean leaders call for a major expansion of Western investment and assistance to ensure the success of "peaceful co-existence." In an effort to back up this call, they urge a wide-ranging resumption of North-South dialogue and propose immediate steps to drastically reduce conventional military forces and curtail military activities on both sides of the DMZ. Much of this scenario is highly positive from a U.S. or ROK perspective. Negative effects might include heightened frictions between South Korea and the United States over economic assistance to North Korea and unfavorable constraints on U.S.-ROK self-defense measures. They might also include increased pressure in both the United States and South Korea for rapid U.S. force drawdowns from the Korean peninsula.

• North Korea peacefully implodes.

Scenario: This is essentially a replay of the East German experience. It was once the desired—and even anticipated—South Korean outcome. Today, concerns over the potentially huge economic costs have dampened South Korean ardor for rapid implosion. Aside from costs, such a development could adversely affect the U.S.-ROK security alliance in at least two major ways: by significantly heightening domestic pressures in both the countries for a total American withdrawal from South Korea; and by removing, without replacing, the central rationale underlying the bilateral security relationship. Further negative spillover would be likely on U.S. regional military planning — with major downward pressures on the U.S. defense budget, global force structure, and future forward-deployed forces — and on South Korean security calculations.

**Critical Assumption #2: The U.S. and ROK can together handle the threat from North Korea.**

Firm maintenance of the U.S. deterrent against North Korean aggression and the continued deployment and exercise of Korean and American forces at robust levels make this appear a safe assumption. Certainly South Korea appears relatively sanguine about this assumption, and the United States officially maintains confidence in its validity. But at least two developments, each based on currently existing trends, could call it into question:

- The United States and the ROK allow their military capabilities to seriously degrade, altering both the prospects for and costs of successful allied defense against North Korea.

Scenario: Pressures to reduce the U.S. budget deficit (with or without a constitutional amendment to balance the budget by 2002) intensify over the next several years, leading to the first significant U.S. force drawdowns from the Pacific, reduced readiness of forces based in the United States, and perhaps substitution of a "one" or "one-and-a-half local war" military strategy for the current "2 MRC" orientation. The United States reaffirms its commitment to South Korea's defense but seeks a more rapid shift—justified perhaps by continued progress in implementing the nuclear agreement with North Korea—to a more "supporting" role on the peninsula. Meanwhile, clinging to its conviction that the presence of U.S. troops precludes any serious North Korean aggression—and with an eye to Korea's presumed military needs *after* unification—the ROK neglects the immediate ground threat from the north in its strategic and procurement policies in favor of the development of sophisticated capabilities (submarines, spy planes, satellites, home-built destroyers, etc.) targeted on potential post-unification adversaries. Morale and cohesion in the South Korean army continue to deteriorate, with mounting shortages of ammunition and spare parts and frequent incidents of insubordination. Interoperability between the United States and the ROK declines as South Korea gives increasing emphasis to technology transfers and domestic production—a problem exacerbated by a reduction in combined training exercises dictated by both political constraints and budgetary reductions. The negative effects of such a development would obviously be severe. At a minimum, prospects for a successful defense against North Korean attack would be diminished. At a maximum, the U.S. assessment of a "reasonable cost" to defend South Korea could be altered, changing thinking in the United States about America's defense commitment to the ROK and North Korea's own "risk/benefit" calculation.

• North Korea uses chemical weapons.

Scenario: Faced with the knowledge that it cannot sustain a long military conflict and must achieve its objectives quickly, North Korea employs chemical weapons as soon as war breaks out on the Korean peninsula. South Korea's inadequate preparation facilitates a rapid North Korean advance down the peninsula, reaching (in a worst-case scenario) the edge of Pusan before U.S. forces can be mobilized. Such a development would have severe adverse effects: militarily, it would necessitate a U.S. amphibious re-entry and costly campaign (requiring virtually the entire available U.S. force structure) to roll back North Korean forces; politically, it would pose for the United States the unpalatable choice of either absorbing enormous U.S. casualties, using nuclear weapons (which could set off retaliatory nuclear attacks by Pyongyang on South Korea and/or Japan), or abandoning South Korea.

**Critical Assumption #3: No political, economic, or military/technological development will enable North Korea to negate this U.S.-ROK capability.**

North Korea's possible use of chemical weapons has just been mentioned. Aside from this possibility, at least two other developments on the Korean peninsula could call this third candidate assumption into question and adversely affect the U.S.-ROK security alliance.

• North Korea intimidates Japan into denying base access to U.S. forces.

Scenario: Either prior to or immediately after the initiation of military hostilities, North Korea threatens to "turn Japan into a sea of fire" if the government permits "imperialist powers or their puppets" to use Japanese territory to support military action against North Korea. Media reports trumpet North Korea's long-range missile capability and warn darkly of "technology marriages" that, like couples, become larger and stronger than the sum of their parts when united (i.e., "marrying" North Korean nuclear and/or chemical weapons with the means to deliver them). Abiding by the U.S.-Japan Security Treaty's requirement for "prior consultations," the United States formally requests use of Japanese bases. The weak coalition government in Tokyo is thrown into chaos and delays a formal response pending further clarification of the situation. After two days of mounting confusion, the Japanese cabinet. . . . In one sense, it is not necessary to know how this scenario plays out: given the critical role of U.S. airpower in the early days of any conflict on the peninsula, significant damage has already been done. In another sense, however, the ultimate outcome is crucial: should U.S. transshipment, resupply, and reinforcement operations be curtailed by Japan, the course of the battle will be directly affected. More important, any such successful North Korean intimidation would spell the end of the U.S.-Japan security alliance and undermine the U.S. position throughout the region. It also would ensure lasting enmity between Japan and the ultimately reunited Korea.

• North Korea locks the United States and the ROK into a "life-support" system which prevents needed allied defense measures.

Scenario: North Korea skillfully manipulates implementation of the nuclear agreement to constrain needed improvements to defense structure (e.g., deployment of additional Patriot missiles, fighter aircraft, etc.) and operational capability (e.g., cancellation of "Team Spirit," etc.) of U.S.-ROK forces. These constraints are bolstered by "self-deterring" actions by both Washington and Seoul designed to avoid antagonizing North Korea.

**Critical Assumption #4: Public support will be sufficient in both the U.S. and ROK to support a close security relationship.**

As noted in the previous section, many of the kinds of developments that threatened public support for the security relationship in the past are no longer major dangers. But other developments are both possible and, if anything, even more consequential than in the past. Resentment over U.S. dealings with the North on the nuclear issue and pressures for South Korean purchases of U.S. military equipment have already weakened support in certain sectors of South Korea for continued reliance on the United States. Opposition to strong U.S. market-opening pressures has also undermined support for the alliance. One interesting aspect of these trends is the increased importance of public opinion in South Korea, reflecting South Korean progress toward greater democratization and desire for a more equal relationship with the United States. But public attitudes remain a critical variable in the United States, as well, as discussed below.

- Nationalist and/or anti-American sentiment becomes dominant in South Korea.

Scenario: North Korea continues to engage in brinkmanship in its negotiations with the United States over implementation of the nuclear agreement. Washington cuts off talks with Pyongyang out of frustration and moves to enlist international support for sanctions against North Korea. The United States also exerts strong pressure on the ROK to rapidly improve its defenses—including significant new purchases of American military equipment—and allow measures to beef up U.S. military capabilities in South Korea. Coupled with a relatively low public perception of threat in South Korea and general preoccupation with *internal* problems, such developments sets off a virulent kind of Korean nationalism that could undermine support for the U.S.-ROK alliance.

- Isolationist sentiment becomes dominant in the United States.

Scenario: The growth of isolationist sentiment in the United States has already been widely noted in public media, and an illustrative sequence of events for how it might develop is probably not necessary. The effect on U.S.-ROK relations, however, is less self-evident.

Presumably, so long as a clear threat exists from North Korea, even an America dominated by strong isolationist sentiment will honor its treaty commitments.  Over time, however, such an America will almost surely become less activist and could begin to redefine its treaty obligations in ways that seek more demonstrable "burden-sharing" from its allies and a less prominent U.S. overseas exposure.  The real danger might come not so much from isolationism per se but its likely co-mingling with strong *unilateralist* tendencies in the United States and the possible rise of nationalism (and perhaps anti-American sentiment) in South Korea.  A sequence of events that constrained U.S. freedom of action with perceived damage to important U.S. interests could well de-link America from Korea's security.  Even short of this, the combination of significantly improved North-South relations—particularly if it leads to a demonstrable reduction in tensions on the peninsula—and the growth of isolationist sentiment in the United States would likely incline the U.S. to re-think its security involvement in Korea, with potentially negative effects on the U.S.-ROK security alliance.

**Critical Assumption #5: Shared U.S.-ROK interests will outweigh potential policy divergencies.**

In the post-Cold War era, the salience of economic interests has risen almost everywhere.  The priority of *domestic* concerns relative to foreign policy matters has also increased.  To be sure, the revival of Russian adventurism could alter this equation, as might the rise of a new threat from a regionally assertive China.  In the absence of some such major threat, however, domestic—especially *nationalist*—concerns will assume new priority in foreign and security policies.  Our ability in the past to assume that commonly shared U.S.-ROK military interests will override divergencies on other issues will be sorely tested.  Aside from the ascendance of economic nationalism in the United States and South Korea, which could undermine a sense of shared interest in both countries, two additional developments could call this assumption into question.  Interestingly, both stem from potential actions taken by the United States.

- The United States irremediably undermines South Korea's position vis-a-vis Pyongyang.

Scenario: Plausible events that could lead to such a development include those stemming from a U.S. effort to placate Pyongyang to ensure successful implementation of the nuclear agreement. While the South Korean government wants to minimize the potential for military conflict, it does not want to see North Korea prosper at its expense. A major U.S. concession that prevents South Korea from becoming the source of any light water reactors provided to North Korea, for example, would be a dramatic political setback to the ROK and precipitate serious rethinking in Seoul about the value of the U.S.-ROK security alliance. Premature steps toward U.S.-DPRK normalization of relations or efforts to integrate North Korea into the international community in the absence of major North Korean policy changes toward South Korea are additional developments that would seriously undermine a sense of shared interests.

- The United States fosters a greater Japanese security role in Korea than South Korea is prepared to countenance.

Scenario: Seeking to scale back and "rationalize" its forward deployments in the Pacific as a budget-cutting measure, America prematurely withdraws troops from South Korea and—as part of a larger effort to "re-invigorate" the U.S.-Japan security relationship—encourages greater Japanese "responsibility-sharing" for Korea. A particularly explosive step would be devolution of responsibility for ground defense and/or reinforcements to Tokyo. Expanding Japan's air defense zone to the 38th parallel or transferring the symbolically important headquarters flag to Japan are other illustrative steps that would be alarming to South Korea.

## PROSPECTS, IMPACT, AND POTENTIAL COUNTERMEASURES

Almost any evaluation of the prospects for and impact of the kinds of developments identified above are necessarily subjective. A whole subset of unspoken assumptions would need to be identified and fleshed out to make any "grading" even remotely "objective." This section makes no pretense at such objectivity. Instead, it presents a strawman ranking and invites the reader to substitute his or her own evaluation. The principal purpose is to stimulate discussion, not produce a "grading" that everyone will agree to. If such discussion helps refine the methodology to produce more useful judgments about those developments that should receive priority attention, so much the better.

## Methodology

The first section of this paper began with an "inward-looking" orientation, identifying a number of candidate assumptions judged critical to the underpinning of the U.S.-ROK security alliance. The second section then looked "outward" and described a number of developments that could materially affect one or more of these critical assumptions. Together, these sections constitute essential steps in what might be called "assumption-based thinking." This approach is somewhat different from that of "assumption-based planning," a methodology developed at RAND by James Dewar and Morlie Levin.[2] But it shares with it an effort to direct attention away from the extrapolation of *external* trends toward potential developments that could upset *internal* plans and operations.

To evaluate each of these potential developments, this section introduces two further variables: *likelihood* and probable *impact*. Each of these variables is applied to the potential developments described in the preceding section and ranked notionally in terms of three categories: "high," "medium," and "low." The results are described in Table 1 below.

A brief explanation of some of the rankings is in order. The likelihood of a limited North Korean military attack is ranked as "low" because of the robustness of the U.S.-ROK deterrent, while some sort of "desperation" attack is a distinct, though certainly not "highly" likely, possibility. North Korea's either formally adopting "peaceful co-existence" or somehow "peacefully" imploding are also judged of relatively "low" likelihood, the former because such a move would seriously undermine the basis for regime legitimacy and open up North Korea to its almost inevitable subversion and the latter because it is

---

[2]James Dewar and Morlie Levin, *Assumption-Based Planning for Army 21*, R-4172-A (RAND, 1992) and James Dewar, et. al., *Assumption-Based Planning: A Planning Tool for Very Uncertain Times* (RAND, 1993).

**Table 7.1.**

**Likelihood and Impact of Potential Developments**

| Potential Development | Likelihood | Impact |
|---|---|---|
| DPRK launches "desperation" attack | Medium | High |
| DPRK initiates limited military provocation | Low | High |
| DPRK threatens to quit nuclear agreement | Medium | Medium |
| DPRK adopts "peaceful co-existence" | Low | Medium |
| DPRK peacefully implodes | Low | Medium |
| U.S./ROK military capabilities degrade | Medium | High |
| DPRK uses chemical weapons | High | High |
| DPRK intimidates Japan | Medium | High |
| DPRK locks U.S./ROK into "life-support" system | Low | Medium |
| Nationalist/anti-American sentiment dominates ROK | Medium | High |
| Isolationist sentiment dominates U.S. | Medium | High |
| U.S. undermines ROK position vis-a-vis DPRK | Medium | High |
| U.S. pushes Japanese security role | Low | High |

hard to imagine key power groups in North Korea being willing to "go peacefully." North Korean threats or actions to suspend the nuclear agreement are easily imaginable, although Pyongyang's interest in attracting foreign assistance makes any such steps counterproductive and hence less than "highly" likely. Even if relatively low in likelihood, each of these potential developments would have significant ("medium" to "high") consequences should they occur.

Perhaps more likely are some of the other potential developments, with the possible use of chemical weapons representing a particularly worrisome problem. Although North Korea is clearly not going to use chemical weapons as part of its regular diplomacy, it is very likely to use them as part of its war-fighting strategy—if for no other reason than because Pyongyang will have great difficulty achieving its objectives without them. Adverse developments affecting both military capabilities and public attitudes in the United States and the ROK appear to have at least a reasonable possibility of occurring. Perhaps to a somewhat lesser (but not insignificant) extent, so too do inadvertent U.S. steps that undermine the ROK's position vis-a-vis North Korea. All of these potential developments, should they occur, are judged likely to have major ("high") consequences.

Again, each of these rankings can be debated at great length. Hopefully, they will help generate not just "heat" but also greater "light."

## CONCLUSIONS AND POLICY IMPLICATIONS

At a general level, the rankings indicated above represent something of a "good news/bad news" situation for the U.S.-ROK alliance. The "good" news is that only one of the adverse developments identified in Section 2 is considered here to have a "high" likelihood of happening, and this only in the context of a conflict that has already started. The small number of high likelihood events reflects judgments about the solidity and resilience of the U.S.-ROK alliance as much as assumptions about North Korean behavior. To be sure, such developments cannot be dismissed entirely: more than half of them are considered to have at least a reasonable ("medium") likelihood of occurring, a relatively high ranking for such adverse developments. But a sensible and far-sighted set of policies can help prevent them from taking place.

The "bad" news is that all of the developments—*if* they happened— would be very consequential. Of the thirteen developments identified, nine are considered likely to have very negative ("high") effects on the alliance, with the other four being of "medium" impact. At least one of these four other developments, North Korea's severing the nuclear agreement, might also be rated as "high" impact were one to assume that such a development would precipitate a sequence of events leading to military conflict. What is striking about the developments is that there are no "freebies"—any of them would have major impact on the U.S.-ROK alliance. This suggests that there is not much room for error in managing bilateral security relations.

Two other broad observations might be offered. First, the widespread focus on North Korea's possible future evolution, while understandable and even essential, should not blind us to less interesting but arguably more important issues. As Table 2 suggests, three fourths of the developments (six of eight) that *combine* either "high" or "medium" likelihood *and* "high" impact are in the bottom part of the table. These have tended to receive considerably less attention in the academic community than the kinds of developments listed at the top of the table, all five of which deal with what may (or may not) happen in North Korea. They also have one additional virtue: they represent potential developments whose outcome we can more readily influence.

**Table 7.2.**

**Combining Likelihood and Impact of Potential Developments**

| Potential Development | Likelihood | Impact |
|---|---|---|
| DPRK launches "desperation" attack | Medium | High |
| DPRK initiates limited military provocation | Low | High |
| DPRK threatens to quit nuclear agreement | Medium | Medium |
| DPRK adopts "peaceful co-existence" | Low | Medium |
| DPRK peacefully implodes | Low | Medium |
| U.S./ROK military capabilities degrade | Medium | High |
| DPRK uses chemical weapons | High | High |
| DPRK intimidates Japan | Medium | High |
| DPRK locks U.S./ROK into "life-support" system | Low | Medium |
| Nationalist/anti-American sentiment dominates ROK | Medium | High |
| Isolationist sentiment dominates U.S. | Medium | High |
| U.S. undermines ROK position vis-a-vis DPRK | Medium | High |
| U.S. pushes Japanese security role | Low | High |

The final observation is probably self-evident: the name of the game is uncertainty. The truth is that no one knows what is going to happen, especially in North Korea but on the Korean peninsula as a whole. Even some of the "low" likelihood developments listed above could conceivably happen, and all of them would be likely to have a significant impact on U.S.-ROK security relations. If there is any general watchword for the remainder of this decade, it is "don't assume—hedge."

## Potential Countermeasures

Developing a serious set of countermeasures for the wide range of possible developments identified above goes beyond the scope of this paper. But at least three broad guidelines for action might be suggested.

First, at the most specific level, *we need to address emerging or potential shortcomings in U.S.-ROK deterrent and defense capabilities.* While the nuclear agreement with North Korea holds the possibility for significant future changes in North Korean policies, for now Pyongyang continues to allocate an extraordinary share of its total resources to military production and to deploy its military capabilities in ways that suggest less than benign intentions. At the same time, the range of adverse trends facing the DPRK makes it an increasingly unpredictable actor. While the general downward trend in U.S. and ROK defense spending may not be reversible—at least in the short term—an effective targeting of existing resources on immediate problems can do much to mitigate the negative ramifications. The ultimate irony would be if both countries allowed either the exigencies of our domestic priorities or preparations for some presumed long-term threat to undermine our ability to respond effectively to potential short-term dangers.

Second, at a slightly broader level, *we need to prepare for countering potential North Korean trouble-making on the nuclear issue.* The signing of the nuclear agreement represents a beginning, not an end. Implementation—if things go well—will take place over a long period of time. It also will involve a series of event-driven decision points whose outcome will affect prospects for terminating North Korea's nuclear program and for changing North Korean behavior. As Arnold Kanter has pointed out, the United States and the ROK need a strategy of implementation that both takes these decision points into account and allows for the inherent uncertainties in negotiating with North Korea.[3] Such a strategy requires the development of credible alternatives at each of the key decision points that would enable the two allies to respond effectively to potential and/or unanticipated developments, especially the possibility of continued brinkmanship in North Korean negotiating and foreign policy behavior.

Finally, and most broadly, *we need to devote greater attention to building public support for U.S.-ROK security cooperation.* The combination of global trends (the end of the Cold War, the increased salience of economic interests, etc.) and domestic developments (South Korean democratization, American weariness with overseas "burdens," etc.) make public attitudes an increasingly important—and potentially volatile—factor affecting prospects for the alliance. While over four decades of close security ties have fostered shared goals and habits of cooperation at the military-to-military level, misunderstanding and disinterest continue to plague public support for the alliance in both countries. Particularly corrosive is an increasing trend toward questioning the intentions of the other partner. Such

---

[3]Arnold Kanter, "The North Korean Nuclear Deal: Making It Work," *The Forum for International Policy*, April 1995.

questioning appears likely to grow, if anything, as both sides move forward in their respective dealings with North Korea.  If the U.S.-ROK security alliance is going to be as healthy tomorrow as it is today, both partners will have to demonstrate sensitivity toward the domestic situations in the other country and implant the roots of the alliance—common values, interests, and national objectives—more deeply in the public consciousness.

# Chapter Eight

# FUTURE DEVELOPMENTS ON THE KOREAN PENINSULA: IMPLICATIONS FOR THE UNITED STATES AND KOREA

## Hyun-Dong Kim

## INTRODUCTION

With the collapse of the Cold War bipolar framework, alliance arrangements and regional security mechanisms are undergoing major change, particularly in Europe.[1] At the moment, it is difficult to predict how these mechanisms will evolve. This is even more difficult to anticipate in Northeast Asia where, unlike Europe, regional security has relied on a mosaic of bilateral alliances, not on a confrontation between competing military blocs.

At present, although there are no signs of a qualitative transformation in bilateral alliance structures in Northeast Asia, past confrontations seem to be easing.[2] Thus, there is still great potential for change in these bilateral alliances, as the end of the Cold War is forcing each country to rethink its own requirements for ensuring security and

---

[1]See in particular *European Security after the Cold War: Conference Papers*, Part I & II, International Institute of Strategic Studies (IISS) Adelphi Papers 284, 285, January and February 1994; Richard L. Kugler, *NATO Military Strategy for the Post-Cold War Era: Issues and Options*, RAND, 1992; Wolfgang F. Schlör, *German Security Policy: An Examination of the Trends in German Security Policy in a New European and Global Context*, IISS Adelphi Paper 277, June 1993; Frederic Bozo, *La France et l'OTAN: De la Guerre Froide au Nouvel Ordre Europeen*, I.F.R.I. (Masson), 1991.

[2]See for the analysis on the regional order and dynamic interactions among nations in Northeast Asia, Barry Buzan, "The Cold War Asia-Pacific Security Order: Conflict or Cooperation?" paper presented at Conference on Economic and Security Cooperation in the Asia Pacific, Australian National University, July 28–30, 1993; Yoichi Funabashi, "The Asianization of Asia," *Foreign Affairs*, Vol.72, No.5 (November/December 1993); and Gerald L. Curtis, ed., *The United States, Japan and Asia: Challenges for U.S. Policy* (New York: W.W. Norton, 1994).

promoting the national interest. Every nation that relied on the Cold War system as a protective shield now feels stripped of that shield and left on its own; Korea is no exception.

In the view of most strategic analysts, the pivotal factor in U.S. relations with South Korea is the North Korean military threat. A rupture in the U.S-South Korean alliance, however, need not be caused by a sudden collapse of North Korea or a desperate action on the part of Pyongyang (e.g. a serious military provocation or a decision to resume its nuclear weapons program). Rather, it may be caused by a clash between the United States and South Korea in the process of redefining post-Cold War American policy toward the Korean peninsula, or in Northeast Asia as a whole.

This process of change, of course, could involve a major shift in U.S-North Korean relations, such as the establishment of diplomatic relations between the United States and North Korea. Such changes, however, would not necessarily create serious near-term conflicts of interest between Washington and Seoul. In this regard, it is important to recognize that both the United States and South Korea want to avoid any weakening of their bilateral relationship. However, given the potential divergence in national interests and foreign policy priorities between America and South Korea, as well as very different positions of the two countries in the international order, it is entirely possible that the two may come head to head on some issues in the future.[3]

The primary purpose of this paper is to examine future developments on the Korean peninsula within the context of changes in the post-Cold War era. More specifically, I will identify the major factors that may affect the U.S.-South Korean alliance, examine how these factors could undermine the alliance, and then assess how they could destabilize political and security relations in Northeast Asia in general.

---

[3]Sang-Woo Rhee, "Whither East Asia?: Ongoing Restructuring of Intra-Regional Cooperative System," paper presented at the Conference of IFANS/IMEMO on Prospects for Russian-Korean Relations in the Context of Summit Meeting, October 1994, Moscow, pp. 11–12. Professor Rhee argues that the American interest in Korea is not "essential" but is "situational." By this logic, once the peninsular situation changes, American policy may undergo significant change.

This paper is divided into two parts. The first part consists of near-term scenarios for the U.S.-Korean alliance. I will examine how emergent changes in U.S. foreign policy could affect not only the U.S.-South Korean relationship, but also U.S. relations with North Korea and inter-Korean relations. I will then focus on specific near-term factors and political flashpoints that could undermine the U.S.-South Korean alliance. The second part consists of mid and long term scenarios. In this section, I will review possible sources of conflict in terms of America's and South Korea's respective strategic interests. From this perspective, I will then explore certain political trends that may negatively influence the U.S-South Korean alliance over the longer term.

## THE NEAR TERM SETTING: POTENTIAL AREAS OF POLICY FRICTION

### America: Redefining a Post-Cold War Order

Since the latter years of the Bush administration, the United States has sought to cope with changes in the post-Cold war era while maintaining its leading role in shaping a new world order. In drawing up a new strategy for its security relations around the world and in Northeast Asia, including Korea, the following factors have been pivotal.

First, the United States is redefining the character of existing alliances in the wake of the collapse of the former Soviet Union and Eastern Europe. In this regard, as U.S. force levels have diminished, the United States is considering a reduction in the number and roles of U.S. commanders in NATO. Through the "Partnership for Peace," the United States is also seeking to restructure its relations with ex-adversaries in the former Soviet Union and Eastern Europe. NATO itself may undergo a change from a collective defense military body to a regional collective security mechanism.[4]

---

[4]See for the detailed analysis, among others, David Miller, "New Look for European Command," *International Defense Review*, 5/1994, pp. 5–7; Paul R.S. Gebhard, *The United States and European Security*, IISS Adelphi Paper 286, February 1994, pp. 38–54; David M. Abshire, et al., *The Atlantic Alliance Transformed*, Center for Strategic and International Studies, August 1992, pp. 32–37; Marc D. Millot, *The Future U.S. Military Presence in Europe*, RAND, 1992, pp. 6–12.

In Northeast Asia, the U.S.-Korean alliance and the U.S.-Japan alliance have lost some of their previous raison d'etre, even though North Korea remains a major security and foreign policy problem. But South Korea and the United States have different views of the threat posed by North Korea. While South Korea still regards North Korea as a major threat to the Korea-U.S. alliance, American officials tend to regard North Korea as a lesser problem than in the past, in part because it has been cut loose by the former Soviet Union, its major benefactor and mentor.

Second, the United States is shifting the basis of its alliance obligations and expectations. Today the United States is less concerned about a long-term contest with a global adversary than with countering new types of military challenges, which do not necessarily involve large-scale conflict. In the past, U.S. military strategy was focused mainly on deterring aggression and defeating enemies through forward deployed forces. However, America is now shifting its focus toward prompt reaction to any outbreak of military hostilities. This requires power projection capabilities and the prepositioning of military equipment to beef up the combat readiness of reserve forces. To this end, military equipment, including fast delivery systems (e.g. C-17 aircraft) must be available at the right place at the right time.[5]

Such changes in U.S. defense strategy and subsequent changes in America's management of its military alliances reveal major potential differences between the United States and Korea. Korea understands that America has to maintain a global perspective in shaping its future military strategy. However, Korea, which has historically maintained a "special relationship" with the United States, expects America to continue to pay close attention to military tensions on the Korean peninsula. This position is based on Korea's assumption and expectation that U.S. forces in Korea are "unmovable" forward-deployed forces that remain vital to deterring North Korea.

---

[5]The White House, *A National Security Strategy of Engagement and Enlargement*, July 1994, pp. 7–9; Les Aspin (U.S. Secretary of Defense), *The Bottom-up Review: Forces for A New Era*, September 1993, pp. 9–12; Larry G. Vogt, "U.S. National Security: Options for the 1990s," paper presented at the 7th Annual Conference of the U.S.-Korean Security Studies, Seoul, November 1992.

Third, with the end of the Cold War, the United States is now focusing increased attention on its domestic concerns. Moreover, America is putting as much emphasis on its economic interests as on its political and security interests. In light of this development, many Koreans believe that the United States would not sacrifice its economic interests for the security of its allies. With an increased emphasis on economic considerations, the United States is insisting on increased "responsibility sharing,"[6] as happened during the Gulf War. As the United States no longer deems the cost of managing its alliances as "leadership costs," and instead expects its allies to voluntarily share costs, alliances have become coalitions. From Korea's perspective, it is not easy to measure and agree upon objective measures of "responsibility sharing."

## Korea: Adjusting to New Realities

South Korea understands that the United States needs to develop different strategies to manage its alliances in the new global environment. However, South Korea finds it very difficult to depart from a peninsula-centered approach, in contrast with the global approach of the United States. The overriding concern of South Korea is that there be no change in America's security policy toward North Korea, which, South Korea believes, still seeks "communization" of the South. To reduce the threat from North Korea, South Korea (in cooperation with the United States) has been attempting to induce Pyongyang to move in a positive direction. Unfortunately, while South Korea feels uncertain about the success of such efforts, the United States seems less concerned about the necessity for North-South accommodation.

There is an inevitable "time lag" between the United States and South Korea as the two countries react to perceived or potential changes in North Korea, the region, and the world. However, the problems created by this time lag are aggravated by the U.S. propensity to treat South Korea less as an equal partner than as a subordinate, even on matters of central concern to Seoul. South Korea clearly regards this American tendency towards unilateralism

---

[6]U.S. Department of Defense, *Toward A New Partnership in Responsibility Sharing,* April 1994, pp. 2–3.

as a source of potential friction. If the United States unilaterally pursues policies without adequate prior consultations with South Korea on issues which Korea deems central to the alliance, major policy conflicts could erupt between the two countries.

However, American unilateralism is nothing new to South Korea. In 1971, for example, when the Nixon Administration devised a policy to end the Vietnam war through reconciliation with China and negotiating with North Vietnam, it also withdrew one of the two remaining U.S. Army divisions from the Korean peninsula. In March 1977, former President Jimmy Carter notified Korea of America's decision to withdraw U.S. ground forces from Korea, although he subsequently reversed this policy decision. Even in the early 1990s, when Korea and the United States agreed on a gradual reduction of U.S. forces through negotiation, this was still regarded by South Korea as an essentially unilateral policy action.[7]

In the past, "junior partners" of the United States like Korea had little choice but to accept U.S. unilateralism. It is, however, far less certain that these nations will continue to accommodate to U.S. unilateralism in the post-Cold War era. Indeed, it is increasingly probable that "junior partners" will begin to raise their voices against U.S. unilateralism for the sake of their own long-term national interests. To maintain close ties in Northeast Asia in the future, the United States will need to put more emphasis on partnership with allies: successful alliances will increasingly depend on the amount of effort American officials are prepared to expend to reach agreements through negotiation and compromise.

Taking the above factors into consideration, we need to examine likely areas of policy friction between Korea and the United States in the coming two to three years.

---

[7]On U.S. unilateralism and its critics, see Christopher Layne, "The Unipolar Illusion," *International Security*, Vol. 17, No. 4 (Spring 1993).

## Diplomatic Normalization Between the United States and North Korea

Korea established diplomatic ties with the former Soviet Union in September 1990 and with China in August 1992 as a result of the "Northern policy" pursued by the Roh administration. The Northern policy was designed, in part, to encourage North Korea to seek diplomatic relations with the West, including the United States and Japan, and to open itself to the rest of the world. South Korea sought to garner support from America and Japan in pursuing its Northern policy, and, in return, to support them in improving diplomatic relations with North Korea. In this regard, Seoul sought cross recognition of the two Koreas by the four major powers, achieving partial success through the simultaneous admission of the two Koreas to the United Nations in September 1991.

However, the stance of the Korean government has changed a great deal since North Korea announced its withdrawal from the Nuclear Non-proliferation Treaty (NPT) in March 1993. Although North Korea subsequently rescinded its withdrawal and was able to initiate direct negotiations with the United States, the hostility between North and South remains undiminished. Despite initiatives from President Kim Young Sam toward North Korea, the leadership in Pyongyang has continued its confrontational stance toward South Korea, and has taken few if any steps to open itself to the outside world. As a result, South Korea has voiced growing skepticism about the underlying purposes of North Korean strategy, especially the North's efforts to undermine close relations between the United States and South Korea.

The North Korean leadership seems to believe that the only way to maintain the current regime is to keep tensions high within North Korean society and to maintain an antagonistic policy toward the outside world, especially toward South Korea. After reaching an agreement with the United States in October 1994 on the freezing of its nuclear weapons program, North Korea seemed more willing to discuss possible improvement of relations with both the United States and Japan. But this shift did not indicate a real change in its basic political line toward relations with the South. Rather, the North is trying to exclude the South from any negotiations over the future of the peninsula; it is also actively seeking to undermine South Korea's cooperative relations with the United States and Japan. Furthermore, even in pursuing inter-Korean economic cooperation, North Korea is trying to estrange the South Korean private sector from the government.

Given these circumstances, South Korea considers North Korea's attitude an incurable "disease." It is not clear, however, that the United States shares this perception. Thus, South Korea must remain cautious, lest the United States play into the hands of North Korea. In other words, through close consultations with America and Japan, South Korea needs to work hard to ensure that every issue related to North Korea be resolved ultimately by the two Koreas. From this perspective, the United States should improve its relations with North Korea only with the participation, consent, and support of South Korea, or, at least in parallel with the improvement of relations between South and North Korea.

Other policy considerations follow from these judgments. How should the United States pace its negotiations of diplomatic normalization with North Korea, if North Korea decides to improve its relations with South Korea during negotiations? What should be the criteria by which to measure improvement of inter-Korean relations? And who should have the final say in cases of disagreement? There will always be room for debate between the United States and South Korea regarding the threat of North Korea and the degree of progress in inter-Korean relations. But, if the United States continues to pursue normalization with North Korea, slighting South Korea's position and interests, it might damage U.S.-South Korean relations. Indeed, South Korea could interpret such a move as an American attempt, not only to open up North Korea, but also to obtain a "North Korean card" to use against South Korea.[8] This might lead South Korea to reconsider the necessity of the alliance itself.

---

[8]The well-known editorialist Kun-Il Ryu used an expression of "playing them both together" in his column "Recent Strange Actions of the U.S.," *Chosun Ilbo*, February 4, 1995.

## U.S. Forces in Korea and Their Changing Role

The continued U.S. troop presence in Korea is necessarily separable from the improvement of U.S.-North Korean relations. It is, however, inevitable that the United States will reduce the number of troops stationed in Korea and readjust their role if the U.S. government believes that the threat from the North has diminished. Even in the absence of shifts in the threat, reductions have been undertaken. In 1988-89, in fulfillment of the Nunn-Warner amendment, the U.S. government undertook an overall reassessment of the role, deployment, and basic structure of its troops stationed in Korea. This assessment was included in the Department of Defense's Report to the U.S. Congress of April 1990.[9] According to the report and related agreements, Korea will gradually take over the leading role in defending itself, with the United States assuming a supporting role. Much has already happened in this regard. For example, the Korean military assumed peacetime operational control of all military forces in South Korea in December 1994; a Korean general was appointed as Ground Component Commander (GCC) in December 1992; Korean troops took the place of U.S. soldiers in the Joint Security Area (JSA) in December 1992; and a Korean general was appointed as the chief representative of the Armistice Committee in March 1991.

According to the 1991 reduction plan, 7,000 U.S. troops in total, 5,000 from the Army and 2,000 from the Air Force, were to be withdrawn by the end of 1992. However, additional withdrawals originally scheduled to begin in 1993 were deferred because of uncertainty over North Korea's nuclear program. Despite the North Korea-U.S. agreement in Geneva and the subsequent accord signed in Kuala Lumpur in June 1995, the United States has determined that no additional withdrawals are anticipated until there is complete resolution of the nuclear issue. The United States, of course, could always shift its position and decide to withdraw more troops, but the newly released U.S. strategic assessment for the region asserts that the

---

[9]U.S. Department of Defense, *A Strategic Framework for the Asian-Pacific Rim: Looking toward the 21st Century*, U.S. Government Printing Office, April 1990.

United States has now completed its post-Cold War force reductions in East Asia and the Pacific.[10]

In the view of many Koreans, however, the possible withdrawal of the U.S. forces from the peninsula is the biggest card the United States can play to put pressure on South Korea. The Korean military, which shoulders primary responsibility for the nation's defense, strongly hopes to keep U.S. troops stationed in Korea because they are deemed necessary to deter North Korea from committing possible reckless acts and to compensate for Korea's inferiority in fire power and intelligence capacities.

A majority of the Korean people also regard U.S. troops in Korea as evidence of the continued U.S. commitment to Korea; at the very least, their presence provides psychological assurance. Accordingly, South Korea has been willing to contribute to the in-country costs of U.S. forces and has also been willing to accept the economic and social consequences of providing base sites free of charge.

Since the end of the Cold War, however, some Koreans have been asking themselves who benefits the most from the U.S. troop presence: the United States or South Korea? This is based on the fact that the purpose of the U.S. military presence in Korea has shifted from deterring North Korea to maintaining an American leadership role as a power balancer in the Northeast Asia region.[11] The fact that the operational scope of the U.S. military has expanded from principally guaranteeing peninsular security to responding more immediately to possible regional contingencies, has fueled Korean doubts about the real benefits of the U.S. troop presence.

In addition, the United States has economic as well as military interests in stationing its forces in Korea. It is true that the presence of U.S. forces in Korea is a vital matter to Korea. However, in stationing its forces in Korea, the United States is clearly serving its larger

---

[10]*United States Security Strategy for the East Asia-Pacific Region*, Office of International Security Affairs, U.S. Department of Defense, February 1995.

[11]Strobe Talbott (U.S. Deputy Secretary of State), "U.S. Policy Goals for Asia-Pacific Region," (Statement at the ASEAN Post-Ministerial Conference, 1994), *Current View*, Vol. 14, No. 4, 1994.

strategic interests. These larger interests will take on greater importance as time goes on.

In the future, therefore, the withdrawal of U.S. forces will become less of a bargaining chip for the United States. Increasingly, the United States will seek to station its forces in Korea as much as, or even more than Korea needs those forces. As a result, the United States will no longer be able to undertake a unilateral withdrawal of its forces from Korea. The Korean government and the public are beginning to realize that Korea is no longer an exclusive beneficiary of the U.S. military presence. Rather, it will be able to negotiate on a more equal footing with the United States.

## The North Korean Nuclear Program

North Korea's interest in developing nuclear weapons reflects a number of possible motivations. Such capabilities would provide a political and psychological safety valve to keep the two Koreas' military forces in "balance;" they would help prevent the collapse of the North Korean regime; and they would diminish North Korean fears of being absorbed by South Korea.[12] Regardless of these or other possible motivations, the United States and South Korea have a common interest in stopping North Korea's nuclear weapons development program. If North Korea were to succeed in acquiring nuclear weapons, they could serve as a major stumbling block to peaceful reunification of the two Koreas, escalate tension on the Korean Peninsula, and provoke Japan to develop its own nuclear program, thereby destabilizing the Northeast Asian region.

In an effort to help stop North Korea's nuclear development program, South Korea successfully persuaded North Korea to adopt the "Basic Agreement of South and North Korea" and the "Declaration of Denuclearization on the Korean Peninsula" at a high level inter-Korean meeting in December 1991. The Agreement and the Declaration took effect in February 1992 after the delegates of the

---

[12]Paul Bracken, "North Korea: Warning and Assessment," Testimony prepared for the Armed Services Committee, U.S. House of Representatives, Hearings on the Situation on the Korean Peninsula, March 24, 1994; Andrew Mack, "A Nuclear North Korea: The Choices Are Narrowing," *World Policy Journal*, Vol. 11, No. 2 (Summer 1994), pp. 27–35.

two Koreas exchanged official documents. On November 8, 1991, President Roh Tae Woo adopted a five-point declaration, stating that South Korea would not develop, possess, store, deploy, or use any nuclear weapons. Furthermore, South Korea gave up reprocessing plutonium and the governments of the United States and South Korea confirmed, in an indirect manner, that U.S. tactical nuclear weapons were no longer deployed in South Korea. On March 24, 1993, however, North Korea declared its intention to withdraw from the NPT, raising suspicion in the international community that it was developing nuclear weapons. After 19 months of twists and turns, the worst-case scenario of a North Korean nuclear crisis was avoided when the United States and North Korea signed an "agreed framework" accord in Geneva in October 1994. An additional agreement specifying some of the steps needed to move North Korea toward denuclearization was signed in Kuala Lumpur in June 1995.

Despite these steps and the agreement between the United States and South Korea on preventing North Korean possession of nuclear arms, there are still potential areas of conflict between Seoul and Washington. Let us examine three such areas. The first relates to U.S. unilateralism. During the Geneva talks, the United States did little to reflect South Korea's position and policy concerns. The fact that North Korea wanted South Korea excluded from the talks was natural; however, the fact that the United States allowed this, was, from the South's perspective, further evidence of its status as a junior partner to the United States. Of course, one reason the United States did not insist on the inclusion of South Korea was precisely because the American and South Korean positions were not identical.[13]

In the eyes of South Korea, North Korea's nuclear program is a matter of life or death: it has a great implications for the present and the future of inter-Korean relations and for the reunification of the Korean peninsula. Therefore, South Korea believes it must be a full party to any negotiation related to North Korea's nuclear program. But in reality, South Korea's ability to gather information on North Korea's nuclear weapons development program is limited. As a result, South Korea had no choice but to depend on the United States

---

[13]See, for example, Jai-Bong Ro (M.P.), "Inquiry to the Government," ROK National Assembly, November 1, 1994.

for information on the status of the North Korean program. Therefore, during the negotiations between the United States and North Korea, all that South Korea could do was to hope that Washington would approach North Korea's nuclear program in a comprehensive context, and would take South Korea's position into full consideration.

Unfortunately, this did not happen. Instead, the United States viewed the North Korean nuclear issue largely in the context of protecting the NPT regime, and gave little thought to peninsular concerns. When the United States appointed a nuclear specialist (Robert Gallucci) to head the American negotiating team--and not a regional specialist, who would have been more aware of and sensitive to South Korean interests--officials in South Korea became quite skeptical of U.S. motives. There was a great deal of fear that neither the Korean Ministry of Foreign Affairs, nor the U.S. Embassy in Seoul would be consulted on a timely basis.

As a result, not only South Korean government officials, but also the general public, openly criticized the United States for leaving the possibility open that North Korea could secretly develop nuclear weapons in the years to come. South Koreans believe that the United States made too many concessions to North Korea, and thus left too much room for North Korea to delay scrapping its nuclear program.

Even assuming that the U.S.-North Korean agreement takes effect, a conflict of interests could still occur between the United States and South Korea. On one hand, if North Korea fully complies with the agreement and removes all suspicions over its nuclear program, South Korea and the United States should not have any major disagreements over the implementation of the Geneva agreement. On the other hand, North Korea is expected to make the most of the Geneva agreement to further its larger diplomatic and political purposes; that is, it will use these negotiations to advance diplomatic ties with the United States and undermine the U.S.-ROK alliance. If North Korea tries to delay needed steps for implementation of the agreement, South Korea will have to change its cooperative attitude toward the accord. In this respect, it is important to recognize that South Korea's role in implementation is critical.

South Korea has made public its intention to bear the bulk of the financial burden of constructing Korean-type nuclear reactors and providing technicians to oversee the project. But if the contract is breached by either the United States or North Korea, the South will have to pull back, and then a major conflict of interest between Korea and the United States may occur. It would be especially so if South Korea is not guaranteed corresponding rights appropriate to its contributions to the North Korean nuclear reactor project.

Finally, South Korea might reconsider its abandonment of nuclear reprocessing, which it declared previously in an effort to stop North's nuclear ambitions. When the Denuclearization of the Korean Peninsula policy was announced in November 1991 by then president Roh Tae Woo, some government officials and experts strongly criticized the policy. For South Korea, which had complied with international supervision of its nuclear activities, the abandonment of nuclear reprocessing would mean the loss of important national interests related to nuclear energy research and development.[14] In this context, many Koreans criticized the United States for forcing South Korea to disregard its national interests in the name of denuclearization. They also pointed out that the United States was biased in its nuclear policy, because it was condoning Japan's nuclear activities, while forcing South Korea to give up nuclear development. This issue is very likely to be raised again in Korea, and might become a major bone of contention between the two countries.

### From the Armistice Arrangements to a New Peace Regime

The two Koreas agreed on the need to devise new peace mechanisms in the Basic Agreement in December 1991. The armistice accord signed in 1953 was basically a tentative one; it guaranteed a ceasefire until inter-Korean conflicts were solved through political negotiations. The Geneva conference on Korea and Indochina in 1954, however, came to a standstill and the U.N. General Assembly Resolution in 1975, which urged the two Koreas to seek a new peace regime, did not bear any fruit.

---

[14]For example, see the opinions expressed at the Conference on Rethinking the Denuclearization Policy in Korean Peninsula organized by the Korean Association of Public Policy Studies, *Korean Journal of Public Policy Studies*, Vol. 1 (Sept. 1993).

Both South and North Korea have set their sights on the reunification of the peninsula. In 1991, they agreed for the first time that the first step toward a reunified Korea would be new peace mechanisms based on mutual political agreement. Recently, however, North Korea has argued that a North Korea-U.S. peace treaty must be signed. North Korea claims that UN and North Korean commanders signed the original armistice accord and that the UN was represented by the United States. Therefore, it asserts that signing a peace treaty with the United States will legitimately replace the armistice accord. North Korea has also put forward another rationale for its effort to replace the armistice with the peace treaty, saying that the end to belligerent relations with the United States should occur in parallel with the two countries officially establishing diplomatic ties.

Whatever rationales North Korea puts forward, its real intention is something different. What North Korea really intends is to eliminate South Korea as a legitimate party to Korean affairs in the international arena. As a matter of fact, South Korea does not recognize North Korea, either by domestic or by international law. Consequently, it is technically impossible for the two Koreas to sign any treaty, not to mention a peace treaty. It is this very niche that North Korea is now playing upon. North Korea is trying to enhance its legal status in the international arena by claiming that it is the only party qualified to sign a peace treaty, and is trying marginalize South Korea, which the North regards as subordinate to the United States.

Despite this, there are no technical difficulties in replacing the armistice accord with a new peace regime based on the Basic Agreement reached by the two Koreas.[15] But the problem is the determination of both sides to make peace. As of now, South Korea has not made its position clear. However, it is assumed that the South Korean government is considering a so-called "2+2 Formula," which would call for two guaranteeing powers, the United States and China, to sanction a peace regime acceptable to the two Koreas.

---

[15]It was known that, in the Report of the Ministry of Foreign Affairs to the National Assembly, the South Korean government was preparing a proposal for a new "peace accord" with North Korea. See *Chosun Ilbo*, October 2, 1994.

It is one of the prerequisites for peace and unification to turn the armistice accord into a new peace regime. In this regard, both the Korean and American governments fully understand the importance of policies related to this issue. If the United States should negotiate a possible peace treaty with North Korea that excludes the South, it can only lead to a harsh response from South Korea. North Korea has been notorious for its reliance on threat and provocation in negotiations; the United States must be prepared to counter such tactics and to ensure that South Korea negotiates with the North as a fully sovereign state.

## THE MID AND LONG TERM SETTING

The near-term prospect of the U.S.-Korea relations covers only the period of the two countries' incumbent presidents. The mid and long term period, however, refers to the period when new administrations will definitely have taken office in the early 21st century. It is very difficult to imagine what the region and the peninsula will be like five to ten years from now. Nevertheless, I will first examine several possible areas that might damage U.S.-Korean relations and then review the issues related to Korean reunification from a Korean perspective.

### Power Restructuring and Dynamics in Northeast Asia

In Northeast Asia, Japan and China are emerging as new major world powers, not just regional powers. On the other hand, Russia cannot exert its influence as much as in the past, nor is it likely to do so in the medium term. Thus, it is the emergence of Japan and China that will have a major impact on the future of the U.S.-Korean alliance.[16]

Japan had to pay a severe price for its conduct during World War II, and with the experience of the horror of atomic bombs, pacifism continues to prevail across the nation. Such factors, combined with U.S. pressure, compelled Japan to adopt a Peace Constitution, which

---

[16]See for the dynamic relations among major powers in Northeast Asia, Monte R. Bullard, "U.S.-China Relations: The Strategic Calculus," *Parameters*, Vol. 23, No. 2 (Summer 1993), pp. 86–96; Gerald Segal, "The Coming Confrontation between China and Japan?" *World Policy Journal*, Vol. 10, No. 2 (Summer 1993), pp. 27–32; Special edition on "Asian Security," *Survival*, Vol. 36, No. 2 (Summer 1994).

has enabled Japan to concentrate on reconstruction and economic development. It has since become among the world's leading economic and technological powers.

Japan's advanced technological base is reflected in its military capabilities. The Japanese army, navy and air force, though small in number, are equipped with high-tech armaments and are extremely well trained. Considering Japan's large reserve force and its ongoing military development, it retains great military potential. However, to numerous Asian countries, which suffered from Japan's aggression during the Pacific War, any significant increase in Japanese defense programs is a source of major concern.

Japan is also actively pursuing permanent membership on the United Nations Security Council (UNSC). Permanent membership on the UNSC would ensure Japan's status as one of the major world powers. This step could also be used to justify the elimination of the obstacles to an eventual amendment of Japan's Peace Constitution, and even the revocation of Japan's non-nuclear policies. Toward this end, Japan has already taken preparatory measures and has been fostering a general atmosphere in its favor at home and abroad. At the same time, Japan's aspirations for a wider international role would depend heavily on development of both civilian and military technology, as in the FS-X case.[17]

From an economic point of view, technological independence might be justified as guaranteeing long-term corporate interests, but from the political and military point of view, it might engender suspicion of Japan's motives. In addition to its pursuit of technological independence, Japan is recently putting far more emphasis on "Asianization." Japan has pursued "Westernization" for more than a century, and many believe it will now try to pursue Asianization in the coming century. These changes in Japan imply that it is making every effort to be a new leader in East Asia and the Pacific, asking for a bigger role in the region. If Japan seeks hegemony in the region, however, it will not be long before Japan comes in to conflict with the United States. If Japan tries to expand its influence mainly over

---

[17]Kenichiro Sasae, *Rethinking Japan-U.S. Relations*, I.I.S.S. Adelphi Paper 292 (December 1994), pp. 22–25, 47–58.

Southeast Asia, where it is currently expanding its economic ties, it is very likely to come into conflict with China.

The growth of Chinese power is also a source of long-term concern to Korea. The effects of Deng Xiaoping's market-oriented economic reforms, which were first implemented in special economic zones in the coastal regions, are now spreading to the inland areas. Given its current growth in trade and in its economy, China may record the world's largest GNP by the year 2020. Of course, this will become a reality only if China maintains political stability and social order after the death of Deng Xiaoping. But China has already become a major power in terms of economic potential as well as military strength. The future of this region will depend on whether these two major powers--Japan and China--cooperate with each other or vie for hegemony in the region. Historically, most of the problems in Korea were caused by its geopolitical location between China and Japan.

In the long run, Korea will feel at ease if the current environment of stability and cooperation continues in the region. If the possibility of conflict between and among various major powers increases as time goes by, however, it will become more difficult for Korea to exclusively support one party. Moreover, if the United States supports one of these parties, Korea's stance might not always be identical with that of America.

What about possible conflicts between Japan and China and between Japan and the United States? If U.S.-Japan relations shift toward head-on competition, and if the United States reconsiders its strategic priority towards Japan, Korea might be compelled to choose one or the other. Currently Japan is employing "smart ambiguity" in order to protect its national interests.[18] If Japan gradually changes this stance into clearer "self-assurance," all kinds of scenarios are possible. For example, if the United States either supports an opponent of Korea, forces Korea to support an ally regardless of Korea's interests, or has a conflict with a nation with which Korea is allied, any of these will severely damage the current alliance. It is very likely that possible conflicts between and among the United States, China, Japan could reshape Korea-U.S. relations, potentially in very damaging ways.

---

[18]See, "Japan's Nice New Nationalism," *The Economist*, January 14, 1995, pp. 13, 19–21.

Relatively moderate conflicts, which are more probable, would also create difficulties for Korea.

In the context of realignment, Korea will have difficulty deciding which of the major powers in the region to choose as a strategic partner. Because the United States has been the only "big brother" to Korea in the region for the past five decades, America will likely remain Korea's first choice. However, the Korean mirror will reflect a new American face and mind.

## The Reunification Process

In addition to the realignment of the power structure in Northeast Asia, the Korean reunification process will also have a profound influence on the future of the U.S.-Korean alliance. Koreans will continue to try to develop a blueprint of a reunified Korea with new values, and appropriate political, economic and social structures. They will also seek to devise basic policy lines and strategies which are most desirable to defend the nation and to maximize national interests in cooperation with external partners.

At present, two major lines of thought are emerging regarding the future of a reunified Korea. One is that Korea should maintain special relations--that is, a strategic partnership--with the United States. The other view asserts that Korea should adopt a neutral or nonaligned position. The former approach seemingly conflicts with the basic premise of this paper, since it implies strengthened relations between Korea and America. If we examine the issue more closely, it does not simply mean more solid ties. Rather, it is based on several preconditions which will be very difficult to realize. The first precondition is that the United States change its traditional attitude, which places priority on Japan. A future strategic partnership between a reunified Korea and the United States will not be an alliance with the United States as a victorious country following World War II, or as a superpower in the Cold War era.

In the past, the United States has sought to utilize the U.S.-Korean alliance in order to ensure the security of Japan, its priority partner. The United States has never recognized clearly and publicly the strategic value of Korea in the region. Will Korea always be secondary to Japan in terms of strategic value to the United States? For Koreans the answer must be no; Koreans insist they will not continue to accept a secondary position. But it is also likely that the United States would find it difficult to accept the Korean view.

The second condition is that the United States recognize the value of a strategic partnership with Korea. If the United States is to form a strategic alliance with Korea in order to secure its long-term national interests, the two countries must transform the alliance into a fundamentally new and cooperative one. Practically speaking, this is no easy task. Should the United States be reluctant to modify its longstanding policies and be unwilling to shed its accustomed mentality, these conditions will not be met. Furthermore, the Korean people's hope for stable, long-term U.S.-Korean relations would be dashed. Whether this outcome will lead to further souring of relations between the two countries is another matter.

The second line of thought—i.e., a neutral or nonaligned but unified Korea—would also have major implications for the future of U.S.—Korean relations. The Korean peninsula has been a historical battleground for foreign powers because of its geopolitical location. Therefore, over the course of history the Korean people have frequently tried to secure a neutral position in order not to be embroiled in the wars waged between foreign countries. However, because Korea has historically been too weak to protect itself, these efforts have been in vain. Even after the Korean War, neutrality was favored by many liberal intellectuals and activists. However, most Koreans were skeptical of neutralism, because they regarded such a policy line as camouflaged "anti-American sentiment."[19] Accordingly, neutralist thoughts have been disregarded.

However, should the prospect for a unified Korea increase, it is likely that neutrality or nonalignment would be hailed as an alternative foreign policy. The underlying reason behind this trend is that active cooperation on the part of neighboring powers is absolutely necessary to achieve Korean unification. The biggest concern of Korea's neighbors is that a unified Korea would evolve into a powerful, hos-

---

[19]In a different context, the idea of a neutralized Korea appeared from time to time even in the United States. See, for example, Sen. Mike Mansfield's report, U.S. Congress, Senate, *Report on the Far East, Part I: Japan and United States Policies*, 86th Congress, 2nd Session, U.S. Government Printing Office, 1960, p. 7.

tile country. Thus, to Korean policy makers, adopting a neutral policy might be viewed as the best alternative to dispel these worries. At the present time, a neutral Korea seems unthinkable. However, if non-alignment can be combined with a nationalistic idea, it is probable that it could evolve into a formidable new way of thinking. Nationalistic sentiments held by most Korean people may lead them to believe that neutrality not only offers the best means of protection, but may also be the best means to unify Korea. A neutral and unified Korea would clearly entail a profound change in Korea-U.S. relations, and would pose a major challenge in sustaining close ties between the two countries.

## POLICY IMPLICATIONS FOR THE UNITED STATES AND KOREA

This paper has sought to identify various factors that may undermine the U.S.-Korea alliance. I will now assess the implications of these factors for the policies and strategies of the United States and Korea. Considering the fact that the United States has a larger voice than Korea in the interactions between the two, we will study the implications for the United States first, and then its consequent implications for Korea.

### U.S.-North Korea Relations

At present, the United States is trying to develop new strategies to cope with the challenges of the newly emerging world order. U.S. policy toward North Korea will be formulated in light of such international conditions. In this sense, South Korea must view U.S. policy development from a new perspective.

In these very sensitive times, the United States needs to clarify its goals in dealing with North Korea, because ambiguity may lead to misunderstanding on the part of South Korea. For example, the United States must choose whether to pursue a two-Korea policy that seeks to maintain the status quo; or to more actively contribute to longer-term peaceful development on the Korean peninsula, or both.

If the United States takes the first path as its goal, U.S. policy would be likely to incorporate the following factors. First, the United States would not make a major effort to diminish military tensions between the South and the North; rather it would remain content with keeping tensions at a manageable level. Second, there would be no need to establish a new peace regime, even without full implementation of the armistice accord system. Third, the U.S. military presence on the Korean peninsula would be maintained as long as possible, enabling the United States to keep both South and North Korea in check. In essence, the United States would move toward a more equidistant policy between the two Koreas.

The advantages of this policy line are:

- relaxing North Korea's security concerns;

- delaying possible aggression from the North;

- receiving favorable response from Korea's neighboring powers (Japan, in particular); and

- securing a favorable leadership position in dealing with North Korea.

The disadvantages of this policy line are:

- upsetting South Korea;

- failing to justify the U.S. military presence in South Korea; and

- arousing the concern of some neighboring powers, in particular China.

In carrying out such policies toward North Korea, the United States would feel less need to seek close consultation and agreement with South Korea. It would become more likely that a deep rift in diplomatic relations between the United States and South Korea would develop.

If the United States adopts the second strategy, however, American polices will be more closely aligned with those of South Korea. Accordingly, close consultation and cooperation between the two countries would be needed, based on a new appreciation and mutual respect of each other. In other words, the United States would not seek its own interests at the expense of South Korea, while South Korea would contribute more to fending off outside aggression, instead of relying exclusively on "big brother."

If the United States pursues both objectives on a simultaneous basis, relations could become much more complicated between the two countries. In the short term, Koreans would understand the reason for changes in the U.S. policy stance. However, if the United States maintains this policy for a longer period, Koreans will perceive it as seeking to prevent reunification, greatly disappointing the Korean people in the process.

## Changes in the Regional Power Structure

In the mid to long term, the United States will have three principal options. The first option is to continue placing top priority on Japan and to regard Korea as a second-order priority. The second option is to establish a new strategy based on the recognition of Korea's strategic value. The last option is to attempt to do both, or to straddle the two objectives.

If the United States maintains its long standing policy line, U.S. policy will help Japan's current trend toward military revitalization, quite possibly thwarting Korea's efforts to build up its naval and air power, on the grounds that Korea is a potential threat to Japan's security. However, if the United States revises its past policy line and embraces Korea as its new strategic partner, then America would then pay greater heed to Korea's judgment in preparing for the post-unification environment. Accordingly, the United States might help Korea increase its $C^3i$ capacities and modernization of military equipment. Also, the United States and Korea would be more tolerant and understanding of each other's views when negotiating issues such as defense burden sharing.

Given the uncertainties about the future, it is safer and more realistic for the United States to adopt the third option. The United States cannot ignore Japan, because, in terms of national power and potential, there is still a considerable gap between Japan and Korea—even a unified Korea. In fact, the United States will not be able to neglect either Korea or Japan. Furthermore, Korea-Japan relations might also improve greatly since the "unfortunate past" is not expected to cast a shadow over younger generations, who are no longer "prisoners of history."

## The Future of U.S. Forces in Korea

Until now, the United States and Korea have maintained essentially comparable positions on the issue of the American military presence in Korea. However, if the United States rethinks its policies toward East Asia and toward U.S. forces stationed in Korea, a conflict of interests between the two countries could arise.

From the U.S. point of view, the presence of its troops in Korea remains important. First of all, the United States needs to keep its military presence in Korea no matter what its policies are toward Pyongyang. If the United States seeks to maintain the status quo on the Korean peninsula, it would need its military presence in Korea to keep both sides in check. If the United States aims simply to maintain peace on the peninsula and prepare Korea for unification, it would still want to keep its troops in Korea in order to discourage North Korea from threatening or attacking the South and to prevent possible chaos after the collapse of the communist regime in the North. Second, the United States needs its military forces in Korea to counterbalance China's military buildup and to deal with potential military hostilities in the region. The U.S. presence on the Korean peninsula could therefore prove useful should unexpected events occur in the future. In the long run, the United States might find its military presence in Korea to be even more valuable than under conditions of a divided peninsula.

As for Seoul, as long as the North continues to pose threats to the South, it will find the U.S. presence in Korea to be essential to maintaining peace. However, as time goes by, U.S. forces in Korea will lose their importance as Korea finds Japan and China to be just as important as the United States in promoting Korea's economic interests. At that time, therefore, the American threat to withdraw its troops from Korea will no longer have much effect on South Korea. In fact, there might come a time when the United States has to persuade the South to allow the American troops to stay on the Korean Peninsula.

The United States and Korea therefore need to begin an extensive and meaningful dialogue at both an official and unofficial level in order to establish a more reasonable and more desirable long-term relationship between the two countries.

# Section V

# The Future of U.S.-Japan Relations

The fifth and concluding session was devoted to a discussion of papers by Courtney Purrington and Myonwoo Lee. Both paper writers foresaw the possibility of an appreciable redefinition of the security relationship, but other participants asserted that the relationship remains highly robust, even in a post-Cold War period of strategic reappraisal. These differing perspectives suggest that the framework of relations (though sometimes seen as psychologically uncertain and even somewhat fragile) is in fact quite resilient, and able to absorb vigorous debate and openly expressed worry about the future. Others suggested that it could only be in the context of a specific, highly negative policy development (for example, appreciable shifts in U.S. forward deployments) that the relationship would undergo appreciable redefinition. As one participant observed, there remains very little support within Japan for a truly autonomous strategic posture. Japanese leaders still see their long-term security interests as best served by continued, close policy interdependence with the United States.

Though both paper writers were attentive to areas of potentially divergent policy interest, the absence of credible or feasible policy alternatives (especially for Japan) appears to mitigate against any sharp shifts in alliance strategy. At the same time, even assuming some increased momentum in favor of multilateral security strategies, there was broad support among the conferees (though perhaps for different reasons) that the United States retain its leadership role in the alliance. But the shifting contours of the post-Cold War world and the heightened salience of economic competition clearly pose a very different challenge to sustaining close security cooperation in the future.

The discussion also highlighted the adaptive capabilities of alliance relations under a range of conditions. Some participants, however, voiced growing concern about the ability of the alliance to effectively withstand a major political or military crisis (e.g. serious instability in North Korea on which the United States and Japan were unable to cooperate effectively).  But these concerns highlighted the necessity of exploring possible changes in the alliance without such change calling security interdependence into question.  Some of these potential changes, for example, would testify to a less hierarchical concept of U.S.-Japan relations than was operative in previous decades. But the challenge for the future would be the redefinition of alliance roles and responsibilities that would enable both countries to ensure the viability and sustainability of their bilateral ties over the longer run.  As one participant observed, irrespective of the growing belief in the pivotal role of China in East Asia's future, the U.S.-Japan relationship remains decisive to maintaining the framework of regional political and security ties, upon which security and stability continue to depend.  Viewed in this context, an attitude of complacency is neither advisable nor prudent, whether in bilateral or regional terms.

Chapter Nine

# THE FUTURE OF JAPAN-U.S. SECURITY RELATIONS: THE CHALLENGE OF ADVERSITY TO ALLIANCE DURABILITY

Courtney Purrington

## INTRODUCTION

The Japan-U.S. alliance has proven a remarkably resilient and durable relationship for nearly forty-five years. Despite its inauspicious beginnings as a negative and temporary alliance designed to supplement the capabilities of two former enemies, the alliance has undergone repeated and successful changes in relation to international and domestic challenges throughout its existence. Indeed, the alliance has adjusted to sweeping changes in the relative power of Japan and the United States over four decades, enabling a shift from highly asymmetrical "patron-client" ties to a more coequal partnership. Moreover, it even survived the disappearance of its supposed *raison d'etre*—the Soviet threat.

This paper addresses whether or not the alliance will remain durable and vigorous after the Cold War. In part, this question simply reflects whether the benefits of alliance maintenance will continue to outweigh the costs to both countries. But it will also depend on whether both allies can continue to adapt to a rapidly evolving security environment in East Asia after the Cold War. Although there remain strong reasons for preservation of the alliance relationship on both sides of the Pacific, there are four major sources of uncertainty for the present U.S.-Japan security relationship that could sap its vigor:[1]

---

[1] Over the longer term, alternative multilateral security arrangements could eventually serve as a substitute for the alliance. In this scenario, the alliance would gradually atrophy because of its success in promoting stability and economic integration within the Asia-Pacific region. This unlikely positive development over the near-to-medium

- Mutual hedging behavior in the Asia-Pacific region;

- Inequities in burdensharing and powersharing arrangements, which exacerbate U.S. isolationist tendencies and Japanese nationalist tendencies;

- Economic friction;

- The potential for divergent responses in a crisis affecting the security of both countries (e.g., a crisis on the Korean peninsula, in the Taiwan Strait, in the South China Sea, or even in the Persian Gulf).

Domestic political change in both Japan and the United States will also affect the durability of the alliance relationship. Even though all of Japan's major parties now support continued maintenance of the alliance, each of these hazards will be strongly influenced by ongoing domestic change in Japan (including political realignment and the shifting balance of power between political parties and the bureaucracy), debate on an appropriate Japan role in Asia, and the future course of deregulation and liberalization efforts.[2] Moreover, the changing domestic context of U.S. foreign policy will also have a pivotal impact.

These hazards represent long-term threats to the durability of the alliance. Such problems, if not addressed, would gradually enervate the U.S.-Japan relationship, by eroding trust and goodwill across the Pacific, upon which the strength of the alliance is predicated. They could ultimately lead to concerns about rising relative gains between both countries (i.e., the concern that differential gains in power will one day be used against oneself). The fourth hazard, which would

---

term, however, is not addressed by this study. Korean unification would be one necessary but not sufficient precondition. Another precondition would be resolution of Japan's territorial dispute with Russia. Finally, resolution of Taiwan's status would also essential. In addition, expectations of long-run and friendly relations among regional actors would be critical.

[2] Growing public resentment against a continued U.S. presence in Okinawa could also weaken the alliance if it led a Japanese Government to demand a removal of the bases from the 'keystone of the Pacific.' Such a danger is likely to be contained unless pro-alliance officials within the government become marginalized, especially if U.S.-Japan differences are exacerbated by bilateral friction and those favoring an exclusive Asian vision for Japan become ascendant.

result from differing responses to "exogenous" events elsewhere in Asia, would most likely render the functioning of the alliance moot.

While the nature of each country's response to regional "hotspots" will be strongly affected by ongoing domestic change, increased consultations and enhanced information flow would help reduce the danger of mutual misperception and divergent responses arising in the event of a regional crisis. Before turning to these issues, however, some contributions from international relations theory that shed light on alliance behavior will be briefly explored.

## THEORETICAL INSIGHTS INTO THE DURABILITY OF ALLIANCES

Alliances perform numerous functions in international politics. Proponents of neorealism, for example, emphasize the aggregation of the capabilities of two or more states *against* an enemy (balancing behavior), or less commonly *with* a threat (bandwagoning behavior).[3] In an anarchic world of egoistic actors, neorealism assumes that the strength of a commitment is based upon immediate calculations of self-interest, so that states will defect from alliance obligations whenever it is to their advantage to do so. These calculations are based on the degree of convergence of security interests, including commonalty of interests vis-a-vis adversaries, the relative importance of precluding an ally's capabilities from falling under control of an adversary, and the degree of a state's strategic dependence on the alliance for supplementing its capabilities.[4]

Neorealism views the origins and durability of alliances as closely tied to the distribution of capabilities and/or threat perceptions.[5] Alliances are viewed as "marriages of convenience," having a limited

---

[3]Japan has historically engaged in bandwagoning behavior with a regional or global hegemon (e.g., China, Britain, and United States).

[4]See Kenneth Waltz, *Theory of International Politics* (Reading, MA: Addison-Wesley, 1979), pp. 166–70.

[5]Stephen Walt, *The Origins of Alliances* (Ithaca, NY: Cornell University Press, 1987), pp. 21–26. A common threat would tend to result in even a more durable alliance than differing threat perceptions among parties to an alliance.  See K. J. Holsti, *International Politics*, 4th edition (Englewood Cliffs, NJ: Prentice-Hall, 1983), pp. 112-13.

life cycle closely linked to the presence of a mutual danger. Shifts in capabilities (or threats) and national objectives will tend to result in changing alignment patterns.[6] With the disappearance of the Soviet threat, proponents of realism would therefore predict the eventual termination of the Japan-U.S. alliance.

But neorealism has less to say about why nations choose to enter into formal alliances, when informal commitments, based upon common interests, could have comparable efficacy.[7] Do formal alliance commitments in fact reduce uncertainty that is inherent in any promissory obligation to render assistance, especially in a world where the interests of two or more states on a given issue are rarely identical?

An institutional theory of alliances furnishes important insights into this question. Traditional realists, such as Hans Morgenthau and George Liska, contend that one of the central benefits of a formal alliance is its "precision," and that ideology strengthens commitment, which more than anything else transforms alliances into social institutions."[8] Neorealism, however, has largely overlooked the role of alliances as institutions, instead treating them as appurtenances to the operation of the balance of power. But as Robert Keohane has

---

[6]Arnold Wolfers, 'Alliances,' in David Sills, ed., *International Encyclopedia of the Social Sciences* (New York: The Macmillan Company & The Free Press, 1968), p. 270. Wolfers' assertion does not rule out, however, that even with the disappearance of a common threat, two or more nations might continue an alliance because of more diffuse security threats.

[7]For example, if the strength of the U.S.-Japan alliance (1960) and NATO were primarily dependent upon a common Soviet threat, why was a formal alliance necessary, if the United States would have invariably rendered assistance to its allies in order to keep their capabilities from falling under Soviet control? A base-lending arrangement would have sufficed during the entire period (along the lines of the 1951 U.S.-Japan Security Treaty).

[8]Hans Morgenthau, 'Alliances in Theory and Practice,' in Arnold Wolfers, ed., *Alliance Policy in the Cold War* (Baltimore: The Johns Hopkins University Press, 1959) p. 186; George Liska, *Nations in Alliance* (Baltimore, MD: The Johns Hopkins Press, 1962), p. 61. Liska argues that shared ideology can strengthen an alliance commitments. See also K. J. Holsti, *International Politics*, pp. 113–14. The research of Glenn Snyder is an exception to this generalization about neorealism. Snyder argues that the degree of explicitness in the alliance agreement is a determinate of choices in the alliance security dilemma. See his 'The Security Dilemma in Alliance Politics,' *World Politics*, Vol. 36, No. 4 (July 1984),pp. 473–74. He also notes that an alliance 'creates or changes expectations about the parties' future behavior.' See 'Alliance Theory: A Neorealist First Cut,' *Journal of International Affairs*, Vol. 44, No. 1 (Spring/Summer 1990), p. 107.

suggested, "alliances are institutions, and...both their durability and strength (the degree to which states are committed to alliances, even when costs are entailed) may depend in part on their institutional characteristics."[9]

An alliance can therefore be viewed as an institution, formed not only when it is believed to be superior, based upon a state's specific needs in the international system, but preferable to arms length transactions in terms of costs, benefits, and risks.[10] Formal alliances help reduce competitive risks (e.g., whether an ally will defect and join an adversary) and coordination risks of security cooperation (e.g., whether an ally will keep security commitments and render assistance in a timely and capable manner).

Although alliance commitments are not legally binding on states and while alliance obligations may not always be fulfilled because of divergent state preferences, the informational and transaction-cost functions of formal alliances can reduce uncertainty in world politics and facilitate more durable cooperation. This does not mean that all formal alliances will prove more durable than informal alliances, just as security cooperation can take place in the absence of institutions. For example, the informal U.S.-Israeli alliance, based upon strong mutual interests, proved much more durable than some formal alliances during the Cold War, such as SEATO and CENTO. But by establishing stable mutual expectations about a partner's future behavior, neoliberal institutionalism expects that formal alliances will prove more durable and stronger, *ceteris paribus*, than informal alliances.

Alliances also contain elements of conditional reciprocity and interject iterativeness into relations between two or more security partners. As each partner seeks to maintain the alliance and to protect and improve the capabilities of its ally, this process will mitigate

---

[9]Robert Keohane, 'Neoliberal Institutionalism: A Perspective on World Politics,' in his *International Institutions and State Power* (Boulder, CO: Westview, 1989), p. 15.

[10]An institutionalist approach to alliances is developed in Courtney Purrington, *Governing An Alliance: The Political Economy of the Japan-U.S. Security Relationship*, Ph.D. thesis presented to the Department of Government, Harvard University, Cambridge, MA (December 1993).

considerations of relative gains in other areas of their relationship.[11] Because obstacles to cooperation are foremost in national security, formal alliances can serve as integrative mechanisms enabling states to overcome the impediments to cooperation and allowing security partners to nest other cooperative endeavors within such a positive-sum framework. By explicitly setting forth standards of behavior, defining what constitutes a violation of alliance norms, rules, and principles, and sharing information that promotes transparency in the strategic decisionmaking processes of security partners, formal alliances extend the logic and longevity of security cooperation.

Under certain circumstances, alliances can even serve as a "basic political framework for cooperation" between states.[12] Such a framework defines longer-term objectives for a relationship toward which shorter-term policies and strategies are expected to be consistent. This is similar to what Robert Axelrod and Robert Keohane define as contextual issue linkage, a situation in which "a given bargain is placed within the context of a more important long-term relationship in such a way that the long-term relationship affects the outcome of the particular bargaining process."[13] Over the course of the post-war period, the Japan-U.S. alliance gradually assumed such a role. To illustrate this transition, the evolution of the security relationship during the Cold War is next examined.

---

[11]As Joanne Gowa has pointed out in 'Bipolarity, Multipolarity and Free Trade,' *American Political Science Review*, Vol. 83, No. 4 (December 1989), pp. 1245–56, there are positive externalities for intraalliance cooperation from an outside threat. But if a state fears that its security partner may defect to an adversary, or its partner represents a long-run threat, externalities can be negative. Indeed, the security externalities of superpower competition were sometimes negative for Japan-U.S. cooperation in high politics issue areas during the 1950s, until the development of a long-run, peaceful shadow of the future and positive alliance. International institutions can influence whether the security externalities of conflicts are positive or negative.

[12]This term is adapted from Alexander George, 'Factors Influencing Security Cooperation,' in George, et. al., *U.S.-Soviet Security Cooperation* (New York: Oxford University Press, 1988), pp. 667–68.

[13]Robert Axelrod and Robert Keohane, 'Achieving Cooperation Under Anarchy,' in Kenneth Oye, ed., *Cooperation Under Anarchy*, p. 241.

## TRANSFORMATION OF THE ALLIANCE RELATIONSHIP DURING THE COLD WAR

The first Security Treaty signed in 1951 emphasized that the security relationship was a "provisional arrangement." The agreement was essentially a "base-lending" arrangement masquerading as an alliance, as part of America's dual strategy in the Far East of containing Soviet and Chinese power, and preventing the resurgence of Japanese power. The United States was given the right to deploy its military forces in and around Japan, both to provide for regional security, and to put down any large-scale internal riots or disturbances in Japan. Reflecting its semi-sovereign status, Japan pledged not to grant base or transit rights without the consent of the United States to any third party. The Yoshida government was willing to agree to such unequal provisions in order to secure its "independence" and because bandwagoning with a Western power was once again in Japan's best interests, at least in the short run. In view of U.S. doubts over Japan's reliability as an ally and initial concerns that Japan might defect from the alliance and choose a neutral foreign policy stance or even align with the Soviet bloc, the United States retained control over Okinawa. Inequitable arrangements in the nature of the alliance and its provisional nature reflected strong, lingering mistrust between two former enemies.

With the eventual emergence of peaceful interactions between the United States and Japan, both countries agreed to revise the unequal terms of the original agreement and signed a new Security Treaty in 1960. This symbolized the evolution of the security relationship into a more positive alliance—that is, an alliance standing "for" and not simply "against" something. For example, both countries pledged to encourage bilateral economic collaboration, to eliminate economic disputes, and to strengthen and uphold democratic principles. But Japan was not obligated to come to the aid of the United States in the event of a crisis outside the scope of the alliance. While this was of little practical significance in the event of armed confrontation with the Soviet Union, since Japan would have been immediately dragged into any such war, it was of practical significance in the event of smaller regional conflicts outside the scope of the treaty (e.g., Vietnam). This difference symbolically represented continuing inequities in burdensharing arrangements.

With increasing indications of Japan's reliability as an ally and pledges by Japan to increase its burdensharing contributions, however, the United States agreed in 1969 to return Okinawa to Japanese control. But U.S.-Soviet detente and the U.S. courtship of China partly postponed the urgency attached to increased Japanese contributions to alliance burdensharing. With detente, heightened Japan-U.S. economic friction, two energy crises, difficulties over nuclear energy relations, and Japan's pursuit of omni-directional diplomacy, the alliance experienced some drift during the 1970s. But alliance relations were eventually strengthened following the signing of "Guidelines for Japan-U.S. Defense Cooperation" in November 1978, which further institutionalized the alliance relationship.

During the 1980s the alliance was reinvigorated by a renewal of the Cold War and by the Soviet military build-up in the Far East. But in view of Japan's rise to the status of an economic superpower, the decade was also marked by increasing bilateral tensions over Japan's burdensharing contributions to the alliance. The alliance was also troubled by increasing friction over a lack of reciprocity in the economic relationship, ballooning trade deficits, and a "hollowing out" of U.S. industries, due to increasing Japanese competition. At the same time, Japan's growing self-confidence provided it with an increased willingness to say "no" to the United States and a desire for a more equal relationship. These tensions came to the fore at the twilight of the Cold War during the FSX fighter imbroglio.

For much of the post-war period, the Japan-U.S. relationship was not unlike patron-client relationships in feudal society. Under such an arrangement, the patron often tolerated imbalances in economic exchanges favoring the client, in return for the client's political and military deference to the patron and other intangible benefits.[14] Such diffuse exchanges were mutually valued, despite the fact that both allies incurred dissimilar obligations. But following major shifts in the international distribution of power in Japan's favor, such a pattern of exchange became a growing source of resentment on both sides of the Pacific. For example, American revisionists criticized

---

[14]Klaus Knorr, *The Power of Nations: The Political Economy of International Relations* (New York: Basic Books, 1975), p. 25; Robert Keohane, 'Reciprocity in International Relations,' in his *International Institutions and State Power* (Boulder, CO: Westview, 1989), pp. 135–36.

U.S. willingness to tolerate "unfair" Japanese trade practices and burdensharing imbalances in order to avoid weakening the alliance. Japanese revisionists complained about Japan's subordination to the United States in security affairs and its pattern of passively surrendering to U.S. trade pressure, in effect rendering Japan a "semi-sovereign" state, whether for reasons of *ongaeshi* (the obligational return of favors rendered earlier by the United States), vulnerability arising from economic and security interdependence with the United States, or because of the economic and political benefits that deference conferred on certain groups in Japanese society.

Despite such major changes in the nature of the alliance relationship during its first forty years, some continuity was also evident. Throughout the period, the alliance served as the key to regional stability in East Asia and mitigated against the need for Japan to again become a "great-power." Japan continued to provide bases for U.S. troops forward-deployed in the Pacific (although instead of receiving rents for U.S. bases, Japan instead began to provide generous host-nation support). Japan also continued to rely primarily on U.S. deterrence capabilities for its security, despite improvements in its own military capabilities. Moreover, Japan remained under no obligation to render assistance to the United States in areas outside the scope of the alliance. The alliance also served as the basis for Japan's ongoing economic and political integration into East Asia. Finally, the alliance promoted increased trust and certainty in relations between two former enemies. Whether or not such functions will continue to persist after the Cold War is the subject of the remainder of this essay.

## POST-COLD WAR ROLES OF THE JAPAN-U.S. ALLIANCE: BENEFITS OF ALLIANCE MAINTENANCE

### Deterrence Against a Common Threat

During the Cold War, the Soviet threat was used as the primary justification by both Japan and the United States for maintaining the Japan-U.S. Security Treaty.[15] Japan played a central role in U.S. regional strategy (both conventional and nuclear) by providing logisti-

---

[15]China was also viewed as a threat during the 1960s.

cal support for U.S. troops and access to bases essential for containing Soviet and Chinese regional power, and by supplementing U.S. naval power (e.g., anti-submarine warfare capabilities). In return, the United States extended its nuclear umbrella over Japan. U.S. conventional and nuclear forces in large part obviated the need for Japan to develop large-scale military capabilities commensurate with its economic capabilities and allowed it to concentrate on economic growth.

With the disintegration of the Soviet system, however, the deterrent value of the alliance has declined. Both countries have largely downgraded the security threat posed by Russian forces in the Far East. In the absence of a Soviet threat, Japan's dependence on U.S. deterrence power is diminished.[16] Similarly, with declining U.S.-Russian competition, the United States derives fewer benefits from its bases in Japan.[17]

## The Alliance as an Insurance Regime

Despite the absence of an overarching security threat in East Asia after the Cold War, the region is still marked by interstate competition over the locus of wealth and power in the international system, sovereignty disputes, risks of nuclear proliferation, and increased arms expenditures that could eventually result in destabilizing arms races. Such centrifugal forces threaten regional ties created by burgeoning intraregional trade, increased foreign direct investment, and heightened technology flows. In order to cope with such fissiparous forces, Japan and the United States are adapting the alliance to lower-profile military roles, including responding to more diffuse threats that might arise within a potentially unstable Asia-Pacific region. Moreover, the Japan-U.S. alliance involves significant investments, or sunk costs that would be lost if both states attempted to reconstruct an alliance relationship should a major mutual threat arise in the future.

---

[16]See Defense Agency of Japan, *Defense of Japan*, 1992, p. 5.

[17]Generous host-nation support by the Japanese Government, however, partly offsets the declining utility of the bases. Moreover, the withdrawal of U.S. forces from the Philippines further increased the value of the bases.

The U.S.-Japan alliance therefore serves as an "insurance regime" that helps moderate mutual insecurity arising in an atmosphere of major uncertainty. In an anarchic international system, particularly in a multipolar system where dangers are more ambiguous, states are uncertain whether alliance partners will fulfill their responsibilities in the event of a crisis affecting their mutual security. With substantial uncertainty about the future strategies of other actors, where states have differential access to information, the Japan-U.S. alliance helps enable both allies to overcome obstacles to collective action, including asymmetrical information, moral hazard, and irresponsibility. Moreover, defection from alliance obligations may entail reputational costs for both states.[18] In addition, continued maintenance of a formal alliance may provide critical time gains for Japan and the United States, enabling them to routinize certain security transactions and to respond promptly to crises affecting their mutual security instead of engaging in ad-hoc negotiations every time a crisis occurs.[19]

The United States and Japan remain confronted with several potential security challenges after the Cold War. These major challenges include Russia, China, and North Korea. The alliance serves a useful hedging purpose should any of these countries pose a threat to regional stability in the future. However, it could also increasingly serve as an important means for ensuring the normalization of these countries as status-quo powers within the Asia-Pacific.

Despite the end of the Cold War, Russia remains a potential threat to both Japan and the United States, especially if nationalist forces within the country attempt to reassert control over other former

---

[18]These costs should not be overestimated in a crisis involving national survival, however, since the high stakes involved would outweigh any potential reputational costs in the calculus of a state.

[19]For example, one reason for Japan's belated response to the crisis stemming from Iraq's invasion of Kuwait was that the Gulf region lay outside the geographic scope of the alliance, necessitating the time-consuming passage of domestic legislation to enable Japan to make non-financial contributions to support U.S.-led multinational troops. Nevertheless, even limited Japanese support for U.S. efforts during the crisis, although criticized for being 'too little, too late,' would not likely have been forthcoming in the absence of a formalized alliance relationship. Instead, Japan would have engaged in 'passing the buck' and would not have defrayed part of the large financial costs of the war effort.

Soviet republics. Except for its nuclear weapons, Russia is no longer a superpower. Its economy is in shambles and its economic output, depending on how one measures it, ranks somewhere alongside middle powers such as Brazil, Britain, India, and Italy. Russia's ability to project military power beyond its territory has largely deteriorated and with the loss of its "near abroad" it no longer threatens Middle East oil supplies. In the next decade, Russia is therefore unlikely to present a global challenge, or even a significant regional challenge in the North Pacific.

Nevertheless, both Japan and the United States remain cautious over Russia's future foreign policy course. So long as the conversion of Russia's military-industrial complex into civilian industries lags, few major changes in the military posture of the Russian armed forces in the Far East occur, and Russia continues to develop advanced weaponry, a latent Russian capability to pose a major threat to the region will persist.[20] Much therefore depends on the future evolution of Russian domestic politics. Moreover, in the absence of meaningful arms reductions in the Far East, continued deployment of Russian SSBNs still pose a *de-facto* threat to Japanese and U.S. population centers. This less prominent strategic rationale for the alliance, however, is much harder to justify to public opinion in both countries. In this respect, Japan's territorial dispute with Russia continues to serve a useful purpose.

The potential rise of China constitutes perhaps the most significant long-term security problem facing both allies in the region. Since Deng Xiaoping launched economic reforms in the late 1970s, China's GNP has averaged nine percent annual growth. In terms of purchasing power parity, depending upon which PPP estimate is used, its economic output now rivals or even exceeds Japan's GDP. Its military spending has largely kept pace with its economic growth. Moreover, China has begun to enhance its power projection capability, including both naval and air power. China has imported advanced weaponry and technology from Russia as it has embarked on a weapons modernization program, given further urgency after the Gulf War.

---

[20]Defense Agency of Japan, *Defense of Japan* 1991, pp. 29–30. U.S. Department of Defense, *Military Forces in Transition* (Washington, D.C., 1991), p. 5. Interviews with Foreign Ministry and Defense Agency officials.

As long as China remains a non-status quo power, its rapid economic expansion and rising military expenditures could alarm other Asian states and result in a region-wide arms race. China claims sovereignty over Taiwan, the Spratly Islands and most of the South China Sea, and even the Senkaku Islands and vast areas of the East China Sea. It has not renounced the right to use force to resolve its sovereignty dispute with Taiwan. Japanese concerns over how China might define its regional objectives as its power grows were exacerbated after China passed a law in February 1992 authorizing the use of force to drive out foreign vessels entering its territorial waters, including the Senkaku Islands occupied by Japan. Within Japan there is concern that the Chinese Communist Party may resort to aggressive regional expansionism in order to reassert its waning authority, as part of a stratagem designed to appeal to nationalistic sentiment and to domestic military interests.

As in the case of Russia, whether or not China becomes a "normal" power within the international system will depend mainly upon the future evolution of domestic politics and economic reform efforts. Other states can only marginally influence such domestic developments by seeking to enmesh China (and Russia) within the international economy and regional security institutions. For this purpose the alliance could serve an important purpose in insuring that both countries respond to potential threats to regional stability in a coherent manner. Thus, the Japan-U.S. alliance remains a useful insurance regime should Chinese economic and military power continue to rapidly expand and China remains a non-status quo power. The alliance essentially serves as a hedge against possible negative developments in China and Russia and obviates against the immediate need for a containment strategy.

The Korean peninsula is also a major potential source of regional instability. But North Korea does not yet pose a *direct* military threat to Japan. Only in the unlikely event that Pyongyang reunites the peninsula by force, develops air and naval power projection capabilities, or develops a nuclear weapon capable of reaching Japan on a Scud-C or successor missile would Japan be directly threatened. Nevertheless, the alliance also provides for intelligence sharing and a forum for consultations and reaching a consensus on problems relating to the Korean peninsula. Moreover, in the event of an outbreak of hostilities on the Korean peninsula, American bases in Japan would likely serve a critical role as they did during the Korean war.

## The Alliance as a Regional Stabilizing Force

The alliance also serves as a regional stabilizing force. The alliance reduces the risks of conflict among the major Asian powers and serves a critical stabilizing role by preventing relative gains concerns from destabilizing the region and by facilitating continued regional economic integration. Abrogation of the alliance, in tandem with a diminished U.S. regional presence, could even lead to the emergence of an East Asian power vacuum and attempts to fill it by either China, Japan, or even Russia.

The alliance also promotes regional stability by reducing concerns about a revival of Japanese militarism. Given domestic constraints on the size and scope of Japan's military, the alliance expands the credibility of Japan's deterrence capabilities, thereby rendering a politically difficult choice of offensive and nuclear weapons unnecessary. The alliance has allowed East Asian nations to trust Japan's growing economic influence and even permitted the growth of its military power without provoking a regional arms race, thereby giving Japan more flexibility with its neighbors and enabling it to emphasize a "trading state" strategy of economic growth and creation of wealth.

Over its four decade history, the alliance has acquired legitimacy among all the major states within the region. Withdrawal from the alliance would entail reputational costs for Japan, especially given the "shadow of the past," and cause other states to question other international commitments Japan has made, thereby undermining the "desire for respect" element in Japanese foreign policy. The alliance is therefore sustained by history, which confers legitimacy on the Security Treaty.

For the United States, the alliance is also valued as a regional stabilizing force. The United States is the only state whose military presence is welcomed by most countries within the region. The withdrawal of U.S. forces from the Philippines has increased the importance of the bases in Japan for maintaining regional stability. Japan is the sole home port to an American carrier in Asia. Moreover, regional stability is of increasing importance to U.S. economic interests, given the importance of the region to U.S. economic interests. The alliance provides the United States with greater leverage within the world's most economically dynamic region. Since East Asian states view U.S. military power as a counterweight to Japan's economic power, they sometimes award major contracts to U.S. companies in order to maintain U.S. influence and interest in the region.

## The Alliance as a Basic Political Framework for Cooperation

Although alliances typically serve a negative purpose of aggregating the capabilities of two or more parties against an adversary, they may also serve positive roles in promoting intraalliance cooperation on non-military issues. As Robert Rothstein has suggested, "an alliance that works reasonably well may reduce the instrumentality of international relations. The mere process of successfully living together for some period of time may have a positive 'feedback' in terms of loyalty and friendship."[21] Although historical instances may be rare, both NATO and the Japan-U.S. alliance are examples of positive alliances. Such alliances include normative elements that are not subject to myopic calculations of interest especially when long-run peaceful relations are anticipated.

The most important task of the alliance in the immediate post-Cold War era (unless a new threat emerges) will be to serve as a basic political framework for cooperation. With the end of the Cold War and the recent power shift in Japan's favor, this role has assumed paramount importance in moderating a search for relative gains on both sides of the Pacific and in promoting bilateral and international cooperation in a post-hegemonic era. There are currently no other organizational alternatives that could assume this critical role. In an emerging multipolar world, the alliance may assume increased importance as a political instrument for maintaining interstate order and avoiding the negative consequences that could result from independent decision making.

---

[21] Robert Rothstein, *Alliances and Small Powers* (New York: Columbia University Press, 1968), p. 55.

Although the positive externalities from the Soviet threat for U.S.-Japan cooperation have disappeared, there remain strong incentives to maintain the alliance on both sides of the Pacific. If this analysis is correct, then both nations should be able to resolve "high politics" conflicts, even though they will be more likely to engage in "brinkmanship" in various bilateral disputes and be less willing to compromise.

The alliance may therefore continue to promote trust, stability, and predictability in U.S.-Japan relations, undermining the appeal of nationalist or special-interest arguments and the salience of relative gains concerns in bilateral disputes. Japan may continue to value how the alliance moderates U.S. responses to economic competition between the two countries, facilitating continued access to the U.S. economy and dispelling Japanese anxieties that the United States will again seek to crush Japan. In turn, the United States may continue to value the alliance for facilitating Japanese trade concessions and channeling Japanese power. The alliance would be seen as helping to prevent the emergence of a new military rival by discouraging Japan from choosing to become a nuclear-armed power with offensive capabilities that could challenge U.S. interests.[22] The alliance would therefore allow the United States to maintain military primacy.

Finally, maintenance of the alliance would also encourage both countries to take into account each other's interests in areas lying outside the formal scope of the security relationship. During the Cold War, the United States promoted Japan's membership in international economic organizations and pressured its European allies to open their markets to Japanese exports. Although such U.S. support is much less important now that Japan is an economic superpower, Japan remains apprehensive about isolation in the world community. In return, more Japanese support or understanding has been forthcoming in the United Nations and other international organizations.

---

[22]See "Excerpts from Pentagon's Plan: 'Prevent the Re-emergence of a New Rival'," *The New York Times,* March 8, 1992.

## COSTS OF THE ALLIANCE RELATIONSHIP

Revisionists on both sides of the Pacific have cogently criticized the costs of maintaining the alliance, although they generally ignore the risks of a major deterioration in relations. For the United States, the costs include giving Japan relatively open access to the U.S. market (in trade, technology and direct foreign investment) that is too often not reciprocated by Japan. For the Japanese, the costs include deferring to U.S. foreign policy goals as a junior partner, to the detriment of its international prestige. Japan is also more vulnerable to U.S. trade pressure because of the alliance relationship. These are costs that could undermine the alliance if not resolved. An examination of whether alternative security arrangements would be less costly for both Japan and the United States is therefore warranted.

### Security Alternatives for Japan

Although the Japan-U.S. alliance remains viable, it is necessary to examine Japan's security options in order to determine whether another alternative would be less costly. There are four basic alternatives for Japan: (1) replacement of the bilateral alliance with a regional security structure; (2) reliance on a U.N. collective security system; (3) a "continental" alliance with Russia or China; and (4) an autonomous security path. The first two options would generally fall within a general scenario of peaceful relations with the United States, while the latter two would invite collision with the United States. Each of these options could also be supplemented with a "nuclear option."

#### • A Regional Security Arrangement

A regional security arrangement could entail a variety of forms. One possibility would be a collective defense system modeled on NATO, including the United States, South Korea, Taiwan and possibly the ASEAN countries. Japan opposed this option during the Cold War out of fear of becoming too closely linked to U.S. global strategy and becoming involved in a Vietnam-type conflict, although it did participate in RIMPAC naval exercises during the 1980s. With a declining Russian threat, deepening Sino-Japanese relations and constitutional restrictions, there are even fewer reasons to expect Japan to choose a formal multilateral alliance, unless a Chinese threat emerges in the region.

A more feasible alternative would be the creation of a CSCE-type regional security community. Recently, Japan has taken modest steps in this direction by initiating the creation of a tripartite organization among Japan, South Korea, and the United States to discuss problems related to the security of the Korean peninsula, including the threat of nuclear proliferation in North Korea. In addition, Japan proposed intensified dialogue on political and security issues between ASEAN and its dialogue partners, which in turn led to the establishment of the ASEAN Regional Forum. But given the wide diversity of interests within the region, and the presence of nuclear-armed neighbors, it would be very difficult to construct a "common Asia-Pacific house" that could guarantee Japan's security in the absence of the Japan-U.S. alliance. In the near future, therefore, any regional security arrangement will supplement—but not supplant—bilateral security arrangements in the region.

### • A U.N. Collective Security System

A second alternative would involve Japan's active participation in a U.N. collective security system. This possibility is noted in Article X of the Security Treaty: "This Treaty shall remain in force until in the opinion of the Governments of the United States of America and Japan there shall have come into force such United Nations arrangements as will satisfactorily provide for the maintenance of international peace and security in the Japan area." Recent government attempts to legalize the participation of the Self-Defense Forces in U.N. peacekeeping operations can be seen as a step in this direction. Japan could remain a trading state while more actively contributing to international security without arousing widespread domestic and international opposition. But abrogation of the alliance and its replacement by a U.N.-centered diplomacy would entail high risks for Japan, unless it could be certain that a U.N. collective security system would provide for its security, especially given its territorial dispute with a nuclear-armed China and continuing problems with Russia.

### • A "Continental" Alliance

A third option would involve a "continental" alliance with China and/or Russia. Such a development would profoundly alter the global balance of power. Given instability within both its large neighbors, such a choice would represent a major risk for Japan. Despite rapidly growing trade and investment in East Asia, Japan's economic interests remain global in nature. Unless in response to a severe loss of markets in North America, Japan would be extremely reluctant to sacrifice its economic and political relationship with its main trading partner, the United States, for potentially unstable and/or minor trading partners.

Moreover, a continental alliance would not likely be capable of sustaining itself. Malevolent pan-Asianism, directed against the United States, would eventually turn inwards and lead to Sino-Japanese confrontation. In the absence of the alliance, which mitigates against a strong legacy of historical mistrust, unresolved territorial problems, and relative gains concerns between Japan and its mainland Asia neighbors, pan-Asianism would likely collapse. Japan therefore cannot easily exploit this "trump card," as suggested by Japanese nationalists supporting an "exclusive" Asia vision for Japan.

### • An Autonomous Security Policy

A fourth alternative consists of different versions of an autonomous security path. One option would involve becoming the "Switzerland of Asia." This option was proposed by General MacArthur in the immediate post-war period and echoed later in the official lines of Japan's opposition parties. Such an option proved illusory, however, since it was only through subordination to America in security matters that Japan could function as a trading state. Moreover, Iraq's invasion of a weak but rich neighbor served as a reminder against the dangers of a "lightly armed" trading state, lacking any international security guarantee. Within Japan, adherents of "one-nation pacifism" are declining with the end of the Cold War. Instead, there is a growing desire for Japan to be a "normal" power and to play a role in international affairs commensurate with its status as an economic superpower.

Another option involves remaining substantially armed, but becoming a neutral trading state. This would require the reorganization of the Self Defense Forces, which is currently interwoven with U.S. regional strategy and lacks independent defense and deterrent capabilities.[23] But this security option is potentially incompatible with a trading state strategy, since abrogation of the alliance could undermine Japan's regional trade relations, due to lingering mistrust of the nation. Given continuing instability within the region and tensions with its nuclear-armed neighbors, the withdrawal of the U.S. nuclear umbrella would likely pressure Japan to "go nuclear."

Finally, another option would be the creation of a regional trading system centered around a Japanese security guarantee and economic power (Japanese hegemony or a "neocoprosperity" strategy). There exists modest support for this alternative, minus a unilateral security guarantee, among some Japanese politicians and within the Finance Ministry and MITI. However, lingering regional mistrust and a legacy of past Japanese conduct in the Asia-Pacific region would make such a security guarantee problematic.[24] Moreover, China and the United States could be expected to challenge any attempt by Japan at regional hegemony. In addition, South Korea and Taiwan would have few incentives to become joint participants in a Japanese "flying geese" strategy and would oppose any major expansion in Japan's involvement in regional security affairs. In the absence of China's implosion and the withdrawal of the United States from East Asia, such an option would be highly unfeasible.

- **The Nuclear Card**

The preceding analysis suggests that various proposed alliance alternatives all entail high security risks for Japan, unless accompanied by major change in the character of the international strategic system (e.g., creation of a genuine nuclear free zone in East Asia) or a Japanese decision to "go nuclear." Accordingly, some right-wing politicians view selection of the nuclear option (i.e., a Gaullist strategy) as a necessary step to obtaining greater international prestige.

---

[23]The Defense Agency has found it impossible to meet even authorized troop levels, which are small compared with Japan's neighbors, due to a lack of interest in a military career among younger Japanese.

[24]See Frances Fung Wai Lai and Charles E. Morrison, eds., *Political and Security Cooperation: A New Dimension in ASEAN-Japan Relations?* (Tokyo: Japan Center for International Exchange, 1987); Robert O. Tilman, *Southeast Asia and the Enemy Beyond: ASEAN Perceptions of External Threats* (Boulder, CO: Westview Press, 1987).

Japan has both the technological capabilities and nuclear material necessary to rapidly emerge as a major nuclear power. Domestic and regional aversion to any revision of Japan's three non-nuclear principles, however, would make such a choice difficult. A "great power" Japan would create regional insecurity and would jeopardize Japan's trade relations with its neighbors. It would therefore likely necessitate a path of formal empire in order to guarantee Japan's access to regional markets and raw resources.[25] But such a step would be even more dangerous since it would also be certain to cause severe conflict with other major powers, especially China and the United States.

## Opportunity Costs: Security Alternatives for the United States

Apart from continued reliance on its partnership with Japan, there exist few security alternatives for the United States in East Asia. Any attempt to use the "China card" would likely backfire, since China would exploit for its own purposes any divisions in the Japan-U.S. relationship. Russia also does not yet represent a long-term reliable partner in the Pacific. Multilateral security dialogues, including the ARF, would at best serve as confidence-building measures and only supplement the stabilizing role played by the Japan-U.S. alliance in East Asia. Finally, any attempt to reassert American primacy in East Asia would likely give rise to malevolent pan-Asianism, including a close Sino-Japanese relationship.

Another option would be U.S. disengagement from East Asia. But as long as U.S. economic interests in the region continue to grow and other East Asian countries, especially Japan, are willing to support U.S. economic, political, and security engagement, the United States would be foolhardy to undertake a military withdrawal from the region, to return to isolationism, and/or to build a North American trading bloc.

---

[25]This idea was captured by Eugene Staley more than five decades ago: 'When economic walls are erected along political boundaries, possession of territory is made to coincide with economic territory. Imperialistic ambitions are given both a partial justification and a splendid basis for propaganda.' Staley, *The World Economy in Transition* (New York: Council on Foreign Relations, 1939), p. 103.

## HAZARDS FOR ALLIANCE MAINTENANCE

### Hedging about the Future of the Alliance Relationship

While both Japan and the United States still seek to maintain and even strengthen their alliance, both countries are also engaged in building alternative relationships should the present structure fall apart. The danger of any hedging behavior, however, is that it could represent a self-fulfilling strategy, by either weakening the incentives for maintaining the alliance, or by creating new sources for bilateral rivalry elsewhere in Asia.

One major goal of Japanese foreign policy after the Cold War has been to strengthen the alliance in order to keep the United States from adopting an isolationist foreign policy and trading-bloc strategy. At the same time, Japan has rapidly expanded its links with the rest of Asia, in part as a hedge against possible U.S. economic, military, and political disengagement from the region. While Japan's expanding influence in East Asia also reflects regional economic opportunities and a desire to maintain the competitiveness of Japanese industries against NIE competitors following the appreciation of the yen, hedging against the potential for future adversity in U.S.-Japan relations is unquestionably an important political factor. However, if Japanese overseas aid and investment lending rules primarily serve to consolidate its influence in Asian markets and to exclude U.S. competitors, it will inevitably heighten economic friction with the United States and lower the incentives for the United States to maintain the alliance. This is especially true in a period in which there is an absence of an overarching strategic rationale to justify continued deployment of U.S. troops in East Asia.

The degree to which Japanese foreign policy either emphasizes or downgrades the importance of the Japan-U.S. relationship vis-a-vis relations with Asia will in large part depend upon the influence of government officials and politicians supporting America's integration within Asia versus those favoring a more Asia-centered diplomacy, or even an exclusive "Asia for Asians" vision for Japan. The future influence of pro-alliance officials within the Ministry of Foreign Affairs versus more Asia-oriented officials within the Finance Ministry and MITI will be an especially crucial determinant.

U.S. economic diplomacy is increasingly emphasizing the importance of APEC and alternative Asian markets to Japan, including ASEAN, China, and India, in part due to the failure of bilateral negotiations to reduce America's trade deficit with Japan ("Japan passing"). While the development of such alternative economic and political ties in part reflects opportunities for the United States elsewhere in the Asia-Pacific region, a *de facto* downgrading in the importance of the bilateral relationship can also be seen as hedging against the possibility of an abrogation of the alliance and worsening bilateral relations.

## Inequities in Burdensharing and Decisionmaking

A central challenge for both allies in the next decade will be to transform the alliance into a relationship in which burdensharing and powersharing are more equitably distributed. This was conveyed vividly during the Gulf War, when severe political stresses were brought to the fore. During the Gulf crisis, U.S. mistrust of its main Pacific ally increased, due to perceptions that Japan's contributions were "too little too late," especially in terms of non-financial contributions. Two major lessons for Japanese diplomacy were drawn from the conflict. First, Japan needs to play a more vigorous role in international affairs, commensurate with its status as a major power. Second, Japan's increasing contributions to the maintenance of interstate order are not appreciated within the world community, especially within the United States, and have yet to result in greater Japanese input into international decisionmaking.[26] Rising Japanese dissatisfaction over decisionsharing in the bilateral relationship are thus a corollary to U.S. dissatisfaction over an equitable division in burdensharing roles and costs, both of which pose a threat to alliance durability.

---

[26]See Courtney Purrington and A.K., "Tokyo's Policy Responses During the Gulf Crisis," *Asian Survey*, Vol. XXXI, No. 4 (April 1991), pp. 307–23; Courtney Purrington, "Tokyo's Policy Responses During the Gulf War and the Impact of the 'Iraqi Shock' on Japan," *Pacific Affairs*, Vol. 65, No. 2, (Summer 1992), pp. 10–21.

## • Burdensharing Inequities

Burdensharing remains a significant potential source of discord that could weaken the security relationship, especially as U.S. diplomacy has emphasized the resolution of economic problems with Japan. It also partly reflects a recent reversal in economic fortunes of the two countries, following the collapse of the Japanese bubble economy. However, the issue could again become significant in the event of a crisis in which Japan's alliance contributions were seen as not commensurate with Japanese capabilities and in an environment of U.S. economic malaise.

Reform of the present bilateral security arrangement would require revision of both its scope and division of labor. A major source of U.S. dissatisfaction is the so-called "security-free ride" Japan is said to enjoy. According to this perception, Japan enjoys immense economic gains from international collective goods provided by the United States, but does not pay costs commensurate with the benefits it derives from the international order. During the military buildup of the Reagan era, when Japan ran huge trade surpluses with the United States, the difference between the security costs the United States paid and the economic gains Japan received were magnified. This perception was reinforced during the Gulf War, when the United States, despite being in the midst of an economic recession, undertook most of the risks in defending Western interests in the Middle East, while Japan largely remained on the sidelines and enjoyed the longest economic boom in its post-war history.

While reform of the present security arrangement will require that Japan pay for more of the costs and the United States receive more benefits, there are limits to increasing Japan's share of the costs. First, with lessening East-West tensions, pressures for a peace dividend are making it more difficult for Japan to import expensive U.S. weapons systems. Second, there are limits to shouldering the costs of maintaining U.S. troops in Japan, as demonstrated by U.S. sensitivities about performing a mercenary role on behalf of Japanese interests during the Gulf crisis. Third, if the military power of the Self Defense Forces (SDF) were further strengthened in conjunction with a gradual, phased reduction of U.S. troops, this would alarm Japan's neighbors and undermine regional stability. Fourth, with the collapse of the Soviet Union, the value of strategic foreign aid to countries such as Egypt, Pakistan, the Philippines, and Turkey, previously seen as a means of increasing Japan's burdensharing costs, has greatly declined. Furthermore, U.S. resentment against Japanese "checkbook diplomacy" during the Gulf crisis also demonstrates the limits to overreliance on such an approach.

Another strategy would entail an expansion of Japan's military roles. One possibility would be revision of the geographic scope or obligations of the present Security Treaty. This could involve replacing present unilateral obligations of the alliance with a bilateral guarantee that would obligate Japan to come to the aid of the United States in a crisis and extending the geographic scope of the treaty to include the entire Pacific region. Any major extension of the military scope of the alliance, however, would present constitutional problems and would be a politically risky step for any Japanese cabinet. As revision of the Security Treaty in 1960 demonstrated, any changes can entail severe domestic political costs. Such a major change is highly unlikely unless a serious external shock again occurs (e.g., on the Korean peninsula), a new challenger state comes to the fore in East Asia, or political realignment in Japan results in the emergence of a dominant political party in favor of Japan becoming a "normal" power.

A strategy of directly addressing imbalances in security costs and benefits may therefore prove difficult over the short term. But if the alliance is regarded as the framework for a global partnership and not simply as a regional security institution, then an indirect strategy, making use of multilateral institutions to increase Japan's global burdensharing costs and roles, might prove more effective. For example, Japan could further increase its contributions to U.N. peacekeeping operations and increase the participation by the SDF in such operations. Such a flexible strategy would expand Japanese contributions to the maintenance of international peace under the rubric of the United Nations and would complement traditional U.S. security roles.

A final strategy would involve linkage of U.S. defense costs with an expansion of Japanese burdensharing in non-military issue areas. Article II of the Security Treaty mandates that both sides seek to eliminate conflicts in their international economic policies and encourage economic collaboration between them. The most effective strategy would be to further encourage U.S. economic integration in East Asia through provision of Japanese capital (e.g., Export-Import Bank loans for development projects in which U.S. companies are principals). This would also address the hedging problem mentioned previously. But implementation of such an integration strategy will in large part depend upon the future course of domestic debate on Japan's future role in Asia.

Increasing Japanese resentment over outcomes in recent trade disputes also shows that there are limits to compensating the United States directly for its security guarantee through bilateral economic concessions. A strategy of expanding Japan's contributions to joint science and technology research, arms control, environmental issues, and defense technology R&D would perhaps be more effective, since such areas are more closely dependent upon continuation of the alliance relationship.

### • Friction Over Governance of the International System

Japanese resentment over "taxation without representation" could turn into anti-U.S. sentiment as the postwar generation comes into power during the next decade. Pride in Japan's economic and technological achievements may give rise to anti-American sentiment in this generation, unless both countries are able to forge a global partnership with an equitable division of responsibilities and costs for governance of the international order. This will be critical to avoiding a repetition of the 1920s, when Japan was cast adrift following the termination of the Anglo-Japan alliance and Western nations were unwilling to accord Japan equal status in the club of major powers, thereby playing into the hands of right-wing Japanese nationalists.

In the Cold War period, the primary threat to the alliance came from nationalism disguised as "one-nation pacifism," while in the emerging international system the primary danger will be nationalism disguised as "one-nation internationalism," i.e., diplomacy ostensibly to contribute to international peace and prosperity, but in reality designed to assert Japanese power. Within the government the influence of pro-American groups has already ebbed and the voices of those advocating a more independent posture in defense, financial markets, and trade are increasingly influential.

Japan shares responsibility for this state of affairs, given that it is a hesitant novice at playing a leadership role and unwilling to play a major military role. During the Gulf War, Japan was criticized for being unable to set forth what principles were at stake and was unwilling to take any substantial human and political risks. While domestic considerations were largely responsible for such possessive diplomacy, Japanese foreign policy demonstrated little evidence of "milieu goals," and remained too preoccupied with the achievement of "possession goals." If Japanese foreign policy remains reactive and purposeless, except for possession-oriented goals, shared leadership will be extremely difficult to achieve. In recognition of this problem, the Japanese Government has begun to actively debate Japan's role in the emerging international system, while also playing a more active leadership role on human rights, arms control, Third World debt, and environmental issues.

The United States also bears some responsibility, due to its ambivalence about sharing decision-making power with Japan. The United States has encouraged Japan to play a larger role in international affairs, but within the framework of the existing alliance. Although the United States has repeatedly called for Japan to increase its burden-sharing contributions, it has been reluctant to share decision-making responsibilities. Thus, the United States needs to realistically address the institutional, political, and psychological adjustments that recent structural changes in the international system necessitate.

## Economic Friction

Economic rivalry between Japan and the United States has been the dominant source of friction in bilateral relations since the resolution of the Okinawa conflict in 1969. Like their predecessors in the Cold War, the Clinton administration and a recent succession of non-LDP governments have sought to keep conflicts over trade and investment from contaminating the security relationship. But economic friction could represent an increased threat to alliance durability after the Cold War. Without a common threat, both states are more willing to engage in tough bargaining over economic issues, as is evident in recent bilateral trade disputes. Over time, these economic grievances could seriously undermine alliance cohesion.

American revisionists correctly point to features of the Japanese "developmental state," such as horizontal and vertical *keiretsu*, the distribution system, administrative guidance, and lax enforcement of collusive behavior by cartels, all of which promote the competitive efficiency of Japanese corporations, or what one economist has called "J-efficiency," thereby posing severe disadvantages for U.S. corporations.[27] But Japanese revisionists also correctly point out how certain U.S. economic practices harm the competitiveness of U.S. firms. In addition, macroeconomic features of the U.S. economy, including its large government deficit and the low savings rate, are a fundamental part of the problem.

While market forces, U.S. pressures, growing internationalization of firms, political change, and even popular demands for deregulation are slowly changing the structure of the Japanese economy, such changes will not reduce the bilateral trade deficit dramatically in the short run. For Japan to play a greater leadership role in the international economy and lessen economic friction with the United States, a major restructuring of its economy is required. For the United States the choices are equally difficult. Any U.S. administration needs to reduce the national deficit, encourage domestic savings, and adopt policies which promote the international competitiveness of U.S. firms in order to increase exports and reduce its enormous accumulated foreign debt. At the same time, achieving greater harmonization between U.S. and Japanese economic practices inevitably will involve a clash between different social structures.

Although the importance of preserving a liberal trading regime and maintaining access to the U.S. market and security protection may provide strong incentives for policy change in Japan, significant changes are unlikely until domestic political realignment results in a stable two or three-party system. Even then the political costs of liberalization could prove too high for any Japanese government to embrace. Until both governments are willing to undertake a major restructuring of their economies, there remains a need for sectoral protectionism. While this represents a temporary "illiberal" expedient, it

---

[27]Kozo Yamamura, 'Will Japan's Economic Structure Change?' in Yamamura, ed., *Japan's Economic Structure: Should It Change?* (Seattle, WA: Society for Japanese Studies, 1990), pp. 13–64. Revisionists, however, largely ignore features of the U.S. economy which give advantages to U.S. firms.

is a necessary step in order to avoid economic tensions which could weaken the alliance. Given the necessity of managed economic relations over the short-run, the alliance will be even more essential in resolving economic conflict. In the absence of a common enemy, however, the alliance will be more taxed than ever in seeking to accomplish this task.

## Divergent Responses in a Crisis Affecting Mutual Security

According to Article IV of the Security Treaty, Japan and the United States will "consult together" at the request of either party "whenever the security of Japan or international peace and security in the Far East is threatened." Although Japan could technically exercise "veto rights" over the operation of U.S. forces based in Japan, it has not done so. Indeed, as a precondition for reversion of Okinawa, Japan agreed to adopt a flexible attitude to the operation of Article IV in the Far East. Furthermore, the 1978 Guidelines for Defense Cooperation specified:

> The scope and modalities of facilitative assistance to be extended by Japan to the U.S. Forces in the case of situations in the Far East outside of Japan which will have an important influence on the security of Japan will be governed by the Japan-U.S. Security Treaty [and] its related arrangements.

Thus, despite the involvement of U.S. forces based in Japan in the Vietnam War, the Pueblo incident, and the Gulf War, Japan has never even insisted on prior consultations during a crisis.[28]   The question is whether this pattern will persist in the future.

### • Korea

Recent tensions on the Korean peninsula has helped strengthen the Japan-U.S. security relationship, by providing a comprehensible rationale for public support. However, future events in Korea could weaken or undermine the alliance. Most dramatic would be a deci-

---

[28]During the Cold War, the Far East was interpreted as including the Korean peninsula and Taiwan (although the United States subsequently pledged to China that it would restrain any Japanese military involvement in matters related to Taiwan).

sion by Japan to insist on prior consultations and perhaps even to refuse to approve the deployment of U.S. troops based in Japan.

The "too little too late" response by the Murayama cabinet to the 1995 Kobe earthquake should not be seen, however, as an indication of how Japan would respond to the threat of conflict in the Korean peninsula. Not only would a more assertive Japanese stance split the coalition government, but even the pacifist-oriented Murayama cabinet would be wary of risking an abrupt end to the Japan-U.S. relationship as long as Japan remains dependent upon the U.S. security guarantee and market. Moreover, the level of U.S.-Japan contingency planning and even joint exercises for such an eventuality is much higher than central-local Japanese planning was for a large earthquake.

But the scope of what Japan would be willing to contribute to allied efforts during a Korean conflict remains uncertain, especially given the current composition of Japan's ruling coalition. In the event of another Korean war, Japan's main contribution would likely be that of logistical support, although it could also provide minesweeping support and perhaps air support over the Sea of Japan. The latter contributions would be necessary in order to avoid an even more serious replay of the Gulf War, when Japan was accused of staying on the sidelines during the crisis. More direct Japanese military contributions, such as ground troops in Korea, however, would be severely constrained by Japan's past historical conduct in Korea.

A more serious threat to maintenance of the alliance would likely arise not from war initiated by the North Korea, but from a scenario in which Tokyo viewed U.S. actions toward North Korea as overly provocative. For example, Japan would likely disapprove of a U.S.-led preemptive strike against North Korea, or the laying of mines around North Korean harbors. Since China would almost certainly oppose such actions as well, such a scenario is highly unlikely.

The most serious threat to alliance maintenance on the Korean peninsula would arise from North Korea's development of a nuclear capability that could threaten Japan. Such an eventuality, or a post-unification decision by Korea to choose the nuclear option, would encourage Japan to withdraw from the Nuclear Non-Proliferation Treaty. This in turn would likely elicit a chain reaction in the rest of

Asia, resulting in a number of new members of the "nuclear club." Whether or not the alliance would in part mitigate against the need for Japan to develop a nuclear deterrent would in large part depend on how Japan viewed future relations with China.

## • China

Despite the importance of Korea to Japanese security calculations, domestic developments in China, and China's external behavior are likely to have a much larger effect on the future evolution of the Japan-U.S. alliance. China's potential rise to power therefore constitutes the single most important issue facing the Japan-U.S. security relationship over the long term. As already noted, the alliance serves an important role as an insurance regime. It is the mainstay of both allies' hedging strategies should China pose a threat to regional stability in the future.

In the absence of a coordinated approach between the United States and Japan, China would likely engage in opportunistic behavior and exploit differences between them. This would likely spell the failure of any attempt at "normalizing" China by enmeshing it within the international economy and international institutions. Instead, the likely result would be a menacing China that would threaten regional stability.

However, without clear evidence of hostile Chinese intentions, such as aggressive behavior in the South China Sea or an ultimatum directed at Taiwan, Japan would be unlikely to support a containment strategy against China. Any U.S. attempt to do so would likely fail and result in severe strains for the alliance. The situation is much different than in 1949 when the United States was a hegemon and Japan a defeated country. In turn, should Japan prove reluctant to engage in the use of "sticks" as well as "carrots" in order to affect Chinese external behavior, especially in the event of rising Chinese military influence on foreign policy, the utility of the alliance could be severely eroded.

## CONCLUSIONS

Despite the end of the Cold War, there remain cogent reasons for continued maintenance of the U.S.-Japan alliance on both sides of the Pacific. The alliance remains useful as an "insurance regime" and as a stabilizing factor in a rapidly changing East Asian security environment. It will therefore most likely remain the keystone of regional stability over at least the near term. Moreover, it will continue to serve as a basic political framework for cooperation in bilateral relations. In the absence of an overarching security threat, however, the costs of the alliance are more difficult to justify to public opinion in both countries. At the same time, however, there will be no discernible alternative security option for the United States and Japan that would adequately ensure the security interests of both countries in the region for at least the next decade.

But preservation of the alliance will entail skilled management of potential sources of adversity for the relationship. It will require both countries to deal with burdensharing and powersharing issues that pose a long-term threat to the vitality of the alliance. It will also require better handling of bilateral economic friction. In addition, it will presume closer and more effective coordination of the East Asian strategies of both countries, especially regarding China. Instead of engaging in unilateral hedging behavior, a coordinated hedging strategy will be necessary concerning common sources of adversity for both countries in East Asia, including the Korean peninsula, China, Taiwan, and the South China Sea.

# Chapter Ten

# PROSPECTS FOR THE U.S.-JAPAN RELATIONSHIP IN THE POST-COLD WAR ERA

Myonwoo Lee

## INTRODUCTION

The collapse of the Soviet Union in 1991 brought about the end of Cold War, which had lasted for more than four decades. No one can be certain about the ensuing international order. Numerous uncertainties abound: these can be seen in the lack of clear direction in American foreign policy, along with the relative economic decline of the United States, in the increasing internal conflicts of the former Soviet bloc countries, in the emergence of regional economic arrangements, such as the North American Free Trade Agreement (NAFTA) and the European Union (EU), and even in the outbreak of territorial disputes between and among various countries.

Various scenarios of a future international order have been proposed by scholars as well as by journalists. Takashi Inoguchi, for example, has identified four possible scenarios: (i) a Pax Americana Phase II, in which the United States maintains its superpower status of the Cold War era while Japan and Western Europe continue to concentrate on their economies; (ii) "Bigemony," in which the United States and Japan pursue a more co-equal status in both economic and military capabilities; (iii) a Pax Consortia, in which no hegemonic power emerges, but with the United States, Japan, and Western Europe sharing power with each other; and (iv) a Pax Nipponica, in which Japan emerges as the sole superpower.[1] One additional possibility omitted in Inoguchi's formulation would be the emergence of inter-

---

[1]Takashi Inoguchi, "Four Japanese Scenarios for the Future," *International Affairs*, Vol. 65, No. 1, Winter 1988–89, pp. 15–28.

national organizations, such as the United Nations, as major actors of unprecedented importance.

Regardless of the dominant pattern that emerges in the future, the relationship between the United States and Japan will prove critical. This article will therefore focus on future prospects for the U.S.-Japan relationship. It will first introduce four possible scenarios for the U.S.-Japan relationship on the basis of American and Japanese foreign policy strategies, in which the roles of these two countries and other actors will be described. Through an examination of the problems that could be encountered under different scenarios, we will then specify the most realistic, or likely, scenario. In the short term, an "asymmetrical" US-dominant relationship is still most probable, but in the medium- and long-term, other types of relationships, such as global partnership and/or regional rivalry may develop.

## THE FRAMEWORK OF ANALYSIS

The future dimensions of the U.S.-Japan relationship will exert a major and potentially dominant effect on the international system over the next several decades. These two states are certain to remain among the most important, if not necessarily preeminent, actors for many years to come. A clear understanding of the possible futures of each country's foreign policy is basic to analyzing global as well as regional futures.

U.S. foreign policy is often said to oscillate between the poles of engagement or expansion and disengagement or isolationism.[2] Japan's foreign policy exhibits a similar duality. Though Japan has been frequently criticized as lacking any ideology or principles, Japanese foreign policy has historically oscillated between "beyond-Asianism" (Datsu-A Nyu-O), through which it endeavored to join the group of advanced and powerful Western nations, and that of "toward-Asianism" (Datsu-O Nyu-A), through which it tried to maintain Asia

---

[2]John Spanier, *American Foreign Policy Since World War II* (New York: Holt, Rinehart and Winston, 1983).

within its own sphere of influence.[3] These respective polarities constitute the basis on which various potential futures need to be addressed.

## U.S. Foreign Policy

U.S. foreign policy goals in the post-Cold War era represent a major issue under debate among academics and policymakers. The positions on this issue are diverse, ranging from those stressing greater interdependence among states, to those denying a decline in American power and asserting the need to retain Cold War-style strategies. These differing views can be roughly divided into two contrasting categories with regard to U.S. policy toward Japan. One proposes that the United States detach itself from Japanese and East Asian security concerns. For example, Edward Olsen argues that there is no need for the United States to be a policeman for the East Asian region, arguing that the United States should disengage militarily from the region.[4]

An alternative position suggests a more positive direction for U.S. foreign policy, particularly toward East Asia. For example, while some commentators urge the United States to develop consistent, long-term policy goals such as the preservation of economic effectiveness and a peaceful environment for democracy,[5] others believe the United States should adopt a more positive and reinvigorated role vis-a-vis Japan and other East Asian nations, citing the growing volume of trade between the United States and the region as evidence for this proposition.[6] Peter Tarnoff and Jeffrey E. Garten, for

---

[3]Yoshimura Michio, "Editor's Introduction," ("Nihon Gaiko no Shiso, Kakusho"), *International Relations (Kokusai Seiji)*, Vol. 71 (August 1982), pp.1–9.

[4]Edward A. Olsen, "A New American Strategy for Asia," *Asian Survey*, Vol. 31, No. 12 (December 1991), pp. 1139–1154.

[5]Theodore C. Sorensen, "Rethinking National Security," *Foreign Affairs*, Vol. 69, No. 3 (Summer 1990), pp. 1–18; James Schlesinger, "Quest for a Post-Cold War Foreign Policy," *Foreign Affairs*, Vol. 72, No. 1 (Spring 1993), pp. 17–28.

[6]Robert A. Scalapino, "Asia and the United States: The Challenges Ahead," *Foreign Affairs*, Vol. 69, No. 1 (1990), pp. 89–115; Robert B. Oxnam, "Asia/Pacific Challenges," *Foreign Affairs*, Vol. 72, No. 1 (Spring 1993), pp. 58–73; Howard H. Baker, Jr., and Ellen L. Frost, "Rescuing the U.S.-Japan Alliance," *Foreign Affairs*, Vol. 71, No. 2 (Spring 1992), pp. 97–113.

example, both identify Japan as among the most important partners of the United States.[7]

## Japanese Foreign Policy Options

The Gulf War of 1991 triggered heated debates on Japan's future international role. Despite payments towards the war effort amounting to $13 billion, Japan was heavily criticized for its uncertain response to these events. This criticism was a source of disappointment to many Japanese. But U.S. dependence on Japanese financing was a reminder of the vital contribution of Japan to U.S. global strategy.

In the aftermath of the Gulf War, a circle of Japanese academics, journalists, and policymakers explored and debated an appropriate future role for Japan. One common theme in these assessments is that Japan's international role should be increased, but there is little agreement on how this enhancement should be realized. On this point, there are two basic views. One urges Japan to become a "real" superpower, not only in the economic sense, but also in a political and even military sense, though still closely aligned with the United States. This approach follows in the tradition of the "beyond-Asianists," since it demonstrates Japan's willingness to increase its global role and responsibilities. The other view stresses Japan's advantages in technology and economic power, and is concerned with Japan's ties to the developing countries, especially those in Asia. Proponents of the latter view argue that Japan should not base its role on an expansion of its military capabilities; rather, they argue that Japan can obtain the status of a superpower by expanding its economic influence in Asia and the developing world. This approach follows the tradition of the "towards-Asianists."

Ichiro Ozawa is the main figure proposing "beyond-Asianism." Ozawa argues that, in order for Japan to sustain its economic well-being and to heighten its political status, it should focus its efforts towards the maintenance of the global free trade system and fully

---

[7]Peter Tarnoff, "America's New Special Relationships," *Foreign Affairs*, Vol. 69, No. 3 (Summer 1990); Jeffrey E. Garten, "Japan and Germany: American Concerns," *Foreign Affairs*, Vol. 68, No. 5 (Winter 1989).

consolidate the U.S.-Japan alliance.[8] At the same time, he argues that Japan must change into an "international" state, that is, a country contributing to the international system, not only in economic terms, but in terms of security and humanitarian aspects, as well. Ozawa asserts, therefore, that Japan must become a "normal" state, i.e., that Japan should carry out all the functions of a great power, including a larger national security role. Former Prime Minister Yasuhiro Nakasone made a comparable argument about the need for the United States and Japan to forge a single community with the same destiny.[9]

Other Japanese commentators, such as Seizaburo Sato, support Ozawa's arguments, at least regarding the necessity of sustaining the U.S.-Japan bilateral relationship; not all, however, share his concern about security.[10] This "beyond-Asianism" might be also called "normal statism." The position of the "towards-Asianists," however, does not necessarily limit Japan's sphere of influence to East Asia. But the focus of their argument is on upgrading Japan's prestige based on the further development of public well-being and the continuation of support to the Third World. For example, Yoichi Funabashi argues that Japan should pursue the goal of becoming a global civilian power with a value-oriented diplomacy.[11]

The value-oriented diplomacy Funabashi articulates includes support of Third World economic development, UN peacekeeping operations, human rights, and environmental protection. Masayoshi Takemura, Finance Minister of the current Murayama cabinet, takes a similar line of argument.[12] This toward-Asianism may also be called "developmentalism."

---

[8]Ichiro Ozawa, *Nihon Kaizo Keikaku* (Tokyo: Kodansha, 1993).

[9]Takashi Inoguchi, "Four Japanese Scenarios for the Future," p. 21.

[10]Eugene Brown, "Japanese Security Policy in the Post-Cold War World: Threat Perceptions and Strategic Options," *Journal of East Asian Affairs*, Vol. VIII, No. 2 (Summer/Fall 1994), pp. 325–362.

[11]Yoichi Funabashi, *Nihon no Taigai Koso* (Tokyo: Iwanami, 1993).

[12]Masayoshi Takemura, *Chiisakutomo Kirarito Hikaru Kuni: Nihon* (Tokyo: Kobunsha, 1994).

Table 10.1.

Four Types of U.S.-Japan Relationship

|  |  | U.S. Foreign Policy Goals | |
|  |  | *Engagement* | *Disengagement* |
| Japanese Foreign | *Beyond Asianism* | Global Partnership | Japan-Dominant Relationship |
| Policy Goals | *Toward Asianism* | U.S.-Dominant Relationship | Regional Rivalry |

Based on these four positions, we can see four possibilities in the US-Japan relationship, as identified in Table 1: a global partnership, a US-dominant relationship, a Japan-dominant relationship, and regional rivalry between the United States and Japan. In the following sections we will look at the characteristics of these four relationships in greater detail.

## FOUR TYPES OF U.S.-JAPAN RELATIONSHIP

### Global Partnership

In the first pattern, the United States and Japan act as equal (or at least highly interdependent) major powers and positively involve themselves with various matters beyond their national boundaries and respective spheres of regional influence. Under this scenario, the international system entails characteristics of what Inoguchi terms "bigenomy."

Most Japanese scholars and practitioners want to strengthen Japan's position in the international arena, regarding the maintenance of the US-Japan alliance as a necessity. They are eager to preserve the alliance, at least for the time being. These commentators share much in common with views of many American observers, who argue that a more economically open Japan and a revitalized United States are in the mutual interests of both countries. The convergence of these arguments on both sides of the Pacific suggest the possibility of enhancing a friendly, more mature relationship between the two countries. But the prospects for such an approach clearly depend on the resolution or management of bilateral trade disputes and the maintenance of the commitment of both countries to a free trade system.

However, the obstacles to global partnership cannot easily be dismissed. That the anti-Japanese mood in the United States has increased as trade conflicts have deepened is an indicator of such difficulties. An early 1992 U.S. public opinion poll, for example, disclosed that two-thirds of the respondents believed that anti-Japanese feelings in America are on the rise.[13] While these figures could be volatile and temporary, a number of influential American scholars and policymakers have voiced growing resentment against Japan; Samuel Huntington, for one, contends that Japan is starting an economic war with the United States.[14]

Despite the absence of a military rivalry between the two countries, it is still very possible that an adversarial relationship, as opposed to a global partnership, could develop should economic quarrels escalate. Under such a "global rivalry," the liberal, free-trade system will be maintained initially, but support for this regime would diminish over time. If either country perceives its interests as being undermined by international institutions, then it is also foreseeable that one or both countries may resort to protectionist measures.

## U.S.-Dominant Relationship ("Asymmetrical" vs. "Symmetrical")

Under a second scenario, the United States, with its military capabilities, maintains a high level of involvement in international affairs as a world policeman, while Japan, with its security alliance with the United States, continues to concentrate primarily on the economic side. This would represent a continuation of the bilateral relationship between the United States and Japan that existed throughout the Cold War era.

This situation may have two variations, depending on the level of future economic growth in the two countries. For example, the

---

[13]*Washington Post*, February 14, 1992.

[14]See David Arase, "Japan's Evolving Security Policy after the Cold War," *Journal of East Asian Affairs*, Vol. VIII, No. 2 (Summer/Fall 1994), p. 402.

United States could still retain its dominant position given its military capabilities, while Japan, with its strong economic performance, becomes a coequal partner in the management of the international system. Complementing each other's strengths, both countries would aim at strengthening the Bretton Woods system through the Uruguay Round of the General Agreement on Tariffs and Trade (GATT) and its development into the World Trade Organization (WTO) system. This situation differs from the aforementioned global partnership in that Japan lacks strategic independence, which would force it to rely more on international regimes in case of major policy conflicts. This might be called a "symmetrical" U.S.-dominant partnership due to the compatibility between Japan's economic strength and the United States' military strength.

However, this scenario poses the question of whether a country without nuclear arms or the capability of neutralizing them can maintain the status of a superpower, not only in relation to the United States, but in relation to various East Asian countries, including at least one with nuclear weapons. The argument of liberal international relations theorists—i.e., that the increasing economic interdependence between states penetrates national boundaries so deeply as to make military capabilities obsolete—assumes major significance in this regard. If this argument does not hold, Japan would retain the status of junior partner, even with its presently increasing international involvement. If this situation is combined with the revitalization of the American economy, the bilateral relationship will turn into an "asymmetrical" one.

## Japan-Dominant Relationship

Under the third scenario, Japan succeeds the United States in global leadership. This would bring about what Inoguchi terms a Pax Nipponica, relying on its exports to sustain its international dominance. But the sustainability of Japan's dominance would be questionable, both because of the nuclear balance and because of the distribution of economic power. Even if Japan were to acquire nuclear arms in order to realize its strategic goals, there still remains the problem of how long Japan's economy could sustain its domination under the corresponding world system. Unless the economic gap between Japan and other potential contenders were to remain quite large, its dominance might not be sufficient or durable. Thus this situation is likely to lead to regional rivalry or to a system which relies heavily on multilateral regimes.

## Regional Rivalry ("Single-Headed" vs. "Multi-Headed")

Under the fourth scenario, the United States and Japan concentrate on enhancing their national power by protecting their respective spheres of influence. This situation corresponds to what Inoguchi labels the Pax Consortia. The trend toward economic regionalism (e.g. NAFTA, the EU, and the East Asian Economic Census, or EAEC) would appear to lend support for this proposition. This regionalization could take various shapes, depending on the leadership in each region. One possibility would be a case in which Germany and Russia emerge as the leading countries of their respective regions—Europe and the former Soviet bloc—and join in the leadership group along with the United States and Japan. It is also conceivable that China would join this leadership group. But there would still be a great deal of potential variability within each regional arrangement, as economic actors of larger size would seek to ensure their prosperity and power. Under certain circumstances, one country would be clearly predominant within a given region (hence a "single-headed" regional rivalry). In other cases, however, actors within each regional structure would compete vigorously with one another or contest the primacy of a single actor (hence a "multi-headed" regional rivalry).

## INTERACTIONS AMONG THE FOUR RELATIONSHIPS

In assessing the opportunities and constraints affecting the position of the United States and Japan under each of these scenarios, we need to examine how both countries might seek to enhance their absolute and relative position. Thus, we need to ask whether the United States can recapture its economic strength while sustaining its present level of military capabilities; whether Japan can become a superpower in terms of military capabilities, possibly including the development of a nuclear capability; and whether Japan can sustain its present economic prosperity and technological advantage should it seek to greatly expand its defense capabilities. There is evidence both for and against these questions. We will divide our assessment into internal and external considerations, focusing on "willingness" and "capabilities" for internal factors and "perception" and "stimulus" for external considerations.

## Internal Considerations

A. *"Willingness" Factors:* In terms of "willingness", we need to ask two main questions: whether the United States is willing to remain deeply engaged in East Asia and whether Japan is prepared to greatly enhance its military power. As discussed previously, there is ample divergence of opinion about the requirements for U.S. leadership in the post-Cold War world. Within the Clinton administration, the basic direction seems to be toward international engagement, though at a reduced level of commitment and expenditure. But many observers argue that there is ample uncertainty in converting key American policy tenets (for example, "the strategy of engagement and enlargement") into a more defined program of action.

Japan's future policy directions need to be examined in relation to its readiness to enhance its defense capabilities and the character of its international participation. Scholars appear quite divided on these issues.[15] Tsuneo Akaha, among others, expresses a rather negative view on the possibility of Japan becoming a nuclear power. David Arase, by contrast, asserts that Japan possesses such a potential (e.g. its recent push toward plutonium production), though he does not predict such a policy breakthrough in the near future, with Japan instead opting for a temporizing policy option.[16]

Although Japan's becoming a nuclear power is far from decided, its willingness to participate positively in international affairs is increasingly evident. The Japanese government's decision to participate in activities following the Gulf War and to send its forces for UN peacekeeping operations in Cambodia, Mozambique and Rwanda reflect Japan's increasing search for a new international role. The current situation in Japanese politics, in which the Socialist Party of Japan

---

[15]Tsuneo Akaha, "Japan's Security Policy in the Posthegemonic World: Opportunities and Challenges," in Tsuneo Akaha and Frank Langdon, eds., *Japan in the Posthegemonic World* (Boulder and London: Lynne Rienner Publishers, 1993), pp. 91–112.

[16]Arase, "Japan's Evolving Security Policy after the Cold War."

revised its traditional anti-U.S. and anti-Self Defense Forces stance, and may enhance this change of policy direction. According to the *Asahi Shimbun,* which posed questions about constitutional revision and the recognition of the SDF, the PKO and nuclear energy to various parties participating in the 1993 election, most reacted positively to these issues.[17] Though the level of support varies, this survey shows that Japan has achieved a working consensus on increased involvement in international affairs.

*B. "Capabilities" Factors:* In terms of "capabilities," we have to seek answers to the following questions: first, whether the United States will be able to revitalize its economy; second, whether Japan is capable of developing much enhanced defense capabilities; third, whether Japan can maintain its economic growth if it decides to adopt a policy of strategic independence; and, lastly, whether Japan can remold its cultural "uniqueness" in relation to its future international role.

In regard to the first question, contrasting views can be found. Those who hold a positive view mention America's potential in scientific and technological development, which is based on openness and pluralism. The recent revitalization of the American automobile industry, the relatively high U.S. economic growth rate of 4.0 percent in 1994, and the share of U.S. manufacturing in the world economy, which reached 22.9 percent in 1990, can be regarded as evidence for this proposition.[18]

Those who hold a more pessimistic view, however, emphasize U.S. domestic ills, e.g., the budget deficits, educational problems, and a diminishing American work ethic. For example, despite bipartisan efforts to reduce the budget deficit, the deficit reached 5 percent of GDP in FY 1992 due to slower economic growth and the rapid rise of health related outlays.[19] (However, recent trends in both political parties suggest that this will remain an increasing preoccupation in U.S. political circles.) Increased labor productivity in the United

---

[17] *Asahi Shimbun,* July 7, 1993.

[18] *Maeil Kyungje Shinmun,* February 6, 1995; *Nihon Keizai Shimbun,* January 1, 1995; *Handbook of Industrial Statistics,* 1992, p. 25.

[19] *World Economic Outlook* (Washington, D.C.: IMF, 1993), pp. 51–54.

States between 1985 and 1990 was also low, at 0.5 percent, which was significantly lower than Japan's 3.5 percent and Germany's 3.0 percent, though a little higher than its own 0.2 percent in the period between 1973 and 1985.[20]

Turning to Japan, few seem to doubt Japan's capability to develop its military potential, including nuclear arms. However, there are serious impediments to such a course of action. Policy change is generally assumed to occur when the need, the solution, and the agent for change are concurrently matched, and none of these can be said to exist in Japan at present.[21] Nuclearization, in particular, would need a tremendous degree of "nemawashi" in the society as well as a resolute leader, even if critical events provide momentum for such a course of action. Considering the time-consuming nature of Japanese policymaking, especially on an issue of such of such extraordinary sensitivity, attitude change would be very protracted. The JSP's recent recognition of the utility of nuclear energy and its acquiescence on other controversial issues (e.g. the legitimacy of the U.S.-Japan Security treaty) seem to be paving the way for a degree of change. However, different groups within the present political process are deeply divided: one group arguing for Japan's becoming a more substantial political-military power and the other proposing that Japan focus on its role as a benevolent aid donor. Without reconciling these differences, it seems extremely unlikely that there will be decisive policy movement.

The third question (i.e., the ability to sustain simultaneously economic prosperity and a much increased defense effort) is not an easy one to answer. In terms of Japan's scientific and technological capabilities, Takashi Inoguchi offers a positive evaluation. He notes that the number of Japanese patents is equal to those of the United States, the number of Japan-based authors' articles in *Chemical Abstracts* exceeds that of the United States, and Japan's seven Nobel Prize winners for the 40-years period since 1945 compared with

---

[20] *Tsusan Hakusho* (Tokyo: Okurasho Insatsukyoku, 1993), p. 374.

[21] For example, John W. Kingdon, *Agendas, Alternatives, and Public Policies* (Boston: Little, Brown, 1984); Harold L. Wilensky, *The Welfare State and Equality: Structural and Ideological Roots of Public Expenditures* (Berkeley: University of California Press, 1975).

U.S.'s five in the first 30 years of this century.[22] We can add to these figures total factor productivity and the contribution of secondary industries to the growth of GDP. Japan's total factor productivity growth reached an average of 1.9 percent between 1985 and 1990, which is higher than the 1.4 percent of the period between 1973 and 1985 or the U.S.'s 0.2 percent in the former period and -0.2 percent in the latter period.[23] The secondary industries' contribution to the growth of Japanese GDP increased at an annual average of 2.41 percent in the period between 1986 and 1990 from that of 1.7 percent between 1981 and 1985, while the U.S. figure rose only 0.8 percent between 1981 and 1987.[24] Moreover, Robert Dekle has estimated that Japan, which achieved a high growth rate of 9.29 percent between 1961 and 1971, would have grown at 8.2 percent even if it had decided to spend for defense at the same level as the United States (6.2 percent of GDP) during the same period due to Japan's high level of private saving and investment.[25]

Reflecting on the U.S. experience and on Japan's economic size and recent recession, however, a more pessimistic conclusion seems warranted. David Arase, for example, predicts that a Japan opting for strategic independence with only two-thirds of the U.S. GNP and a rapidly growing Chinese economy may be trapped between too little growth and too little military and political capability to establish even regional predominance.[26]

The last question also reflects an issue posed by Joseph Nye: that is, whether Japan has the "soft" power with which a hegemonic power or a superpower must be endowed.[27] Japanese authors usually regard democracy and the free trade system as the guiding values for

---

[22]Inoguchi, p. 25.

[23]*Tsusan Hakusho*, 1993, pp. 373–377.

[24]*World Tables* (Baltimore and London: The Johns Hopkins University Press, 1993), pp. 32–33.

[25]Robert Dekle, "The Relationship between Defense Spending and Economic Performance in Japan," in John H. Makin and Donald C. Hellmann, eds., *Sharing World Leadership?* (Washington, D.C.: American Enterprise Institute, 1989), pp. 127–149.

[26]Arase, p. 417.

[27]Joseph S. Nye, Jr., "What New World Order?" *Foreign Affairs*, Vol. 71, No. 2 (Spring 1992), p. 86.

the future of Japan and the world. These views do not contradict each other at least on the surface. However, how Japan's self-consciousness about its distinctive international and cultural identity would persist under changing international conditions remains far from certain. For example, McCreary and Noll argue that behind the stalemate of the trade issue between the United States and Japan lie profound cultural, psychological and structural impediments.[28] These limitations are often described in terms of tribalism, inferiority complex, and sense of victimization ("higaisha ishiki"). These authors assert that without changes in these fundamental conditions, expectations about trade negotiations yielding satisfactory results could prove an illusion. This shows that Japan faces a formidable task if it tries to export its values abroad, even as it has sought to pursue a more flexible and adaptive policy.

## External Considerations

*A. "Perception" Factors:* Whatever form the U.S.-Japan relationship may take in the future, it depends not only on domestic factors but also on international acceptance, especially the responses of Japan's neighbors in East Asia. Any move by Japan toward hegemonic or regional superpower status would encounter severe criticism from other Asian countries. South Korea and China have repeatedly expressed their apprehension about the role of Japan in East Asia, not to mention the possibility of Japan possessing nuclear arms. This concern can be seen in their reluctance to acknowledge Japan's participation in UN peacekeeping operations and their coolness regarding Japanese membership on the UN Security Council. Their worries are not simply driven by past memories, but also by remarks coming intermittently from the nationalistic cabinet members and by views expressed in Japanese textbooks.

But the picture is not all bleak. The Southeast Asian countries have largely recovered from their anti-Japanese feelings of the seventies, and are encouraging Japan's willingness to act as the region's spokesperson. Malaysian Prime Minister Mahatir's encouragement

---

[28]Don R. McCreary and Chris J. Noll, Jr., "Cultural, Psychological, and Structural Impediments to Free Trade with Japan," *Asian Perspective*, Vol. 15, No. 2 (Fall/Winter 1991), pp. 75–98.

for Japan to play a more positive role is a good example. Despite their apprehensions, South Korea and China also need Japan; for example, China is in need of capital for economic growth, particularly if its relationship with the United States encounters increased difficulties; South Korea also still relies greatly on Japanese capital goods. This contrasting evidence underscores the suggestions of some Japanese commentators that a more transparent Japan could earn increased trust from its neighbors.[29] But this may not prove easy, since there is also the factor of ambition, to be discussed in the next section.

The United States is also not immune to criticisms from Asian countries. Although most Asian states recognize the necessity of the U.S. military presence for regional stability, they fear U.S. "hegemonic" pressures or economic penetration. This seems to be the underlying reason for the ASEAN countries professing different views on Asia Pacific Economic Cooperation (APEC) and the willingness of some states to turn to Japan as their spokesperson. China's reluctance to participate fully in multilateral security fora reflects comparable unease about U.S. domination.

Therefore, even if U.S. pressures aimed at reviving its economic strength succeed, excessive unilateral pressure on economic issues may backfire and give Japan more room to emerge as an alternative power. One reason for the US-Japan security alliance (especially as viewed by other East Asian countries) is to prevent a recurrence of Japanese expansionism.[30] If this is still true, the United States needs to take more careful actions toward East Asia if it is to avoid highly adverse responses to its policy goals.

*B. "Stimulus" Factors:* South Korea's and China's uneasiness toward an enhanced Japanese regional role also reflects their own ambitions (especially China) to emerge within the region, and to check and balance against Japan. The China factor has two aspects: military expansion and economic growth. The shape of post-Deng China remains uncertain at present. However, it is possible that one or more contenders for leadership may ignite nationalist sentiment as a way

---

[29]Atsumasa Yamamoto, *Multilateral Activities for Stability in the East Asia-Pacific Region* (Tokyo: Institute for International Policy Studies, 1994).

[30]Nathaniel B. Thayer, "Beyond Security: U.S.-Japanese Relations in the 1990s," *Journal of International Affairs*, Vol. 43, No. 1 (1989), pp. 57–68.

of consolidating their power base. Any moves in this area will affect Japan's posture and may test China's relationship with the United States as well as its future relations with ASEAN.

On the other hand, China, presently experiencing an annual growth rate of 10 percent or more and perceiving the possibility of a Chinese economic zone, may emerge as a major economic pole in its own right. Its advent as an economic power will also influence the bilateral relationship between the United States and Japan. For instance, if China is able to manage current difficulties with the United States and continues to develop at a fast rate, it may emerge as a regional superpower. This would provide an opportunity for the United States and Japan to rethink their respective relationships with China, which may induce both states to diminish their relative importance to one another.

The other important factor is North Korea. This concerns two areas of major potential instability: nuclear arms and domestic politics. Despite the October 1994 and June 1995 agreements between the United States and North Korea, it is still unclear how the agreed-on measures will be pursued. On the other hand, it is also not clear how long the Kim Jong Il regime will last. Its durability has to be viewed in terms of a power struggle and a tumbling economy. The United States and Japan both acknowledge that the stability of the Korean peninsula is vital to the security of Japan and the region as a whole. However, if the North Korean nuclear arms question is not resolved and North Korea's domestic instability heightens, these developments will challenge the effectiveness of bilateral relationship between the United States and Japan. Under such circumstances, Japan could rethink its strategic options. For example, Japan recently stated that it was prepared to send PKO forces in case of crisis in Korea. But other courses of actions may also result. In the event of an impending crisis of the peninsula, any hesitation by Japan to provide logistical support for the U.S. forces will put into question its credibility as a partner of the bilateral relationship. The hesitation may come from the notoriously time-consuming nature of Japanese policymaking or from its strategic concerns.

## Possible Courses of Future Development

Of the four main issues identified in this paper, internal capabilities and perceptions seem to have the greatest capability for influencing the short-term outcome of the U.S.-Japan bilateral relationship. The factors of willingness and external capabilities can only be tested over a long period of time. The recent growth of the U.S. economy, in contrast to Japan's experience of recession, suggests that the realization of the U.S.-dominant relationship in the Cold War period remains more feasible, at least in a short-term perspective. Japan's opportunity to pursue strategic independence, which would be needed for a true global role, still seems very unlikely. Slower economic growth will also make Japan depend more on the United States rather than on a regional-based strategy.

Of the two types of U.S.-dominant relationships, the "asymmetrical" pattern is likely not only because the American economy seems to have revived, but because the economic gap between the two countries needs to be substantially widened in favor of Japan for the realization of a "symmetrical" pattern. However, it is difficult to predict how long this trend of U.S. economic growth will continue. Most recent economic trends, such as GNP growth and trends in the U.S. automotive industry, lead to a more positive evaluation for the United States and a more negative one for Japan—even allowing for the latter's continuous trade surplus with the United States and despite America's domestic problems such as the budget deficit. If this trend continues, then, the "asymmetrical" US-dominant relationship will last for quite some time.

A more "symmetrical" U.S.-dominant relationship, though conceivable, would take much longer to realize. It is also possible that other types of relationships could replace the "symmetrical" pattern due to unexpected conditions in the medium-term perspective. An abrupt shift in the short-term perspective could come from North Korea, or from the territorial disputes with China and Russia that reflect problems of domestic instability and nuclear arms.

Japan may have two options if a more negative scenario emerges. One is to rely on the United States in which case the "symmetrical" relationship will revert to an "asymmetrical" one. This course of action, however, would depend on the U.S. willingness to remain deeply involved in such regional concerns, and second, whether Japan with its successful economy can expect an undiminished U.S. security guarantee.

Japan's other option would be to pursue strategic autonomy, including development of nuclear weapons. As mentioned previously, under "normal" circumstances, this possibility remains highly remote. However, should there be an abrupt change in external conditions, the domestic mood may also compress the time needed to build the consensus for armament. The "symmetrical" relationship would then be replaced either by global partnership or a Japan-dominant one. It is also possible that these two scenarios occur sequentially. In either event, Japan's international influence would grow appreciably. Given Japan's limited economic size, however, the Japan-dominant relationship would initially take the form of a "single-headed" regional rivalry. In a longer-term perspective, a "multi-headed" regional rivalry would be very likely, since China could be expected to emerge as another regional superpower.

## KOREAN VIEWS ON THE U.S.-JAPAN BILATERAL RELATIONSHIP

The United States and Japan have been the most important countries economically and politically to Korea for decades. Their importance, however, has different connotations. America has been perceived by most South Koreans as a "friendly" state that liberated and protected South Korea from Japanese occupation and the communist threat. Meanwhile, Japan has been the target for dislike (or even hatred), but at the same time the object of envy; it is a country from which Korea has much to learn and to overcome. Given this difference in perception, a U.S.-dominant relationship, whether it be "asymmetrical" or "symmetrical," would be preferred by Koreans.

In addition, such a scenario would better serve the goals South Korea is presently pursuing: economic development and the peaceful unification of Korea. The U.S.-Japan security alliance would be maintained under this relationship, which in turn would bring about stability in the region and, for Korea, act as a buffer against a possible North Korean attack and renewed Japanese expansion.

Any type of Japan-dominant relationship would be far less attractive to Korea. Japan's acquisition of nuclear arms would increase rather than decrease regional instability in East Asia, including the Korean peninsula. It could also exert a negative influence on the feasibility of Korean unification, since Japan's armament could trigger an arms race on both sides of the peninsula, quite possibly prolonging the division of the peninsula.

In order to make the U.S.-dominant relationship a more viable option for the region, multilateral efforts between the concerned parties are needed, even if they may take time to develop. This reflects the simple fact that the problems confronted in the region are multilateral, interrelated, and therefore need to be approached on a comprehensive basis. For example, efforts between the United States and Japan to address China's future political-military development necessarily include China as well as the other regional countries, since their national interests will all be affected in the process. The same conclusion holds for the problem of North Korea. In this respect, the United States should place relatively more weight on multilateral approaches, since over the long run they provide the best means for addressing the region's future.